BISLEY 19

Robert E. Howard's

CONAN

ADVENTURES IN AN AGE UNDREAMED OF

System Design
Benn Graybeaton, Nathan Dowdell
& Jay Little

Line Development
Jason Durall & Chris Lites

Writing
Mark Finn, Richard August,
Chris Lites, Rachael Cruz & Jason Durall

Approvals
Patrice Louinet & Jeffrey Shanks

Editing & Proofreading
Sally Christensen & Ian Finch

Cover Artwork
Simon Bisley

Interior Artwork
Jorge Barrero, Shen Fei, Nick Greenwood,
Gunship Revolution, Antonio José, Matthias
Kinnigkeit Fares Maese, Ed Mattinian,
Stark & Michael Syrigos

Cartography
Jose "Gigio" Esteras & Tobias Tranell

Art Direction
Mischa Thomas

Lead Graphic Design
Michal E. Cross

Layout
Thomas Shook

Additional Graphic Design
Dan Algstrand & Malcolm Wolter

Produced by
Chris Birch

Operations Manager
Garry Harper

Community Support
Lloyd Gyan

Publishing Assistant
Sam Webb

With Thanks to
The Robert E. Howard Foundation,
Professor John Kirowan, H.P. Lovecraft,
Fred & Jay at Cabinet Entertainment

Published by
Modiphius Entertainment Ltd. 3rd Floor,
Ashbourne House, 35 Harwood Road,
London. SW6 4QP, United Kingdom

TABLE OF CONTENTS

CONAN THE THIEF

> *"Well," Conan was recovering some of his resilient confidence, "there's no assurance that the thief will throw it away. If I know thieves — and I should, for I was a thief in Zamora in my early youth — he won't throw it away. He'll sell it to some rich trader. By Crom!"*
>
> — **The Hour of the Dragon**

A WORD FROM SHEVATAS...

Let me speak to you as an equal, for I sense in you a kinship. I would never accuse you of purloining this fine volume. It no doubt fell off a book-seller's cart, or perhaps was a gift from a colleague. Far be it from me to ask questions. I am more than passing familiar with this work, though, and can acquaint you with its contents.

Conan the Thief is filled with adventure, danger, and ideas. When Robert E. Howard wrote Conan's tales of thievery, he thrust his unruly barbarian into a short-lived career of certain peril and desperate adventure. Equipped with this volume, the gamemaster can inflict the same upon the player characters, filling them with dread and challenging their very lives, with fortunes riding on their wits and skill.

If you have the nerves for such guidance, these pages contain everything required for creating and running games in which the player characters are desperate thieves. The world is awash with such men and women, their purses as empty as their stomachs. But cunning, speed, and dexterous hands can change one's fate, should surety guide them. This volume is the complete guide to doing just that.

Now... get going, quickly. The watch is after you!

Chapter 1: Thief Characters

New archetypes, life paths, talents, specialized equipment and weapons, and other vital ingredients for character creation and improvement.

Chapter 2: Gazetteer

Here are the cities and kingdoms of the Hyborian Age where thievery is at its most rampant — from fabled Zamora where every shadow is an assassin, rustic Brythunia, staunch Nemedia, to Shadizar the Wicked, where every street is redolent with depravity. This chapter is filled with incident, action, and information for thieves seeking fortune.

Chapter 3: Events

The world is filled with madness and adventure — and thieves can be involved in anything and everything. This section is a collection of ideas, occurrences — both trivial and significant — in which rogues might become embroiled.

Chapter 4: Myth and Magic

It is a time of powerful sorcery and deadly incantations which can rip asunder the veil of reality itself, plunging both wizards and their victims into dreadful darkness. Strange gods and stranger religions also take root in the minds of men and women everywhere — some for good, others for ill.

AN EXTRACT FROM THE FOREWORD TO THE NEMEDIAN CHRONICLES: A PROPOSED CHRONOLOGY

...many have of course attempted to place specific dates on those events transpiring in the Hyborian Age as recorded in the Nemedian Chronicles. His peripatetic wanderings, guided only by his own instinct, are without parallel. Specifically, the life of Conan drove many scholars veritably insane in their attempts to chronologize it. I, myself, cannot pretend to have been untouched by this mania.

When first I encountered the "The Nemedian Chronicles", I, too, labored night and day to apply to them those sequences of numbers which make the past history, instead of consigning it to the realm of "once-upon-a-time". It is tempting, even for those who have pretensions toward scholarly detachment, to wonder if, should he have lived in another time, might he have faced the mighty Achilles in battle? For, if the German excavator is correct in his grandiose speculations, then it seems true that the "fleet-footed" King of the Myrmidons also drew breath beneath the sun, as I believe Conan of Cimmeria did. And what a battle that would have been to witness.

The reader must forgive me this digression: there is a point to this rambling and I will come to it. It is, I now believe, senseless to try and precisely date the events of the Hyborian Age so that they effectively cohere with our current notions of the earth's epochs. Instead, we should understand the Hyborian Age, and specifically, the life of Conan, as being divided for us thematically.

Yes, again I must apologize to my colleagues who dabble in the Classical field, for I wish to borrow their techniques.

Conan's life should not be approached as a series of dates for, quite clearly, this is not how the historians of the Hyborian Era understood it. Indeed, the classicists may rest easy, for Herodotus is still the Father of History. The nameless Nemedian chroniclers, however, understood time as something other than a linear series of events. Perhaps their notion of time was quite different from ours. Instead, let us see the life of Conan as the sequence of things he was and did. So, to the purpose of this monograph: before the glory of the throne of Aquilonia and the many triumphs of the battlefield, Conan was a thief. He was the lowliest kind of footpad and cutpurse. These aspects of the "Chronicle" are often overlooked, but should not be: the underworlds in which Conan once moved are as interesting as any of the palaces and great courts he later visited and ruled. It has ever been the dream of the schoolboy to take what he pleases: to be free of those great moral constraints we would place on him. In our own age, do we not worship the graven images of Billy the Kid and Jesse James?

Why then, would we not worship that legendary barbarian all the more for what he was as a young man, when he was merely Conan the Thief?

Prof. John Kirowan (PhD, FRS, FRAI, FRGS)
Guest Lecturer, Department of Anthropology
Miskatonic University
Arkham, Massachusetts

Chapter 5: Encounters
Within this section are descriptions of remarkable and terrifying figures that might offer thieves help or deadly hindrance, as well as a variety of strange and dreadful creatures to trouble even the most courageous of rogues.

Chapter 6: Hither Came Conan...
Just who was Conan when he ensured his survival by undertaking daring raids on the palaces of the rich and the towers of the mighty? This section describes Conan, with a summary of his adventures when he was a young and callow thief, though lethal as ever!

Chapter 7: The Way of Thieves
How do thieves become thieves? How do they carry out their specialized trade? What organizations do they band

themselves into — and how might thieves join? All this and more is contained herein. This is the gamemaster's personal toolbox. Read it, steal from it, mix it up, and forever fill games with larcenous fun.

Chapter 8: Heists
Find here the means to quickly assemble a host of adventures for thieves, using a few dice rolls. With this section, the gamemaster will never be short of an adventure again — and the thieves will never run out of things to steal.

Chapter 9: Heroes of the Age
Created by backers of the *Robert E. Howard's Conan: Adventures in an Age Undreamed Of* Kickstarter campaign, these characters are provided for use as player characters or non-player characters to encounter.

THIEF CHARACTERS

Native rogues were the dominant element — dark-skinned, dark-eyed Zamorians, with daggers at their girdles and guile in their hearts. But there were wolves of half a dozen outland nations there as well. There was a giant Hyperborean renegade, taciturn, dangerous, with a broadsword strapped to his great gaunt frame — for men wore steel openly in the Maul. There was a Shemitish counterfeiter, with his hook nose and curled blue-black beard. There was a bold-eyed Brythunian wench, sitting on the knee of a tawny-haired Gunderman — a wandering mercenary soldier, a deserter from some defeated army.

— "The Tower of the Elephant"

Civilization can be a complicated, overbearing place. It is constructed on a code of unfairness, or so it seems to some who visit it for the first time from the barbarian kingdoms of the north. It protects the weak and restrains the strong. It prizes obedience and order, organizing men and women according to such arbitrary divisions as age and wealth and learning; it sanctions rudeness and ignorance by condemning the honest pursuit of vengeance against those who offend you. And in return it offers what? Poverty, paltry food, and the tyranny of those whom the unguessable laws of a city have placed in power over you.

What should you do then, if you are one of those without the security of wealth? Accept the depredations of those wealthier than you, stronger than you, or invoke the spirit of those barbarians who take what they want through force of will. For that is what the thief is, in truth. He is civilization's barbarian, the return of the wild to the tamer regions of the world, the authentic nature of humankind liberated from the shackles with which city walls and tall houses seek to restrain it.

THIEF HOMELANDS

Thieves can be from anywhere in the Hyborian kingdoms and beyond, as the forces that drive one to thievery are universal to most human societies. Players can choose to roll randomly or pick their character homeland as described in *Step One: Homeland* on page 13 of the **Conan** corebook, though this sourcebook focuses primarily on countries with thriving thief traditions, societies, and the environments they prosper best in — countries such as Zamora, Corinthia, Nemedia, and Brythunia. To get the most out of *Conan the Thief*, those homelands are recommended.

THIEF CASTE AND STORIES

Most thieves are products of their environments. Live long enough among the cesspits of the Maze and everyone finds their fingers a little lighter and their eyes a little more attuned to who hasn't protected their coin purse properly. It is always possible, of course, that being raised in great wealth will produce the urge to steal, that sleeping each night on the silken sheets of Vendhyan royalty will create a lust for the unobtainable that might only be sated through theft. But, just as there are some born to power and prestige, so too are some born to rob and steal. In every society, there are intergenerational gangs of criminals, places where you learn the arts of larceny in the cradle and are tutored in robbery, as a squire is the sword.

Player characters wishing to join these intergenerational gangs should first consider their castes. For most, the only caste that makes sense is that of Outcast (see page 20 of the *Conan* corebook), but in regions where such gangs proliferate, the gamemaster may also allow player characters to be from the Outlaw caste, described below.

Should player characters be from the Outlaw caste, they can choose not to roll Education but instead roll to see what their apprenticeship was like. Once the player characters' stories are rolled, they gain the option of rolling an Apprenticeship.

OUTLAW (CASTE)

Caste Talents: *Tradesman, Vagabond*
Skill Gained: Society
Social Standing: 0

OUTLAW STORIES

Roll	Event	Trait
1–3	Nobility in All But Name	Isolated
4–6	With Overflowing Pockets	Bedeviled with Requests
7–10	Honor Is Key	Known and Respected
11–14	A Family of No Standing	Mistrusted
15–17	A Victim of Justice	Branded
18–20	An Example Must Be Made	Hunted

Nobility in All But Name

How did you end up like this exactly? Less than a generation ago, your family was wealthy and respected, simply waiting to be awarded the land and title which would have officially elevated them to the aristocracy. And then it all vanished. The money, the acclaim, the servants, the houses, and the bright and glorious future. Now all you have is a gnawing hunger in your belly and a chip on your shoulder. Unsurprisingly, where you live now, your accent, and your mannerisms mark you as a former member of the detested elite. You are alone — you learned your trade the hard way, and only recently have you fallen in with a group you might call friends. Your loyalty to your fellow player characters is absolute and unyielding but, where anyone else is concerned, you might be something of a liability.

THIEF ANCIENT BLOODLINES

The *Ancient Bloodline* talent (described on page 17 of the CONAN corebook) indicates that one or more of a player character's high attributes is due to the influence of a lineage descended from the powerful ancestors of old. These manifest in certain ways during the course of play, and are powerful indicators of the hold the dim and forgotten past has over the present. A player character with this talent might choose to amend it on the character sheet (to "*Ancient Bloodline: Zamorian*", for example) or can use the basic description from the CONAN corebook, unmodified. Each homeland represents a specific ancient heritage, described below.

- **BRYTHUNIA:** The Brythunian heritage is almost entirely Hyborian, a remnant from that tribe's wandering. When this talent comes into play, the player character feels a powerful sense of pride and connectedness to the Hyborian people, almost to a fault. Others will get a sense of this direct lineage to the primary Hyborian bloodline.

- **CORINTHIA:** Though the origin of the Corinthian people does not extend beyond the Cataclysm, they were nonetheless a flourishing kingdom when the empire of dreaded Acheron rose and fell. A Corinthian exhibiting the effects of this trait will feel a flush of satisfaction and a slight superiority, and others might sense a bit of arrogance.

- **NEMEDIA:** Born out of the ashes of ancient Acheron, this country's descendants are inheritors to the rich tradition of knowledge and scholarship that the land is known for. When this talent manifests, the player characters may feel the weight of antiquity and a sense of the immensity of time press upon them, while others beholding them may feel detachment and aloofness.

- **ZAMORA:** These folk are descended from the Zhemri, one of the races that came into being after the Cataclysm. Whenever this talent manifests itself, those nearby will experience illicit sensations of bygone times, hints of some ancient depravity and debasement. For a thief-based campaign, this is not necessarily a bad thing.

The *Ancient Bloodline* talent is in all other respects identical to the version presented in the CONAN corebook.

With Overflowing Pockets

Too much money and too little sense. That might have been your family's motto. Money was easy to come by — clever trading, greasing the right palms and, of course, not being averse to stealing and killing when required — and you made the most of it. It made you popular, but it also drew attention. The kind of attention that can help a young thief on his way to fame and glory, and the kind that can result in a young body swinging slowly from a gibbet. It really isn't easy to tell which is most likely; what is easy to guess is that people are going to be coming to you for loans whenever they need it. A slow week in the thieving world is likely to see a host of foreigners suddenly claiming a deep and abiding friendship with you and your family. You might be able to call in some of these favors in the future — but people are quick to forget. Anyway, now you're trying to make it on your own. What makes you think you can rely on the family money?

Honor Is Key

Honor and reputation is everything. It always has been. You would never step away from a challenge, and this led you into some unfortunate situations — you've got a network of scars all over you and a number of tales which end bloodily as a result. You also have, however, a reputation and a standing amongst thieves which, if not yet entirely secured upon your own merit, has the authenticity of a long-earned family guarantee. That's the thing with inter-generational thievery; it's not as though you are likely to suddenly betray the principles you were raised with. You understand the way things are done and why they are done that way. Yes, maybe sometimes they may seem imperfect, but these are traditions for a reason. You know them, you've learned them and by Bel's keen ears, you'll uphold them. It's honor, after all.

A Family of No Standing

Someone in your family talked. Sometime in the past they offered someone up in exchange for their own life. People remember. It wasn't you that made that choice — and maybe you never would — but the memory lingers in close-knit communities like those of thieves. You've been allowed into the fold but there are still whispers when you pass by. There are still those who openly curse your family's name. Your mates would never do so — they know you and your loyalty to them — but those voices still whisper.

A Victim of Justice

They caught you. They made sure that everyone knew they caught you. Your skin is permanently scarred with the mark of your failure and their triumph. The thick, black weals rising from your flesh bears that most accusatory of epithets: thief. Of course, you are a thief and damn the gods themselves if they think you'll be ashamed of that fact, but still… it doesn't help to advertise in this business. And now, no matter how many successful heists you manage to pull off, no matter how wealthy you become, the mark of your failure will never leave you. None of your family bore this mark. You have failed in a way that they did not. Now you must succeed as greatly as you once failed.

An Example Must Be Made

The problem with coming from a lineage of thieves is that sometimes you don't get a say in the crimes you're held responsible for. And that's what's happened to you, pursued by those who accuse you for a crime you did not commit. Or maybe you actually did it. It honestly doesn't matter. Your name is the same, your reputation identical to those who took part. Vengeance is coming. And it's going to get you if you aren't smart. It's faster and more dangerous than the implacable men and women on your trail. Start running… you've got a long way to go yet.

THIEF ARCHETYPES

Players may choose any one of the following archetypes during character creation. As with the archetypes in the corebook, this merely determines the path of your character at the beginning of the game. Where your character decides to go once the game starts is something the players and gamemaster will explore together. War stories and training details can likewise be embellished or altered to reflect a life spent learning the trade of thieving, at the gamemaster's discretion.

TAURUS SPEAKS

"Ho, so you're not some run of the mill cutpurse, are you? Well, you'll have no trouble plying your… ah… more specialized trade here, but remember this, my young friend: everyone is a thief at some point in their lives. Everyone".

"The first time you haven't eaten in three days, you'll forget all about that fancy equipment and those lovely clothes and you'll wonder how fast you can snatch a loaf of bread from the marketplace and make away with it. It's not always finesse that gets the job done".

ASSASSIN

Killers from Zamora, skulking in the dark, striking silently, and leaving no trace save a bloodied corpse are the stuff of legend — a bogeyman conjured up by superstitious governesses to scare young lords and young ladies into obeying their elders. These whispered deeds of death imply that the assassins are something more than human. Not surprisingly, these legends come from the assassins themselves, who understand the value such tales have on the uninitiated. The upper-class nobles who look past the legends pay well for the services of these killers.

Operating primarily from the city of Shadizar, the assassins known as the Black Hand hire out to whomever has the most gold, and they pride themselves on their "fealty to the coin", meaning that they will honor any contract to completion, provided that the money is right. Legends around the origin of their name vary widely. Some say the hands of these assassins are permanently stained from handling deadly plants used in their vicious poisons. Others claim they wear one black glove at all times to identify fellow members. Only members of the Black Hand know the truth.

Assassins who ply their trade outside of Zamora are either self-taught or have broken away from the Black Hand for one reason or another. Occasionally, this causes friction between the freelancer and the Black Hand, especially if the freelancer encroaches on the Black Hand's market in a given area.

PLAYING AN ASSASSIN

Because of their violent reputation and legendary prowess, most assassins choose to pass themselves off as a more innocuous profession when dealing with others. Doing so allows them to hide in plain sight, and often makes it easy to get close to their target. Many assassins learn the art of disguise for just such a purpose. If the assassin is a member of the Black Hand (page 32), then they are considered a Patron and will periodically contact the character with contracts to carry out.

CAREER SKILL: +2 Expertise and +2 Focus in Stealth
CAREER TALENT: *Living Shadow* (page 85 of the CONAN corebook)
MANDATORY SKILLS: +1 Expertise and Focus to Acrobatics, Alchemy, Ranged Weapons, and Observation
ELECTIVE SKILLS: +1 Expertise and Focus to two of the following skills: Melee, Society, or Survival
EQUIPMENT:

- Two weapons of choice
- Choice of a padded jerkin (Armor 1; Torso, Arms) or a mail vest (Armor 3; Torso; Noisy)
- Fine traveling clothes
- Alchemist's kit
- Traveler's survival kit
- A riding horse or donkey

OPTIONAL:

- Faction membership in The Black Hand (see page 32)

BLOODY RIGHT HAND

Everyone needs a bastard; everyone who runs the streets knows the type — the dangerous ones, the ones without any fear or pity behind the eyes. The kind of person who doesn't ask "Why am I breaking this arm?" but instead ponders "In how many places?" This is the bloody right hand; the thief, enforcer and general purveyor of bad news found in every back alley in every city in every kingdom in the world. That's not to say there aren't regional differences; an Aquilonian right hand is likely to wield a cosh instead of a knife and to rely on intimidation more than violence. A Zamorian equivalent is likely to have half a dozen knives and be more than prepared to sheathe them in prospective targets.

Talented in a number of areas and with a willingness to attempt any crime, no matter how dangerous and difficult it may be, the bloody right hand is a survivor, capable at everything and of anything. Able to sense which way the tides of power are flowing — a notoriously difficult thing to do given how fast power dynamics can alter — the bloody right hand is loyal, as far as it suits him, and deadly, when given the opportunity. And every head of a thieves' guild employs a bloody right hand, in one way or another. It teaches the reality of thieving, more than it teaches the art.

PLAYING A BLOODY RIGHT HAND

You are the proverbial jack of all (criminal) trades; you have a grasp of how to achieve anything you might be tasked with. Sure, you might not be as fancy at climbing over a wall as a master thief but you're a damn sight cooler when fists and knives start flying. Perhaps you don't vanish into a crowd with the well-practiced skill of a spy, but you do well enough at hiding in plain sight and you'll be damned if the spy can pick three pockets at the same time. You're the backbone of the underworld. You're invaluable and never to be underestimated. Perhaps you felt it was time to break away from the crime lord you're serving — time to explore the world a little for yourself. Perhaps you see a route to the top opening up, if you can get some loyal men and women on your side. Perhaps you finally said "no" to one last murder. Who knows? Only you do. But the bloody right hand is going to make damn sure that he and his friends make it out alive.

CAREER SKILL: +2 Expertise and +2 Focus in Melee

CAREER TALENT: *No Mercy* (see page 73 of the CONAN corebook)

MANDATORY SKILLS: +1 Expertise and Focus to Observation, Parry, Ranged Weapons, and Thievery

ELECTIVE SKILLS: +1 Expertise and Focus to two of the following skills: Command, Persuade, or Stealth

EQUIPMENT:

- Two daggers or a sword
- Heavy clothing and a brigandine vest (Armor 3; Torso)
- Clothes and accouterments for a second identity
- Thieves kit
- Traveler's survival kit
- Riding horse or donkey

FENCE

There is always a middleman. How does the graven image of Ibis come to be in the hands of the wealthy, decorous nobleman? Does he buy it from a thief in an alleyway encrusted with grime and the sour vomit of a Nemedian mercenary? No, of course not. He has it brought to him by the fence. The man or woman who knows everyone. From the crudest street thug to the most eloquent scholar, the Fence is welcomed by anyone with something illegal to sell or who wants to buy something which can only be acquired through somewhat dubious means.

Fences are intelligent and subtle — or at least the best ones are. They survive by always knowing the right card to play at the right time, the right thing to say at the right moment. They know who can find just the right tool to pick that exquisitely complex lock or which brothel owner will hide a wanted thief in return for that little jade amulet. Canny, tough and ruthless, Fences are invaluable assets to their friends and companions and dangerous enemies to their foes. Because, if a fence can't beat you in a sword fight, he'll know just the person who can.

PLAYING A FENCE

As a fence, you're a strategist and a planner. You can gain access to places, using your reputation and innate capacity to gauge what a person wants and giving it to them in order to do so. You have an excellent sense for how much an object might be worth, of its history and provenance. You are an expert in thievery — though your practical skills might not be up to much, you make up for that by being accomplished in a number of other areas; moving between the very rich and the very poor has given you an unusual mixture of skills but that only means you can do things which no one expects you to be able to do.

CAREER SKILL: +2 Expertise and +2 Focus in Insight

CAREER TALENT: *Sixth Sense* (page 68 of the CONAN corebook)

MANDATORY SKILLS: + 1 Expertise and Focus to Lore, Observation, Persuade, and Thievery

ELECTIVE SKILLS: +1 Expertise and Focus to two of the following skills: Craft, Melee, and Society

EQUIPMENT:

- A single melee weapon (something dignified and unobtrusive: a dueling sword or dagger)
- Traveling clothes (nondescript, blending in anywhere)
- A magnifying glass
- Traveler's survival kit
- Riding horse or donkey

HIGHWAYMAN

If the skills gained in the Maul are likened to wielding a rapier, then the highwayman's technique is a blunt instrument. Using charm, intimidation, and the threat of violence to accomplish his goals, the highwayman takes what he needs to survive from unwary travelers, traders, caravans, and merchants.

There's a name for these bandits in every country. In Brythunia, they are called brigands. In Corinthia, they are outlaws. Nemedia calls them road agents. Whatever the term, the highwayman operates on the fringes of society, and rarely alone. All jackals hunt in packs.

Playing a band of highwaymen is certainly an option for a group of players, and not all of the players need to take this archetype. A sorcerer can travel within a gang of outlaws, as can a soldier or scholar. Otherwise, it is assumed that the highwayman is between gangs for a reason. This would relate to their war story, and likely provides a hook for future adventures. With the Road of Kings running through Zamora, Corinthia, and Nemedia, there are plenty of opportunities for like-minded individuals with the right amount of daring and bravado.

PLAYING A HIGHWAYMAN

Fellow thieves will surely not mind someone with the highwayman's abilities sharing the road with them, provided that everyone keeps one hand on their coins and the other away from their swords. Other types of characters may not be as forgiving, especially if there's a run-in with bandits in their backstory.

CAREER SKILL: +2 Expertise and +2 Focus in Persuade

CAREER TALENT: *Force of Presence* (page 76 of the CONAN corebook)

MANDATORY SKILLS: +1 Expertise and Focus to Command, Melee, Parry, and Thievery

ELECTIVE SKILLS: +1 Expertise and Focus to two of the following skills: Animal Handling, Linguistics, or Survival

EQUIPMENT:

- Two melee weapons of choice

- A suit of mail armor (Armor 3; All Locations; Noisy) or brigandine long coat (Armor 2; Torso, Arms, Legs) w/helmet (Armor 3; Head; Heavy)

- Plain traveling clothes

- Traveler's survival kit

- A cheap riding horse

MASTER THIEF

Far more severe than a mere honorific, the master thief has certain obligations and traditions to uphold. His code of honor is legendary, after all, and reflects not only upon himself but every other who make their living through relieving others of their wealth. Of course, this code of honor is a strange, confusing thing to any who aren't thieves. For instance, master thieves may never turn down an opportunity to steal, or sacrifice another thief in order to preserve their own lives. Master thieves are not simply thieves with greater skills than another: they are masters of thieves, the aristocracy of the underworld, and they must act like it. Master thieves are planners and plotters, whether working alone or with a hand-picked crew. Becoming a master thief requires the dedication of a lifetime — it is a path that must be decided upon at a young age and pursued with the diligence that sorcerers must commit to their study of rites and rituals. Agility, intelligence, and the means by which even the most highly guarded of locations can be broken into... all of this a master thief must learn.

Very few master thieves can call themselves thusly and not be Zamorian by birth. Those that do had to prove themselves and test their mettle at least twice, if not three times, before being grudgingly allowed to use the title.

PLAYING A MASTER THIEF

The master thieves of Zamora live by a code of honor. This allows for a measure of respect in certain quarters, and healthy contempt elsewhere. Master thieves all have a certain swagger, a confident bravado that makes them good as leaders of a small bands of thieves, or self-reliant in solo situations.

CAREER SKILL: +2 Expertise and +2 Focus in Thievery

CAREER TALENT: *Thief* (page 88 of the CONAN corebook)

MANDATORY SKILLS: + 1 Expertise and Focus to Athletics, Command, Observation, and Stealth

ELECTIVE SKILLS: +1 Expertise and Focus to two of the following skills: Acrobatics, Craft, or Persuasion

EQUIPMENT:

- Melee weapon of choice
- Padded Jerkin (Armor 1; Torso, Arms)
- One piece of unique thief equipment (one-shot, non-lethal)
- Thieves' kit
- Plain traveling clothes

RELIC HUNTER

Nemedia is the cultural center of the Western kingdoms, with vast holdings of ancient artifacts and lore that they have successfully used to model their civilization upon. The church of Mitra is especially eager to acquire these cultural relics, for posterity, you understand. And in doing so, it becomes necessary to employ certain people, with an eye for treasure and a vast network of contacts, to collect these precious objects.

The relic hunter is well-versed in the lore of the ancients and smart enough to know how to avoid trouble, most of the time. Rubbing shoulders with smugglers and less-trustworthy thieves is dangerous work, and the relic hunter can navigate those troubled waters with relative ease. Their knowledge of high society can be an asset in these situations.

PLAYING A RELIC HUNTER

Relic hunters are opportunistic to the point of ruthlessness. Whether working for a wealthy collector, the church of Mitra, or a head of state, their eyes are always on the prize, and they are not above withholding delivery of an antique if the price doesn't suit them. Not all relic hunters are untrustworthy, but there is always something in it for them in every job — be it wealth, renown, personal leverage, or all of the above — relic hunters make a note of every angle and plays the odds until they are in their favor.

CAREER SKILL: +2 Expertise and +2 Focus in Lore

CAREER TALENT: *Scribe* (page 72 of the CONAN corebook)

MANDATORY SKILLS: + 1 Expertise and Focus to Counsel, Observation, Society, and Thievery

ELECTIVE SKILLS: +1 Expertise and Focus to two of the following skills: Acrobatics, Craft, or Stealth

EQUIPMENT:

- A sword or two daggers
- One set of expensive clothes and a more common set of digging garments
- Mapmaking tools
- Excavating tools
- Traveler's survival kit
- Riding horse or donkey

SPY

In the civilized kingdoms of the world, there is overt diplomacy, often carried out in arranged marriages, exchanges of gifts, and bequeathing holdings. Then there is covert diplomacy, conducted by men with no name, who pry secrets from unwilling lips and bring them back to their masters to use as leverage in the next round of negotiations. Wherever there is politics, there is a need for spies. Spies and thieves spend a great deal of time together and, for those thieves who can restrict their urge to pilfer from pockets (unless absolutely necessary), spying can provide a path to a slightly more respectable way of life. If you survive long enough, of course. Thieves guilds also use spies, to ensure that the nobility isn't considering doing anything stupid like "cleansing the streets". Influence is power and spies are the ones who use it best.

Nemedia and Corinthia are hotbeds of political activity, and thus, are rich in opportunities for spies. Brythunia, too, makes use of spies on occasion. Zamora uses them extensively; in fact, Zamorians use spies in place of any other kind of diplomat, preferring instead to bribe and cajole through the judicious use of illegal trade and goods than negotiate like any other nation. In Zamora, the underworld is understood more than any other place on the continent, and the spy also knows that it is far more effective at ensuring deals get made, and adhered to, than other more traditional forms of diplomacy.

PLAYING A SPY

Good spies reveal nothing, give up nothing, unless it directly benefits them. Often, a spy will bait others into doing his job for him. The mission is all that matters, and there is nothing a good spy wouldn't do to obtain the information required. This would include betraying a colleague, if the stakes were high enough, but spies do their utmost to avoid this: they pick their comrades carefully, ensuring that their goals are aligned. And, if their comrades don't have any agendas beyond getting rich, so much the better.

CAREER SKILL: +2 Expertise and +2 Focus in Observation

CAREER TALENT: *Sharp Senses* (see page 74 of the CONAN corebook)

MANDATORY SKILLS: +1 Expertise and Focus to Linguistics, Persuade, Society, and Stealth

ELECTIVE SKILLS: +1 Expertise and Focus to two of the following skills: Lore, Melee, or Thievery

EQUIPMENT:

- Melee weapon of choice
- Heavy clothing
- Thieves' kit
- Set of plain clothes
- Traveler's survival kit
- Riding horse or donkey

THIEF EDUCATIONS

Players desiring more suitable educations for their thief characters may roll a d20 or pick an education. However, unlike those in the *Conan* corebook, these backgrounds represent specific training at the hands of a skilled type of thief. However, these are not mandatory. Player character thieves are nonetheless able to choose from educations in the corebook, as well as these.

THIEF EDUCATION			
Roll	Master	Roll	Master
1–2	Fence	11–12	Standover Man
3–4	Burglar	13–14	Spider
5–6	Confidence Man	15–16	Bandit
7–8	Rustler	17–18	Quack Physician
9–10	Lock Breaker	19–20	Thug

FENCE

You either worked for a local fence, paying attention the variety of items being brought in almost as closely as those who sought to sell them, or you dealt with a fence that took a particular liking to you, teaching you how to identify valuable items, to bargain for a good price, and to re-sell them without earning the attention of the law.

Mandatory Skills: +1 Expertise and +1 Focus to Lore, Observation, Stealth
Elective Skills: +1 Expertise and +1 Focus to two of the following skills: Animal Handling, Insight, or Society
Talent: One talent associated with any of the above skills
Equipment: An additional 3 🦅 in Gold (1 Gold minimum) and one item of value that cannot be easily sold. The gamemaster should determine the exact item, its worth, and its original owner(s).

BURGLAR

You spent your formative years as an apprentice or assistant to a burglar, as part of a small gang of thieves that focused on burglary, or you figured it out for yourself. You've learned how to case a potential site, search for traps, watch for guards, and how to get in and out without notice.

Mandatory Skills: +1 Expertise and +1 Focus to Athletics, Acrobatics, Stealth

Elective Skills: +1 Expertise and +1 Focus to two of the following skills: Discipline, Society, or Thievery
Talent: One talent associated with any of the above skills
Equipment: An additional 1 🦅 Gold (1 Gold minimum), a pry bar, and lockpicks.

CONFIDENCE MAN

Whether it was family or strangers who taught you how to spin elaborate lies and convince others to trust you, you learned the subtle art of persuading people to act against their best interests, spending money on junk or otherwise behaving in a manner contrary to their beliefs.

Mandatory Skills: +1 Expertise and +1 Focus to, Insight, Observation, Persuasion
Elective Skills: +1 Expertise and +1 Focus to two of the following skills: Alchemy, Athletics, or Healing
Talent: One talent associated with any of the above skills
Equipment: Three sets of clothing to help you blend in with your intended marks: noble, tradesman, and peasant.

RUSTLER

Unlike other thieves, you spent your youth in the countryside, working with a group of cattle — or horse-thieves. You learned how to find them and to move with stealth into their barns, corrals, or pastures and lead them away without detection, and to train them for later re-sale.

Mandatory Skills: +1 Expertise and +1 Focus to, Animal Handling, Craft, Survival
Elective Skills: +1 Expertise and +1 Focus to two of the following skills: Athletics, Melee, or Resistance
Talent: One talent associated with any of the above skills
Equipment: One riding horse, mule, or cow (pick one). A saddle and tack, if appropriate.

LOCK BREAKER

Many are the thieves who use brute force to get what they want, while your apprenticeship was spent poring over locks and other mechanical devices, learning how to disable and dismantle them. While others learn to steal and escape quickly, yours is the art of stealing and leaving no trace there was ever a theft.

Mandatory Skills: +1 Expertise and +1 Focus to Craft, Discipline, Thievery
Elective Skills: +1 Expertise and +1 Focus to two of the following skills: Alchemy, Lore, or Stealth
Talent: One talent associated with any of the above skills
Equipment: Locks, lockpick set.

STANDOVER MAN

Early on in life, you fell in with a standover man — someone who extorts money from tradesman through intimidation, usually a threat of violence. You went along as your mentor did their rounds, going from shop to shop and getting payment in return for being left alone. Sometimes it was necessary to show reluctant victims that it was no idle threat, but most of the time, the looming specter standing over them as they counted out their protection money was enough.

Mandatory Skills: +1 Expertise and +1 Focus to Discipline, Insight, Thievery

Elective Skills: +1 Expertise and +1 Focus to two of the following skills: Melee, Parry, or Resistance

Talent: One talent associated with any of the above skills

Equipment: An additional 3 ♆ Gold, an easily concealable hand weapon, and an apple taken from a vendor's stall.

SPIDER

To thieves, a "spider" isn't someone who climbs walls — it's someone who sits in the middle of the web, watching and waiting, then pouncing when prey comes along. You apprenticed with just such a mentor, learning how to cultivate sources, leads, connections... how to barter for information and how to create a web of contacts that could get you what you want, and to help you get what others want.

Mandatory Skills: +1 Expertise and +1 Focus to Observation, Stealth, Thievery

Elective Skills: +1 Expertise and +1 Focus to two of the following skills: Command, Insight, or Persuade

Talent: One talent associated with any of the above skills

Equipment: Fine set of clothing, fake documents or badge of office, contacts high and low.

BANDIT

Out in the countryside with a gang of like-minded thugs, you and your allies preyed upon travelers, merchant caravans, and others who dared leave the safety of cities and their estates. You learned how to pick those ripe for looting, and those to avoid.

Mandatory Skills: +1 Expertise and +1 Focus to Discipline, Resistance, Survival

Elective Skills: +1 Expertise and +1 Focus to two of the following skills: Ranged Weapons, Society, or Stealth

Talent: One talent associated with any of the above skills

Equipment: Wineskin and dried meat, heavy cloak, walking staff.

QUACK PHYSICIAN

You learned the healer's art alongside one who sold false remedies to unwitting peasants, sometime even pretending to be miraculously cured. Occasionally you and your mentor treated some of the high and mighty, relieving them of their imagined pains as easily as you did their coin. Despite selling little more than flavored oils and wines, you nonetheless learned a bit about actual medicine.

Mandatory Skills: +1 Expertise and +1 Focus to Counsel, Healing, Persuasion

Elective Skills: +1 Expertise and +1 Focus to two of the following skills: Alchemy, Lore, or Sorcery

Talent: One talent associated with any of the above skills

Equipment: Additional 2 ♆ Gold, healer's kit, 4 bottles of false cures.

THUG

At the basest level of thievery looms the thug, a brute with little finesse, style, or training, used as henchmen and muscle by criminals across the continent. Maybe a family-member was a thug, showing you the ropes, or you joined the entourage of a gang leader and learned the brutal techniques of thuggery there.

Mandatory Skills: +1 Expertise and +1 Focus to Melee, Ranged Weapons, Resistance

Elective Skills: +1 Expertise and +1 Focus to two of the following skills: Command, Discipline, or Persuasion

Talent: One talent associated with any of the above skills

Equipment: Blunt weapon of choice, leather jerkin (Armor 2; Torso), at least one intimidating scar.

THIEF WAR STORIES

Instead of a war story (determined in *Step Eight: War Story* on page 40 of the **Conan** corebook), thieves usually have heists of note, particularly big scores that they are known for and helped shape their worldviews. Thief characters can roll on the *Heists of Note* table, pick a desired result, or can choose instead to have a war story from those provided in the **Conan** corebook.

	HEISTS OF NOTE	
Roll	**Select Heists of Note**	**Skill Improvements**
1–2	Sacked a Mystery Cult Temple	+1 Expertise and Focus to Melee and Sorcery
3–4	Robbed a Merchant Caravan	+1 Expertise and Focus to Animal Handling and Persuade
5–6	Stole a Mysterious Object for a Stranger	+1 Expertise and Focus to Discipline and Insight
7–8	Robbed a Drunk of an Expensive Piece of Jewelry	+1 Expertise and Focus to Observation and Society
9–10	Sold Forged Goods in the Market	+1 Expertise and Focus to Athletics and Craft
11–12	Plundered a Merchant Vessel at Sea	+1 Expertise and Focus to Ranged Weapons and Sailing
13–14	Performed as "Angry Drunk" and "Out of Control Lover" While Robbing Tavern Folk	+1 Expertise and Focus to Parry and Persuade
15–16	Served a Nobleman as His Thief of Choice	+1 Expertise and Focus to Insight and Society
17–18	Survived a Horrible Gang War	+1 Expertise and Focus to Parry and Resistance
19–20	Planned and Executed Several Thefts with Skill and Precision	+1 Expertise and Focus to Stealth and Thievery

THIEF TALENTS

The following talents are especially useful for thief player characters, but might be allowed for others, at the gamemaster's discretion and if the prerequisites are met.

ATHLETICS TALENT
Perfect Cast

Prerequisite: *Strong Back*
Experience Point Cost: 200

You are highly skilled throwing rope where you want it to go, whether with grappling equipment or not, and securing it in advantageous spots. When climbing, you can reduce or increase the Difficulty for Athletics tests by one step. Everyone climbing the rope suffers the same bonus or penalty, which is decided when the rope is cast.

You can attack with a noose as if it were a regular ranged weapon. A noose counts as a Garotte with the Thrown (C) quality.

ALCHEMY TALENT
Poisoner

Prerequisite: None
Experience Point Cost: 200

You've made a study of toxic plants and animal venoms and can distill their essences down to a single dose, to be administered by mouth or at the end of a weapon. You have access to lotus powder petty enchantments and all other venoms. When using this petty enchantment, you may attempt higher Difficulty tests to increase the power of a particular enchantment, as if possessing the *Master of Formulae* talent for the poison. You may experiment during your downtime between adventures, to find and/or create other poisons with different effects, such as blindness (for example).

Such research requires a Daunting (D3) Alchemy test, and requires three times the amount of ingredients that the poison might need. Successful poison creation makes enough poison to coat a dagger blade or a handful of powder; in other words, a single dose, which is enough to affect a human-sized living creature. Once applied to a weapon, it must be used within a few hours or it will lose its potency. Powders will last much longer but are more difficult to administer and must either be fed to a character or released as a gas. Readying a poison to be released as a gas requires an additional Daunting (D3) Alchemy test to prepare the mixture. Once the mixture has been prepared, deploying it is managed as a standard Ranged Weapons attack which releases the poison with the Area quality. This test cannot be dodged with Acrobatics, but can be avoided with a Defend Reaction using the Alchemy skill.

This talent can be taken as an alternative to the *Alchemist* talent as the first step in the Alchemy talent tree (on page 58 of the **Conan** corebook).

LORE TALENT
Excavator

Prerequisite: None
Maximum Ranks: 3
Experience Point Cost: 200

You are trained to recognize, identify, and retrieve the relics of the past. When searching for any treasure or artifact, or when attempting to identify their use or value, any Difficulty test is reduced by one step. Additional ranks in this Talent generate 1 Momentum per rank in any related Difficulty test.

OBSERVATION TALENTS
It's a Trap!

Prerequisite: Observation Expertise 1
Experience Point Cost: 200

You can spot covered pits, pressure plates, fulcrums, and other constructions designed to keep thieves out of burial chambers and treasure rooms. With a successful Challenging (D2) Observation test, you can detect any nearby traps as a Minor Action. With this talent, as a Free Action you may then trigger these traps as an offensive weapon — using your foe's own weapons against them.

Architect

Prerequisite: Observation Expertise 1
Experience Point Cost: 200

You can sense changes in elevation, discrepancies in room size, spot camouflaged doors, and other hiding places that are built into a structure. If and when you walk past a secret space, the gamemaster is obliged to disclose that an entrance is concealed nearby. In return, the gamemaster adds 1 Doom to the Doom pool. This talent only reveals that a hidden space exists; it offers no indicators of what that hidden space contains.

Human Compass

Prerequisite: *Architect*
Experience Point Cost: 200

You have an innate sense of direction and can always find north, even with no visible markers. Whenever you are lost, you may add 1 to the Doom pool to be immediately given the correct direction to follow. This instinct is unerring — but might lead you into trouble if you aren't careful!

PERSUADE TALENT
Intimidate

Prerequisite: None
Experience Point Cost: 200

You can use your physical presence or carefully chosen words (or both) to compel obedience from others, whether through the threat of violence or social humiliation. Whenever making an appropriate Social test under these conditions, you generate 1 automatic success.

THIEVERY TALENTS
Jury Rigger

Prerequisite: *Journeyman, Master Thief*
Experience Point Cost: 400

A master thief works faster than lesser thieves and has developed shortcuts to getting the job done. With success on a Challenging (D2) Thieving test, you can work without thieves' tools. You must substitute more common items in order to complete the task. This success is only good for a single use and ruins whatever makeshift tools were being used in the process. Any Momentum from the test can be spent to provide an additional use per point of Momentum.

When you have access to your tools you gain bonus Momentum equal to your Skill Focus in Thieving, which may only be spent on reducing the time taken to complete the task.

Smuggler

Prerequisite: *Master Thief*, Craft Expertise 1
Experience Point Cost: 400

Smugglers can modify existing objects and structures to hide contraband and leave no trace that a hiding place exists. When making a test in order to hide any small item upon your person (or, when hiding a Medium — or Large-sized object onboard a wagon or a ship, for example), you automatically generate a number of successes equal to your Craft Skill Focus, to better avoid detection.

Picker of Locks

Prerequisite: *Master Thief*
Experience Point Cost: 400

The ability to open locked doors is, perhaps, the most important skill a thief can possess. Where some might be able to break open a door with strength alone, or others steal over a wall without rope or equipment, the safest and surest way into or out of anywhere is through the door. Whenever you fail a Thievery test, you can choose instead to succeed — at a price. In order to automatically succeed, you can add Doom to the pool in an amount equal to 1+ the Difficulty of the test.

SAMPLE CHARACTER NAMES		
Homeland	Male	Female
Brythunia	Kormark, Finnian, Gilduin, Golven, Griffeth, Jagor Watkin, Kervran, Kireg, Lennick, Maddock, Morvand, Pierig, Prothro Davies, Segalen, Tadek, Telor	Aliss Manoun, Amiere, Anwyn, Brynir, Catelinne, Cati, Estir, Glynnis, Gweneth, Lina Flavier, Lonore, Maegan, Merial, Rhiann, Siriol, Tonwen, Sibille
Corinthia	Ambrus, Anatar Lillus, Borus Gergo, Gorgar Sotir, Hegerus, Horvath, Latka Petir, Kordes, Makar, Orban, Vasmus, Milonas, Zalvatos	Cirsten, Divina, Evelina, Idania, Idola, Jarmila, Kotas Athan, Rea, Saffeera Nanos, Sica, Valetis, Vass Petra, Veres Farago, Xandra, Yalena, Zofia
Nemedia	Aractus, Bruccus, Castus, Fauthis, Galarius, Karthis, Larellis, Lucius, Maximus, Peddollus, Quintus, Septaius, Sevarus, Tiberas, Tranicus	Archaria, Augusta, Calva, Camilia, Festinia, Genesia, Lecintia, Lutatia, Munia, Octavia, Ripana, Saesta, Tadia, Vesnia
Zamora	Abdullah, Darvish, Dharsin, Fatari, Hamal, Hoonam, Kameen, Malir, Rubihir, Razavi, Sakara, Sorna Khan, Zafar, Zakosa Jagar, Zamehr	Banu, Behram, Cawasi, Fakkia, Farim, Govadia, Javadi, Kabellah, Kadin Boman Ravak, Namerian, Shapurana, Shendi, Veena Commis, Yamina

THIEF NAMES

The names below expand those provided those on page 48 of the **Conan** corebook, and can be used for players, as well as the gamemaster for non-player characters.

THIEVES' KITS

The collection of gear assembled for a particular job is collectively known as a thieves' kit, covering everything from lockpicks to lampblack. Whether secreted on the thief's person or in the kit itself, a kit can store three resources called Essentials in addition to the basic tools. These resources can be expended to provide an additional +1d20 on a Thievery skill test or can be expended individually to perform a trick of the trade.

A thief can plan ahead and attempt to procure exotic equipment for specific jobs. Such purchases do fill a slot in their thieves' kit, nor do they replenish a slot. The item is listed separately in the inventory and used when needed.

TRICKS OF THE TRADE

Aside from the standard tools in their kit, a thief may need more specialized gear from time to time. These specialized items are collectively known as "tricks of the trade". Thieves are not required to determine which tricks they have on them until they need to use them. Below are some sample tricks, but thief player characters are encouraged to work with the gamemaster to create personalized thematic tricks to capture the player characters' particular style or represent their level of ingenuity. These can also include alchemical items (for the relationship between thieves and alchemists, see page 106 of this book). These items can also be used as melee weapons in a way that common tools cannot.

THIEF EQUIPMENT		
Equipment	Damage	Effect
Pig Spit	—	Difficulty of Grapple escape reduced by two steps
Marbles	1 ♅ (see notes)	Surprises pursuer, requiring Average (D1) Athletics test to avoid if walking or Challenging (D2) if running.
Tripwire	1 ♅ (see notes)	Entangles target, stops pursuit for one action
Smoke Stick	—	Observation test Difficulty raised by two steps
Sutli Bomb	+1 ♅ mental	Stun, Blinding

Pig Spit

This thick, viscous oil is rubbed on the thief's exposed skin. The effect is twofold. If the thief has to wriggle into or out of tight spaces, the pig spit makes the test one step easier. Also, when the thief is grappled, the oil reduces the Difficulty of escaping the grapple by two steps. The thief may still take damage, but it is next-to-impossible to hold onto him.

Marbles, Tripwires, and Grease Pots

There are many ways that a cunning thief can cause a pursuer to fall behind him. Whether a well-timed handful of marbles dropped on a flat surface, a tripwire placed earlier, or a clay pot filled with slippery oil — the effect is the same. Every pursuer crossing the trapped zone must make an Acrobatics or Athletics test to avoid falling. The Difficulty of this test is equal to the number of Essentials used. Failure means the pursuers are knocked down and take 1⚔ damage. If the intended victim is if running, the Difficulty of the test is increases by one step, and can increase by additional steps in narrow entrances, poor lighting, or other concealment (such as grass). If the intended victim reduces their movement to slowly cross the affected zone, the gamemaster may decide no test is needed.

Alternatively, the thief can deploy caltrops. These small spikes count as Improvised weapons, and instead of causing a fall, will inflict 3⚔ damage to the pursuer, with any armor protection reduced to 1 point (regardless of how heavy a suit of armor is, it inevitably has leather boot soles).

More complicated to set up, but guaranteed effective, the thief hammers the tripwire into the wall and stretches it across an opening. A Daunting (D3) Awareness test spots the tripwire beforehand. Otherwise, anyone crossing the threshold is knocked prone. Anyone following behind the person who fell must make a Challenging (D2) Acrobatics or Athletics test or become entangled. Entangled characters require a Standard Action to extricate themselves from the tangle of cord and bodies.

Hidden Plate

By hiding a simple, clay plate against the torso, a thief can prevent immediate harm without needing to invest in the expense of armor. When used, this trick grants 1 Armor Soak to any blow that hits the torso location. This soak stacks with heavy clothing, but not with armor. Once used, the plate is cracked and offers no additional Soak value.

Smoke Stick

This mixture of alchemical elements, contained in a thin copper tube, has a startling effect when crushed beneath a foot. It releases a thick fog which fills an entire zone, raising all Observation tests by two steps of Difficulty for four standard turns. In order to use this item, it must be crushed, requiring an Average (D1) Brawn test.

Sutli Bomb

This unassuming little thing — a wreath of jute twine spun around a small alembic — is most commonly found in Vendhya, used in celebrations at the coronation of a new king or queen. When thrown at the ground with sufficient force, the alembic explodes, activating a curious powder within it, igniting the jute and causing a blinding flash of light and a deafening roar.

HIDDEN WEAPONS

Hidden weapons usually serve to foil pursuit, distract, or deliver a poison, powder, or other substance. They are small, portable, and easy to dispose of. Examples include caltrops, poisoned thorns, or thin clay pots that shatter on impact and splash enemies with their contents. Hidden weapons gain no damage bonus, and cannot be used to Parry an attack. Most of these weapons are available in sturdier versions for 4 Gold apiece. These versions are not Fragile.

COMMON POISONS

All poison is rare, and all poison is considered a one-shot item. It can be purchased or crafted by an alchemist. Poison in a powder or gas form can affect human-sized opponents in a single area, and as many as three human-sized targets at the gamemaster's discretion, but the Difficulty to

HIDDEN WEAPONS				
Weapon	Reach	Damage	Size	Qualities
Blowgun Dart/Poison Thorn	Range C	1⚔	1H	Fragile, Hidden 1, Non-lethal
Boot Blade	1	2⚔	—	Hidden 1, Persistent
Caltrops	1	2⚔	1H	Hidden 1, Piercing 2, Thrown
Clay Pot Grenade	Range C	1⚔	1H	Hidden 1, Spread 2, Thrown
Needle Ring	1	1⚔	1H	Hidden 1, Piercing 3
Push Dagger	1	3⚔	—	Fragile, Hidden 2, Vicious 1
Thumb Blade	1	2⚔	1H	Fragile, Hidden 3, Unforgiving 2

POISONS	
Poison	Effect per Ingredient or Trick used
Bile-Maker	Incapacitates victim due to vomiting and dehydration (one dose does 2⚔ damage per ingredient used)
Snake Venom	Poison (1 dose does 3⚔ Persistent 1 damage per ingredient used)
Sun Dust	Blurred vision increases the Difficulty of all tests requiring sight by one step (1 day per ingredient used)

SWORDS AND DAGGERS							
Weapon	Reach	Damage	Size	Qualities	Availability	Cost	Encumbrance
Dueling Sword	2	3🔥	1H	Parrying, Unforgiving 1	2	5	1
Katar	1	3🔥	1H	Parrying, Unforgiving 1	2	5	1

FLEXIBLE WEAPONS							
Weapon	Reach	Damage	Size	Qualities	Availability	Cost	Encumbrance
Garrote	1	2🔥	2H	Grappling, Hidden 2, Unforgiving 3	3	5	—

manufacture it is increased by one step, and one Wealth level higher in order to purchase. The *Poisons* table has examples of poisons player characters can research or create, and the **Conan** corebook has more information on poison.

CREATING NEW TRICKS OF THE TRADE

There are many useful items not covered, allowing player characters and gamemasters the agency to create their own useful items and kits. Player characters needing gear should tell the gamemaster what they want and the gamemaster then determines its feasibility using the guidelines above.

A new trick is always considered a one-shot item. If the player character seeks reusable equipment, then it is purchased as normal. A new trick of the trade confers one of three specific bonuses: bonus Momentum, a re-roll of 1d20, or reduced Difficulty.

Anything that can be scrounged together with common implements and objects does not count as a thieves' tool and does not use a slot in a thieves' kit. This only applies to specialized items that, while not alchemical, are still unusual, rare, and difficult to obtain.

Three examples of how specialized thieves' tools are used to help with a specific test are listed below. Each tool works differently to aid thieves in their endeavors. Creating any of these requires a single use of an Essential.

Grappling Hook

A length of rope attached to a climbing iron, anchoring it in place for lengthy climbs. Thieves can re-roll 1d20 when making a Climbing test using this device. The grappling hook's bonus is in addition to any bonus gained from a climbing kit and spikes.

Loaded Dice or Marked Cards

Useful for amassing some quick traveling funds, or any number of confidence schemes, these items provide 1 additional Momentum on a successful Gambling test.

A Small Flask of Aragh-e Sagi

A potent and rough liquor, *aragh-e sagi* can make even the most intolerant guard more pleasant. When shared, *aragh-e sagi* can loosen the tongue of those willing to talk. *Aragh-e sagi* provides 1 additional Momentum on successful tests to gain information using the Persuade skill.

THIEF WEAPONS
Dueling Sword

These light blades are carried by nobles and only rarely see combat. Though a dueling sword may be decorated with gems and precious metals, these lethal blades are as capable as any other sword, and are occasionally better-made.

Katar

With blades mounted horizontally to the hand instead of vertically like most common knives or swords these knife-like weapons are unusual but no less dangerous. The ability to "punch" with these blades allows for a rogue to penetrate deeply into a foe's body.

Garrotte

Innocuous lengths of wire studded to promote bruising and prevent the target from breathing, these weapons are deadly in the hands of one stealthy enough to get close and apply the right pressure to the neck. The garrotte is applied over a series of turns until the victim is dead.

CHAPTER 2

GAZETTEER

Torches flared murkily on the revels in the Maul, where the thieves of the east held carnival by night. In the Maul they could carouse and roar as they liked, for honest people shunned the quarters, and watchmen, well paid with stained coins, did not interfere with their sport. Along the crooked, unpaved streets with their heaps of refuse and sloppy puddles, drunken roisterers staggered, roaring. Steel glinted in the shadows where wolf preyed on wolf, and from the darkness rose the shrill laughter of women, and the sounds of scufflings and strugglings. Torchlight licked luridly from broken windows and wide-thrown doors, and out of those doors, stale smells of wine and rank sweaty bodies, clamor of drinking-jacks and fists hammered on rough tables, snatches of obscene songs, rushed like a blow in the face.

— "The Tower of the Elephant"

The kingdoms of Zamora, Nemedia, Corinthia, and Brythunia represent some of the larger struggles of power in the Hyborian Age. As East meets West, the rich subjugate the poor and barbarians clash with civilization. Each kingdom possesses a unique identity and problems specific to the regime, but they are alike in a one way: what they lack in military might, they more than make up for in guile and cunning.

Zamora is best-known for its two sister cities, Zamora the Accursed and Shadizar the Wicked. This country is famous for its thieves, who claim to have perfected the subtle art. Zamora is an old kingdom, one that was ravaged by many wars and strange sorcery thanks to its location. Zamora's long-standing ties to the kingdoms in the east have eroded, accounting for only a glimmer of its former prestige. The nation's primary export is skulduggery.

Corinthia is largely composed of city-states wielding considerable economic power in overlapping regions. These cities — Magyar, Stregos, and Krotoa — were cultivated by expatriates from Koth, Zamora, Stygia, and elsewhere, people tired of oppressive regimes, high taxes, and religious intolerance. The city-states grew out of these trading ports and now hold considerable economic power, but very little political power, due to constant infighting between various factions.

THE LANDS TO THE EAST

These four countries represent the discordant viewpoints and cultures in the Hyborian Age, specifically the differences between new political regimes on the ascent and the decadent cultures whose time has passed. In the cycle of barbarism versus civilization, Zamora, Corinthia, Nemedia, and Brythunia represent the faded luster of older cultures. But the old snake still has venom, and these four kingdoms will not go quietly into the night.

Political control is a key component in each of these nations. Power is tenuous and fleeting. The fate of a political coup often rests along the edge of a sword. Agents of every stripe, both overt and clandestine, cross paths with one another on the open road and in the banquet halls. They break bread as often as they break bones.

Power and influence are major resources that change hands frequently, and certain types of people could make much of this. Whether it's stealing important documents from couriers or simply taking advantage of the political chaos to line one's pockets, there's no shortage of jobs for people possessing certain less-socially-acceptable skills and talents...

Nemedia is an old kingdom, built upon the foundations of earlier peoples. Large stone and brick structures have been repurposed for these blonde-haired, blue-eyed Northern descendants and their adopted and occasionally invented culture. Years of wars and border disputes in every direction have forged the Nemedian army into a formidable defensive force.

Brythunia is a land of extremes — of cold, of cruelty, of ferocity. The conquering Hyborian savages moved south into new lands and forged small fiefdoms for themselves where they could continue their ancient tribal feuds in relative peace. The lords cling tenaciously to their scraps of land and fight tooth and nail for every inch of dirt. Western influence brought a semblance of order to the wilderness, and political business is now handled through marriage and, occasionally, a good old-fashioned raid to grab some hostages for trade.

All four countries, while being very different in peoples and cultures, have a kind of shared history in that they are both conquerors and the conquered. Warfare, insurgent occupancy, and political violence figure heavily into their communal past.

These countries also represent, rather broadly, the gateway from the west to the east by way of the ancient trade route known as the Road of Kings. While not strictly at odds with one another, the uneasy truce and fluid alliances between the city-states in Corinthia and the trade centers in Zamora and Nemedia allowed a thriving black market to emerge. This is the underside of civilization, where anything can be bought and sold, from family heirlooms to human life. In a time of general unease, plots are sketched out and plans hatched.

There is always need for someone willing to do what needs to be done, be it for personal gain, for gold and jewels, or for some noble ideal. That these actions go against the laws of the land is immaterial. This world is brutal and harsh. The master thieves of Zamora and their loose affiliation of tricksters, brigands, murderers, and burglars have no end of business opportunities in such troubled times...

ZAMORA

Located on the Eastern flank of Great Western Powers, Zamora serves as a gateway to the East and also as a barrier, due to the mountain ranges that surround the west, north, and east that keep this ancient civilization shrouded in mystery and intrigue. Zamora shares a border with Brythunia in the north, Corinthia in the west, and Koth in the south. To the east, held in check more by a fear of Zamora's sorcerers than the nearby mountain range, are the Turanian steppes.

Despite the fearsome climate — dry and arid, rimmed with foreboding mountains and cliffs — the kingdom is moderately populated, with most of the people in or around two major cities. These are Zamora the Accursed and Shadizar the Wicked. A third city, Yezud, is much smaller in comparison but steeped in mystery and rumor. Between these cities are a number of villages and farms that serve as rest stops for the travelers, pilgrims, and merchants that crisscross Zamora on their way to better fortunes and nicer climes.

TURANIAN PREJUDICE

Although the last occupation of Zamora by the Turanians ended a great many years ago, Zamorian memories are long and they are slow to forgive. Their cosmopolitan reputation notwithstanding, any Turanian player character making a Society test against a Zamorian must attempt it at one step of Difficulty higher. Should the player character fail the test, they are unable to interact with the Zamorian citizen in a peaceful manner. An angry Zamorian would rather draw a dagger and curse than tell some Turanian son-of-a-jackal where the nearest temple of Bel is to be found.

ZAMORIAN HISTORY AND BACKGROUND

Zamorians can trace their lineage back to the Thurian Age as descendants of the Zhemri people, about which nothing is known except that which may be mirrored in Zamorian culture. Zamora has twice been under the control of foreign invaders, and as a people, they vowed there would never be a third instance. To this end, Zamora developed a number of covert and overt countermeasures against foreign occupants. Some think this is the beginning of Zamora's culture of vice, in particular that of thieves in Zamora the Accursed and the assassins in Shadizar the Wicked.

Zamora is politically neutral to Brythunia, and friendlier with Corinthia and Nemedia, thanks to the Road of Kings, a major trade route that runs through those countries. Publicly, Zamora is cordial to Koth, but secretly they are close allies. Koth has designs on the southern portion of Zamora, and Zamora relies on a close relationship with Koth to better know when Koth intends to disregard their alliance and attack.

To this day, Zamorians despise their previous conquerors: the Hyrkanians and, more recently, the Turanians.

Zamorians are dark-complexioned with dark brown or black hair. The men are barrel-chested and the women voluptuous. They are physically similar to Zingarans, with whom they may share their lineage. Despite their turbulent history, Zamorians are happy and positive as a rule, to the point of being over-confident and boastful.

MAJOR CITIES OF ZAMORA

At one point in the development of Zamora it was considered a sacred land, and the city of Shadizar was built up as a gathering place for the various temples and their followers. During the two occupations of Zamora, as prayers for deliverance went unanswered, many turned away from the old gods and embraced a more licentious lifestyle that ensured their survival.

Zamora the Accursed and Shadizar the Wicked benefit from the close proximity to the Road of Kings; because of this, they are major centers of commerce and recreation, respectively. Yezud is far enough away from the Road of Kings that getting there requires intention on the part of the traveler. Thanks to the Spider-God cult, there is no shortage of pilgrims making that regular journey. Yezud also serves as an out-of-the-way meeting place for people who prefer to do their business away from prying eyes.

Villages and trading posts dot the rude trails leading off and away from the Road of Kings and the ancient roads, now all-but-obliterated by the desert winds. Many of the farms nestle between the hills and abut the mountains and cliffs, the better to catch the rare rainfall.

ZAMORA THE ACCURSED

Zamora is also the sitting capital of the King, Jaagir the Formidable. Though somewhat curtailed by the influence of the sorcerer Yara, who has held his court hostage for years with his foul magic, the king enjoys a free hand oppressing the people of the region. Himself a very pious

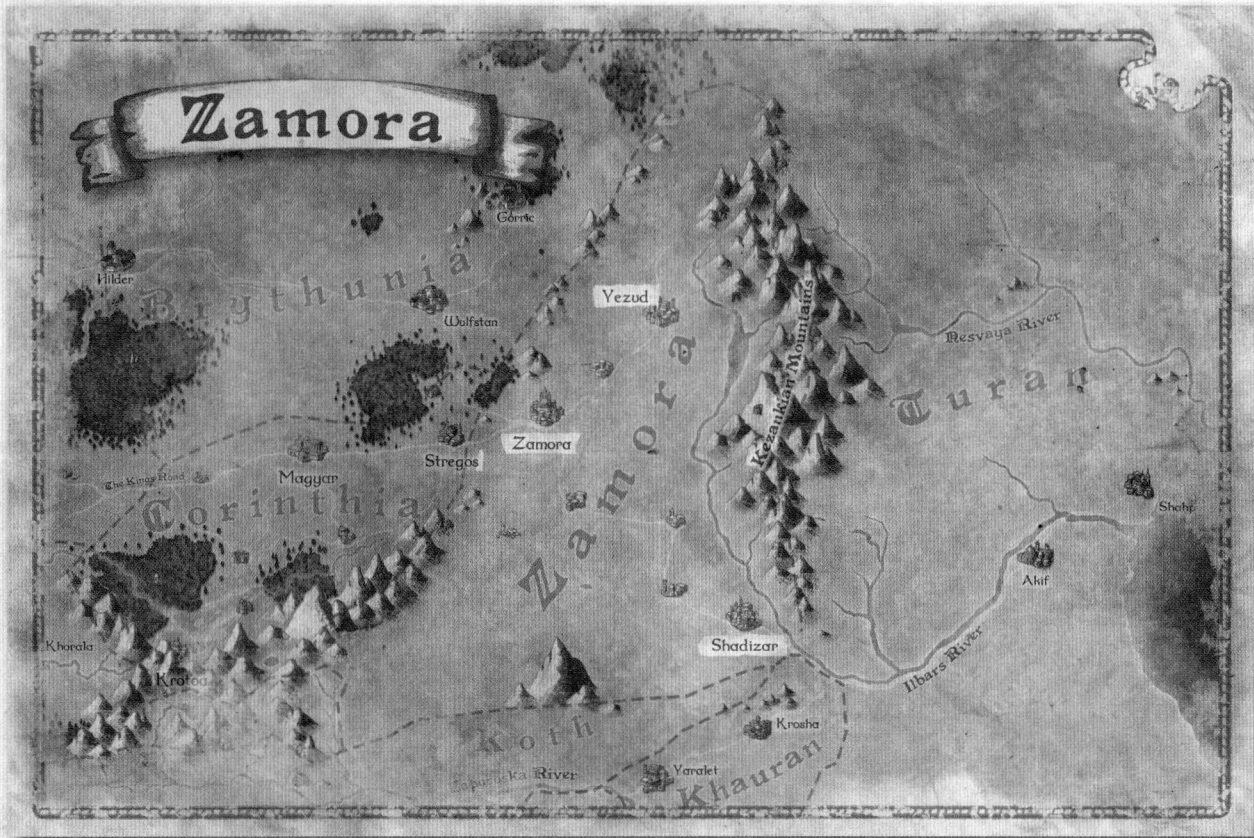

man, and also paranoid and secretive, he is rarely seen in public and keeps a wary distance between himself and his subjects, preferring instead to let his vassals, wazirs, and loyal guards carry out his wishes and enforce his polices.

Accursed Zamora is an ancient city, once a shining example of civilization and piety for the kingdom. But that was ages ago, and now many of the massive temples that once were the hallmark of the city have been torn down or repurposed. All of the gilt has long since been scraped off of the tall fluted columns by thieves' knives, and all of the precious stones pried out of their settings around the high domed roofs by eager and desperate hands. Only the palace remains untouched, walled off, high on one of the hills that bracket the city, overlooking the rows of brick and wood structures that are now crammed between the ruins of much greater buildings. Zamora the Accursed is a city of extreme poverty and obscene wealth.

Centuries of warfare, sorcery, revolt, and rebuilding lend a haphazard feel to the Zamorian skyline. The city lies roughly parallel across a sloping hill, with the capital high above and the remnants of old town below. The streets are wide and paved, though they may be in need of repair, depending on where you are in the city. The neighborhoods are identified through street names and prominent businesses, and these smaller collections are contained within the districts outlined below. Residences in Zamora the

Accursed are found in every district, though they may not be directly accessible from main thoroughfares.

Zamora the Accursed is where thieves from all over the region — and every corner of the map — gather to trade lies, hone their craft, spend their money, and pick up work.

The Main Gate

The walls of Zamora have long ago fallen into disrepair, but the main gates on the western road leading into town are still standing; fifteen feet tall at the top of the stone spires, jutting five feet above the packed earth and stone walls, with niches for lanterns held in place with hooks and chains. There are always at least two guards present; four or more during the caravan season, but the guards only stop and question people they deem suspicious. And these suspicions, by the way, can be easily alleviated by the application of gold into a guardsman's hand.

Anyone entering the city as part of a merchant caravan or within a train of travelers won't be stopped and questioned. Lone travelers or anyone who looks suspicious will be asked their business. Four guards are usually stationed here, in shifts. The rest of the city watch patrols the various neighborhoods in groups of two. Depending on the neighborhood, sometimes multiple patrols will be assigned.

The city watch will only investigate overt acts of thievery; people who are new to the city, the young, and the inexperienced will be chased vigorously through the crowds, with weapons drawn and much fanfare. Caught thieves will be paraded before the sullen crowd, as if daring the population to call Zamora "the City of Thieves". It's all theater, and everyone knows it, but they play their parts, all the same.

The Market Place

Here is the source of commerce in Accursed Zamora. Whether you need to hire transportation, buy a new sword, purchase nice clothes, or restock your provisions, the market is the place to do it. Not only is the main market here, but also the homes of just about everyone who works in the district. Player characters attempting to sell items might not get a fair price for their treasures, but then again, they won't get robbed at dagger point, either.

City guards are present and they make an effort to be vigilant, but they cannot be everywhere at once. For that reason, many merchants employ hired muscle to help them with shop security.

Most common items, gear, and weapons and equipment can be found among the many stalls. Prices will be somewhat higher, and customers are expected to haggle down to something close to the listed value (but not always).

The Maul

The smallest district in Accursed Zamora is no less densely packed, being a carved-out niche of the temple district and the market district. It's only four blocks long, and spans the adjoining streets on either side of the main thoroughfare. It is impossible to see from the roofs because of the covered awnings and leaning boards that block out the sun and also prying eyes. First time visitors who venture out of the Maul will invariably get lost in the snarl of cul-de-sacs and alleys and will certainly encounter some of the locals, who are happy to lead them back to the main street, for a small donation, of course. The length of the Maul is lit with lanterns and torches, creating stark pockets of warm light and pitch black shadows. The paved stones have long since been worn away or pried up, since the packed dirt makes less sound when walking.

Not everyone in the Maul is a thief by trade; some are thieves only in the eyes of others. Mercenaries, sell-swords, and other strong arm thugs can be found easily enough in the taverns and drinking halls. Anyone with a larcenous intent will eventually make their way to the Maul to conduct their business. And the traders know exactly how much they can cheat the thieves of Zamora without fear of reprisals. That *esprit de corps* does not apply to merchants outside of the Maul, however, and they are more likely to prey upon a desperate thief in need of quick cash.

City Of ZAMORA

1	Market district
2	The Maul
3	Inner district
4	Temple district
5	Palace district
6	Old Town
7	Tower of the Elephant
8	North Gate
9	South Gate

The main avenue in the Maul is famed for its array of taverns, inns, and recently dead bodies; to some it has become known as Crookback Street, though whether such a name is likely to stick, who can say? It was originally an outdoor market with small buildings and vendor's stalls on either side. At some point in the city's long history, a series of arched frames were placed regularly down the street, with stretched canvas tarps covering them. Over the years, the tarps have been replaced by wooden planks, cloth sacks, and other patchwork repairs, maintaining the cover, if not the integrity, of the enclosure. Narrow buildings and small kiosks crowd the street on both sides of the street, selling all manner of dark delights from pleasurable company to deadly poisons. Here the trade craft of the thieving profession is out in the open, and guards are paid well to never turn down the darkened street, where disagreements usually are settled among peers.

Even more narrow side streets lead deeper into the district to other less reputable and more unsavory establishments. Slaves are bought and sold out of sight and assassinations plotted and paid for. Back alleys wind and turn, like a labyrinth, depositing wanderers onto side streets outside the Maul, or worse, right back into it. Despite these narrow confines, the denizens of the Maul all display a relaxed, if not unguarded, demeanor. The laughter is free and easy, but there's always one hand resting on the pommel of a dagger or sword.

In the center of the Maul is the remnant of the original market, now a pavilion of debauchery. Most of the businesses on either side of the stalls and tents are solid stone, with domes and arches and other trappings to remind people that the city was once a better place. The largest tavern is located here, a cheerful nest of cutthroats and brigands called The Serpent's Pit, where characters can carouse and try to find gainful employment.

Other establishments around this open-air market sell goods and commodities at a hefty mark up. Haggling is expected here, and considering that so much of the merchandise is stolen, the profits are high. Specialized thieves' tools are available at listed prices.

The Capital District

This fortress-like mansion looms high over the city, surrounded by tall, sturdy walls, and buttressed on three sides by the city guard's barracks and town armory. The king's personal guard lives inside the walls, and they — along with the king — are seldom seen. Also included in this district are the blacksmiths, butchers, and other essential shops that service the guards and the castle, as well as the wealthiest members of Zamorian society. In the capital district, the shop keepers and artisans will not waste time with anyone who does not look and act like a member of the upper class. Any disguise or ruse that is less than perfect will ensure that prices for goods and services are doubled, or even tripled.

The Temple District

The large, boxlike structures with domed ceilings that line the Royal Road leading up to the always-closed gates of the capital have seen better days. Those temples closest to the King's presence enjoy a measure of traffic from citizens and visitors alike. The priests of Anu and Bel, and a host of other gods and goddesses, fling incense about and say their prayers and chant their songs and ring their bells dutifully, if not piously. At the far end of the street, near the east gate, is the cult of the Spider-God, fresh from Yezud, attempting to curry favor with the rogues that skulk there looking for unwary zealots to rob. In the center of the district is a tall, smooth, featureless tower, surrounded by high walls and many guards.

Not far from the East Gate entrance is an open courtyard with statues and a central fountain that now merely trickles water. This is the Courtyard of the Philosophers, and it is here that the clergy and the unhinged gather daily to debate the laws and scriptures and edicts of their gods and religions. One or two city guards are on hand in case an argument escalates into a physical squabble. There is no temple or church in Zamora that is not well-protected from thieves. Any character attempting to rob a church is in for a surprise. Even small, unpopular religions like the church of Ibis have guards on hand in the evening to deter anyone from trying to make off with the week's offerings.

The Tower of the Elephant

This is the home and lair of the wizard Yara, known colloquially as the Tower of the Elephant. Yara is a priest, and also a sorcerer of renown and is unequivocally the political power in Zamora. He is widely feared by all, including the king. It is no secret that he has the king's ear and is the true power behind the throne. This allows Yara to conduct his research and experiments with impunity and to act as he pleases. The tower stands high above the city, a tempting prize for many a thief who has attempted to penetrate its defenses and lost their life. Interfering with any part of Yara's operation, even unknowingly, would invite a powerful enemy who would make life very difficult for the player characters.

The tower remains the most famous point in the city, and still draws crowds of admirers, despite its reputation. It is not simply the astonishing architecture of the place which has so secured its infamy — the strange odors and sounds which regularly emanate from the enormous, crystal edifice and spread across the city like storm clouds are also loathed and feared by residents in equal measure. The interior of the tower is, likewise, a mystery. Its corridors are never the same, with some claiming that the tower can be seen to rotate at night, twisting itself into impossible geometries as though it were alive. Others claim the tower is sentient; after all, they reason, it was raised in a single night — perhaps it simply walked here, an animate edifice which Yara tamed for himself. Stranger things have been known, they will say (though do not ask them to name one). Some say the round, smooth-walled tower is haunted by ghosts, summoned by Yara, and no one can dissuade the thieves of Zamora from this story. More than one thief has fallen from the walls, or been found dead in the garden (mauled by a strange animal), or simply gone mad from the effort. City guards swing by the abandoned garden on their patrols, but don't stop to investigate unless they hear or see something. The gardens teem with terrifying creatures: lions and other, crueler, stranger things which those who have glimpsed them claim could not have been real. Whether they are or not remains to be discovered by men and women bold — or reckless — enough to enter those eerie grounds.

Old Town

This portion of Accursed Zamora was razed to the ground in the dim past by countless invaders. These ruins have been reclaimed and repurposed by the working poor and the lower classes. As many as fifteen or twenty families may live in a single, partially demolished temple with a wooden roof and tarps to keep the occasional rain at bay.

Parts of Old Town rise up over gentle rolling hills and mounds, and few remember that it's these mounds that are actually the rubble of larger buildings, such as temples and museums, that were destroyed so long ago. Some of these ruins actually extend beyond the walls of the city to the north and east — for the walls now protecting the city are new, rebuilt over the destruction. These ruins on the outskirts of the city hide deep, dark secrets. The general population considers them to be both haunted and cursed, and will not willingly venture into them. There are at least four entrances to the crypts below Old Town, and one of these leads to the ruins on the other side of the wall. What is below Old Town is mostly cleared out, except for a few lingering animals who call the crypts home. But there are a few places not discovered that would be ideal for adventurers to explore and possibly loot.

The Ruins

Zamora is an old city, ravaged by wars, sorcery, and neglect, and there are portions of the ancient city that are now little more than a rough foundation for the current residents. These ruins extend well outside the partially collapsed city walls on the south and east sides of the city. There is no shortage of caves, tunnels, or even sewer mains that lead down into the dusty and crumbling remnants of the city. Some of the sites are rumored to be as old as the Zhemri culture, but this may be nothing more than idle gossip among thieves.

YARA

Yara famously reaps the consequences of his malice and lust for power at the climax of Howard's "The Tower of the Elephant". While the above is written with the idea that the player characters explore the tower before Conan visits, when you set your games is entirely up to the gamemaster.

Depending on the point at which the adventure takes place, the player characters might attempt to conduct their own heists in the Tower of the Elephant, pre-empting the activities of Conan and Taurus of Nemedia. Alternatively, they might have to rescue a fellow thief from the clutches of Yara's guards. If the gamemaster prefers to set an adventure after Conan's visit, then the player characters might be raiding the grounds for jewels, magical artifacts and other remnants which Yara's demise has left free for those daring enough to claim them. The strange maulings that still occur from time to time in the tower's precincts could be the result of a single lion left untouched by Conan and Taurus. Or it could be the vengeful ghosts of the lions poisoned by Taurus, or something sinister once under Yara's control, now set free by his death. It could also be nothing more than a rumor.

Perhaps the player characters can investigate the elevated garden that surrounds the tower. Once, perhaps, it was a crown jewel set in the city of Zamora, but, after Yara's death, thieves might grow bold and steal over those walls once thought to mark the boundary between life and death itself. Then all that is left is to make off with the gems once set into the top edge of the tower.

As though things are ever that simple…

There is still much to explore amid the ruins outside of Zamora, and these are the perfect settings for novice thieves in need of experience. Does an ancient cult gather here, to enact hideous rituals in worship of unimaginable gods? Has a princess been kidnapped and hidden away in the ruins, or does a bandit chief use these ruins as the staging post for his raids on caravans? Who knows? The point is, it might be worth your characters' while finding out.

SHADIZAR THE WICKED

The sister city to Zamora the Accursed, Shadizar is neither as war-torn nor as restrictive, thanks to being out from under the thumb of the king. Once the religious center of the country, the temples have since relocated to Zamora, and their current occupants are far less pious but just as desirous of freely offered coin.

The city was originally designed in the shape of a wheel, with the various temples in the "hub" at the center, and the major streets radiating out from the center like spokes. Those temples are now houses of prostitution, gambling halls, and the homes of Shadizar's infamous assassins.

The streets themselves act as *de facto* districts, and like businesses and institutions are grouped along parallel roads. All of the major thoroughfares run into the city center, where they terminate into an open area that at one time was the cultural center of the city. Now, those buildings serve another purpose. Cross streets and side streets abound, and they are where the citizens live in modest to ramshackle homes made of brick and clay.

The City Gates

Three gates provide access to Shadizar from various trade routes entering the city, and they are all regularly guarded and well attended to. Few are stopped on the way into Shadizar unless they show open hostility or malice.

North Gate

The road leading up to the north gate is known as the Pilgrim's Path, a tongue-in-cheek reference to the number of acolytes to and from Yezud who use this road.

The north gate enters into Nobles Street, a large boulevard of exquisite homes for the wealthy. These houses are well kept, and their owners represent very old families who have lived in Shadizar for hundreds of years. Some of the more successful merchants and priests also call Nobles Street their home.

West Gate

The road that feeds into the west gate is known as the Merchant's Way, and it leads travelers straight to the Road of Kings and Zamora beyond. Caravans are a regular sight along this highway.

The west gate transforms into Market Street, the source of commerce in Shadizar. Here, one may purchase goods and supplies, food and drink, and anything else player characters may need. As Market Street continues into the heart of the city, the shops become more gaudy, shopkeepers more aggressive, and the merchandise more scandalous. At the point where Market Street terminates into the city center, a regular slave auction is found with people buying criminals and hostages with years left still to pay on a sentence or a debt.

South Gate

The southern road leading into Shadizar is called the Sand Road, and it was once the main trade route before the Road of Kings was established. Now, it is primarily used for caravans from the south for which Shadizar is their final destination.

The south gate opens onto Maker Street. This street is also a wide boulevard, much like Nobles Street, lined with master craftsmen and their wares; blacksmiths, leather workers, wheelwrights, brewers, coopers, and all other manufacturers make excellent goods and furnishings. Artists, too, have shops and studios here and produce artwork, tapestries, sculptures, and more.

Nobles Street

Nobles Street and the streets on either side of it are where the upper class conduct their business. There are temples here; smaller, less stately than the giant structures that mark the city center, but they are in good standing and carry modest congregations. Guards are always present during daylight hours, and regular posts and patrols at the major intersections ensure that revelers don't take a wrong turn and disturb the sleeping, or mistake one of their stately manors for a house of ill repute.

Temple of the Spider God

In the middle of Nobles Street, not quite in the bad part of town and just on the other side of the respectable businesses, is a large square stone structure that now serves as the temple of the Spider-God cult. The torches in the iron sconces are always lit, and acolytes scurry in and out of the temple at all hours of the day and night, going about

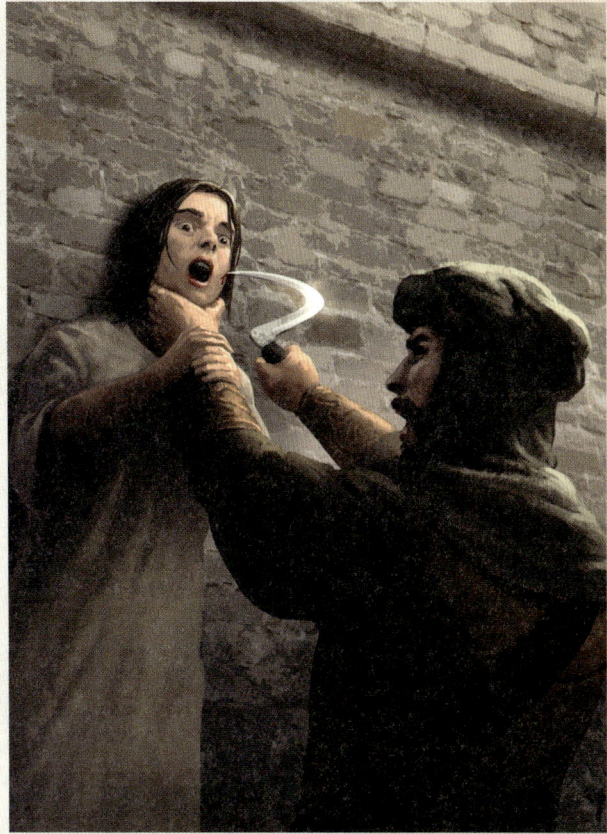

City of Shadizar

1 Temple of the Spider God
2 The Heart of Shadizar
3 Hall of the Black Hand
4 Dagoth Hill
5 The King's Hall
6 The Temple of Gold
7 The Slaughterhouse
8 North Gate
9 South Gate
10 West Gate
11 Black Hand Safe House
12 Noble Street
13 Fleck Street
14 Lantern Street
15 Maker Street
16 Market Street

the business of the cult and occasionally escorting dazed travelers into the building.

It's rumored that one of the giant spiders from the Zamorian hills is installed in the upper chambers of the building. Some will even brag of having seen it, along with a sufficiently lurid description of the monster. Locals shun this building, much in the same way that many of them do not go into the city center without a good reason. Cultists wear gray robes and are polite, inviting and, if their intended victim is weak-willed, insistent that they explore the temple and experience the wonders of the celestial spider (see page 73 for more on the Spider-God cult).

Fleck Street

This avenue runs northeast from the center of town and contains Old Town. Most of the working poor, the servants, and the regular citizenry who are trying to get by live in these wood and stone buildings. There are several small open air markets and stalls nestled in-between the densely packed houses that sell fruits, vegetables, and even chickens and eggs.

Lantern Street

Lantern Street runs in a southeast direction from the city center. It's named for the colorful lanterns that adorn these ramshackle hovels and create a carnival-like atmosphere at night, but make no mistake: those lanterns advertise something very specific, and the color of the lantern tells the regular patron what to expect inside the building in question.

Many who live in this area of town also work there. Its reputation as a district of ill-repute ensures that a steady stream of guards, well-to-do travelers, politicians and priests — all with a pretense of having other business to conduct — make sure they take a stroll down Lantern Street and spend an agreeable hour or two.

Maker Street

The street running due south of the city center is known as Maker Street, and it's where one can find no end of fine art, both beautiful and blasphemous, in the form of elegant tapestries, hand-dyed silks, paintings, statuary, jewelry, and much more. Even mundane items are decorated with intricate carvings and delicate stains and paints adorn furniture, leather, armor, and even weapons.

All prices for mundane items are doubled here, and uncommon or unique items cost five times more than the listed prices. This does not apply to thieves' tools, or other tools of the trade, which cannot be obtained here.

As Artisan's Row moves closer to the city center, the statues become more lewd, the paintings more suggestive, and the artists more depraved. Visitors to Shadizar walk only as far as their comfort level, and then turn around when their sensibilities have been strained past the point of decency and personal morality.

Market Street

Every block on Market Street is grouped around a different commodity. Woodworkers are near the front gate, as are stonemasons. Farmers and florists are located centrally, about halfway down the wide street. Food traffic and carts move slowly, as pedestrians clog the thoroughfare and the streets, crisscrossing in all directions and heedless of the right-of-way. The locals know the trick of taking parallel streets to the block where they need to shop, and then retreating when they have made their purchases.

Closer to the city center, the merchandise changes and so does the character of the street. Stolen goods are openly hawked in rickety stalls and shabby tents, and used items like leather jerkins with only a single knife thrust through the breast are available for sale at cut-rate prices. At the edge of Market Street, facing the city center, is an auction block used for trafficking human lives. The men who run the auction block have a contract with the city to sell petty criminals to traveling merchants, wealthy farmers, and flesh peddlers when the jails are overcrowded.

Each block on Market Street leading into the city center is grouped around what is sold. Livestock and food, for example, is closest to the outside of the hub. Vegetables are on the next block. Textiles, rugs, and silk after that. Rare and wondrous items are in short supply, for what foolish merchants would paint targets on their back? But common items are easily obtained at fair prices. Seedier commodities, and seedier merchants, are located closer to the city center. At least one block in this area could serve as a clearinghouse for folks unloading stolen goods.

The City Center

Known as "The Heart of Shadizar" (and a black heart it is), this wide, open island is circular as is the street that surrounds it. Here's where the major thoroughfares terminate from as far off as the city gates, and other smaller streets branch out from this circular hub, as well. In the circle, all things are permitted and all vices encouraged. The guards are paid well to stay clear of the city center, and murder and robbery is commonplace. It's the city center that gives Shadizar its reputation for wickedness.

There are several noteworthy businesses and institutions here. This is the place where player characters are likely to get in the most trouble, guaranteed. Any newcomers into the city center are watched as closely as predators watch potential prey. Eventually, someone or something will test the players and, if they don't respond accordingly, it will color all future business in Shadizar — especially with

the criminal element. Whether they are propositioned, challenged, insulted, or just ignored, the underworld of Shadizar expects a certain response from fellow predators... and an entirely different response from prey.

The Black Hand Safe House

This unassuming grog house serves overpriced, watered down ale and spirits to newcomers. But, if you know what to order, and know the words to say, you can get a message to the Black Hand. You might request an audience, get paid, or avail yourself of any number of other functions that go with being a dead drop for a group of secret assassins.

The bar, known as The Thundercloud, has several regulars who know exactly what the place is and what it's used for. That does not prohibit them from drinking, dicing, and in all other ways making full use of the place.

The Hall of the Black Hand

Once the home of a local potentate and self-appointed "savior of Shadizar", this large, square building was fully claimed by the Black Hand. It was taken from its previous owner at the point of a knife (a knife that, a few weeks later, was inserted into his spine) and brutally converted from a luxuriously appointed residence into something resembling a fortress. Murder holes were bored through thick walls, defensive spikes planted on top of walls once decorated only with ivy, and doors reinforced with layers of iron and steel. Few enter the Hall itself: indeed, there are almost none who can attest to the door ever opening, yet the lights always burn in the windows and sometimes revelry echoes from within. More often, though, the building stands in ominous silence. Thieves speculate that the Black Hand must have a sewer entrance, though none will confirm this — preferring to live instead of proving a theorem. Though the whole city of Shadizar knows the building to be the Hall of the Black Hand, none acknowledge it to be so. Asking a local tavern-keeper or passing merchant for directions to the Hall will result in muttered repudiations of any such place and a hurried cessation of chatter. The Black Hand has eyes and ears throughout Shadizar, and they are ruthless in dealing with any who betray their secrets — no matter how obvious these secrets might be. That being said, directions can be obtained by asking locals *"Where should I avoid?"*

Domain of the Black Hand

Astute observers will note that there is no eastern gate leading out of Shadizar. In fact, there was a gate, but it has long since been bricked up and mortared over.

Traveling east from the city and into the southern end of the Kezankian Mountains, there is a desolate-looking temple that appears abandoned and neglected. The outer courtyard is strewn with rubble, and there are many stories told of this place: haunted, cursed, or merely unlucky. It all means the same thing — travelers avoid this place or risk life and limb.

But beyond the courtyard, through hidden stairs in a concealed alcove, there is much more to this place. This is the meeting place for the Black Hand, the assassins who call Shadizar home. Here is where new "brothers" are initiated and all business relevant to the guild is conducted, including trials and punishments for any member who disobeys the code of conduct or fails to resolve a contract.

It is, of course, off-limits to any non-members, and anyone stumbling into the place find themselves quickly subdued, drugged, robbed, and removed from the hall with no memory of what happened (see *Dagoth Hill*, below). If the intrusion calls for more harsh measures, the Black Hand has no problem with killing someone and leaving the body in the streets of Shadizar for the watch to find.

Anyone wishing to join the Black Hand must first meet them in Shadizar. Only those that meet all the criteria and pass the tests are allowed access to the Hall of the Black Hand. They are blindfolded on their initial visit. After they are initiated, they are allowed to know the route in and out of the hall, as well as the secret means of accessing Shadizar from the east gate.

THE BLACK HAND

Known more by rumor and reputation, The Black Hand is rarely called by their full faction name — usually just "assassin" is enough to conjure up images of melting shadows, grisly murders, and horrific poisons.

In truth, the assassins are principled in their dedication to duty. They see themselves not as dealers of death but as instruments to be wielded by other, greater men. Black Hand assassins have no personal agenda, and they willingly practice detachment and emotional distance from others to better make the taking of life more abstract.

There is an apprenticeship to becoming a member of the Black Hand, and it's not easy to join. Traditionally, the assassins grow their ranks by taking in orphans, often as infants. They are raised at the Hall of the Black Hand (see page 31) and are educated by the elders of the hall. If they show aptitude for the physical demands of an assassin, they begin that training at the age of 10. Those that don't are allowed to continue their studies and become elders themselves. Anyone not adopted into the faction must prove himself or herself before being allowed access into the inner workings of the order. They

must perform at least one assassination as part of the vetting process. Killing is the business, after all.

The Black Hand has its home and traditions in Zamora, and their feelings about honoring contracts are as adamant and inflexible as those of the master thieves. They do not always accept contracts, relying on their own judgment and occasionally the input of the master assassin.

The master assassin is the final arbiter in all faction business. His real name is unknown to the Black Hand assassins. It's possible that one or two elders knows the master's true identity.

Once indoctrinated into the faction, the assassin swears from this moment forward that they are anything but. The secrets of the Black Hand are to be kept secret at all costs, under pain of death if need be. The faction's enemies are legion. A player character wishing to join the Black Hand should use the guidelines for joining the Thieves' Guild (see page 107 for more information) suitably tweaked for the slightly deadlier circumstances concerning trained killers.

Dagoth Hill

East of Shadizar, this ancient burial site is a day's ride from the city and said to contain the remains of pre-human monsters in its packed earth mound. Tall, flat stones carved with unusual symbols sit atop the hill at strange angles, neither tombstone or monument. The stories surrounding the site are weird and fantastical; sleeping women ravaged by demons, weary travelers losing an entire day upon first staring at the standing stones and so forth.

Whether there is anything valuable or any truth to the rumors that hang over Dagoth Hill, this is where the Black Hand dumps interlopers who stumble upon their headquarters, or who they deem unworthy of an audience. Anyone waking up amid the standing stones in the middle of the night is bound to make haste for Shadizar and count their blessings that they are still alive to tell the tale.

"The King's Court"

This open-air market is home to the thieves and rogues of Shadizar. "The King's Court" is little more than a collection of tents and tarps, smoky oil lanterns, and a ramshackle bar. Thieves lounge about on the grassy hillside or try to talk business at one of the crude tables.

The "King" himself is a loud, crude master thief named Hazeer, who runs the bar and oversees operations while making sure the only people drinking in the King's Court are those who work at night. His "court" is a motley gang of thugs and killers from the grimiest corners of the civilized world. They are fiercely loyal to Hazeer and obey his every command.

If any group in Shadizar is going to be a problem for the player characters, it's the King and his court. Hazeer, the leader of the band of miscreants, is used to people paying him the appropriate amount of respect, whether or not he rightfully earned it. Any player characters failing to show the proper feudal spirit are called out by the King and harassed by his men. These men may attempt to find out the player characters' business in town for the entire time they are in Shadizar.

"The Temple of Gold"

This former temple of Anu was converted into a gambling hall, where all kinds of games of chance and other betting sports are played. Some of the games are actually honest, though it's not readily known how to tell the difference, so sharp are the dealers and gamesmen.

Cards, dice, darts, throwing knives, and other such sports are easy to fall into. More exotic attractions take place below the former temple. To gain access to these requires a patron or a friend who can vouch for a person, or personal wealth readily on display.

"The Slaughterhouse"

Next to the Temple of Gold is a ruin, one of the few casualties of war over the years. This once-great temple has been partially reconstructed and refurbished, and now serves as an arena where blood sports are regularly held. Boxing, wrestling, and when grudge matches, armed combat, all are conducted in the middle of a howling crowd. The smooth stone floors that once held prayer mats are now permanently stained with dried blood.

Formal challenges among rivals are fought here in the open with the stakes clearly stated, so that the witnesses corroborate the victors' story or help uphold the decision in the event of a non-lethal encounter.

Anyone fighting in the Slaughterhouse under contract that does well, or exhibits puissant skill, is quickly bought and sold to the Nemedian flesh-peddlers who haunt the Slaughterhouse looking for new talent to exploit in Hanumar and elsewhere. Player characters can try to pick up a purse of gold if they don't mind fighting to the death. The patrons of the Slaughterhouse expect to see blood and react poorly if someone's hand is stayed from a killing blow.

YEZUD

After the first occupation of Zamora, the monarchy determined that it would move the remnants of its culture, the Library of Zhem, out of harm's way and keep it from being destroyed by uncaring interlopers. They built Yezud on an area of steep elevation, with five towers facing all directions to aid as both a lookout and for defense. Once completed, they moved the Library of Zhem there to keep it safe behind the high stone walls.

When the Hyrkanians took Zamora, they did considerable damage to the city. Shadizar saved itself by submitting unconditionally. Only Yezud stood in opposition, and the Hyrkanians were never able to take the outpost because of its excellent defensive position.

In the intervening years, the military outpost grew into a thriving refuge for political outcasts, religious zealots, and refugees seeking a temporary respite. Though Yezud is still connected directly to the Capital City, the Spider-God cult has virtually taken over the walled enclave, and they now send envoys and emissaries to Zamora the Accursed and Shadizar the Wicked in the hopes of spreading their foul teachings.

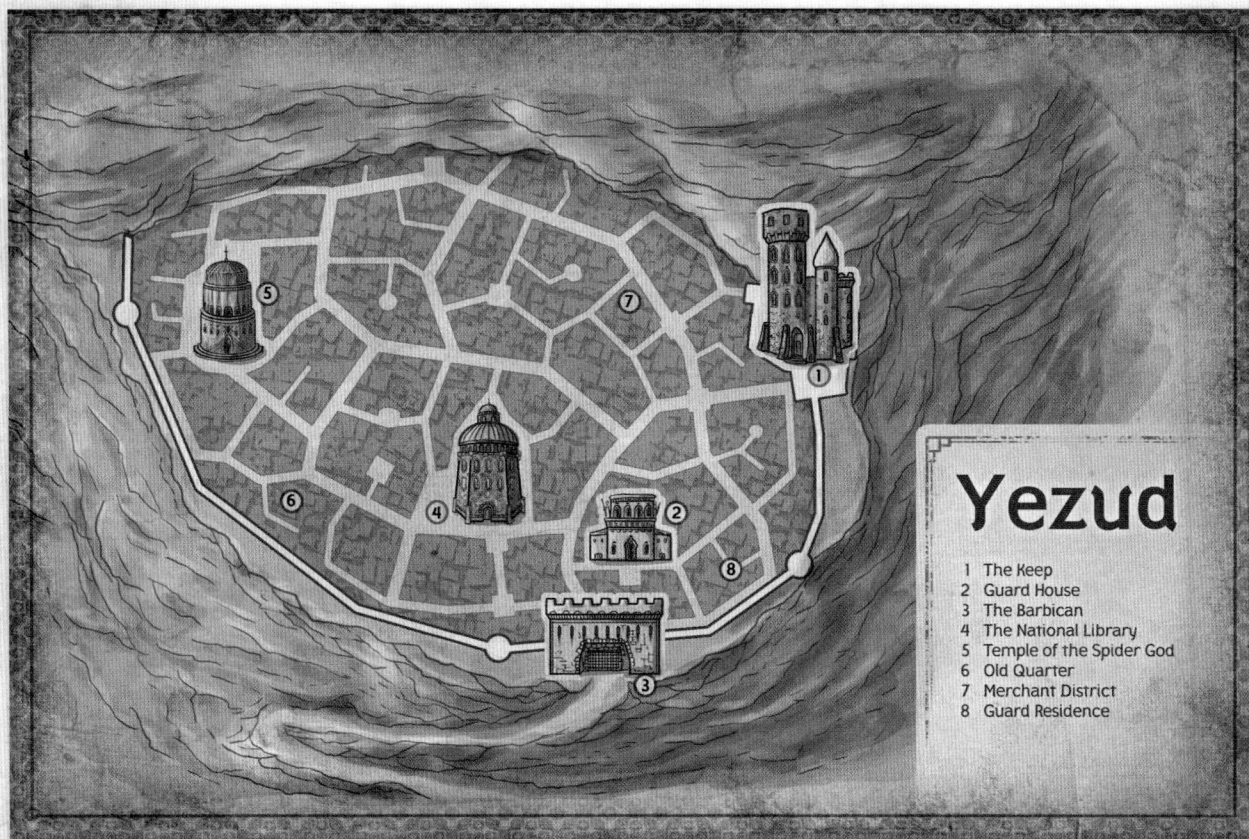

Yezud

1 The Keep
2 Guard House
3 The Barbican
4 The National Library
5 Temple of the Spider God
6 Old Quarter
7 Merchant District
8 Guard Residence

The Pilgrim's Road

This road is the only way to get to the city, hugging the gentle elevation and curving around to the guard house, facing west. It is a well-trod path, and there are offerings to the gods, set up on makeshift altars, along the ascent. Wine and water skins are found hanging from poles at regular intervals. Initiates and acolytes refill these routinely. It is highly likely that anyone traveling the Pilgrim's Road will encounter acolytes from the Spider-Cult god either coming from or going to Yezud. They are all polite and well mannered, but traveling with them will be an unnerving experience. They watch everything and everyone, constantly, and engage in conversation only when spoken to. No cultist attacks people traveling on the road without a specific order from the High Priest himself.

Bandits frequent the Pilgrim's Road, and cultists rush to defend anyone attacked during their travels. Saving travelers is a great way to change people's minds about the sinister motives of the Spider-God Cult, after all.

The Barbican

The only way into the city of Yezud is a gated barbican some three stories tall. A contingent of the city watch is always in and around the structure, asking questions of newcomers and making certain that the traveler's intentions are mundane.

Windows along the second story are usually filled with one or two archers. Stairs leading up to the top of the guardhouse reveal several casks of oil and a cache of lanterns, torches, and the like to set them on fire once dropped. These defenses have not been needed in decades, but they are still maintained.

The city guard is loyal to the governor, but suspect that the high priest of the Spider-God cult has compromised him. Speculation runs rampant among the ranks. Between the gate house and the barbican, there are no fewer than eight city guard on duty at all times — an ancient arrangement from the old wars, when lookouts were paramount to the city's defense.

The Outer Walls

The city of Yezud cuts into a steep hill, overlooking the southern valley. Around this city are stone and mortar walls, twenty feet high and ten feet wide with parapets built up on the outer side some four feet high in places. The city guard routinely patrol the walls from both inside and out, treating Yezud like the outpost fort it has always been. Ramps inside the walls lead up to the parapets, allowing crossbowmen plenty of positions from which to rain death down on invaders. These walls cannot be climbed without specialized equipment, being smooth and offering no cracks for handholds.

The Spires of Yezud

Facing north, south, and west are three spires connected to the outer walls. They tower over the rest of the city, a hundred feet high, with domed roofs and intricate carvings on the exterior. These spires were once lookout perches, but are now rumored to be infested with spiders, and citizens and soldiers alike shun them.

The Keep

Located on the east wall, this nigh-impregnable edifice of veined rock and mortar is as imposing as it appears. From within the tower walls, Verham Shadan, governor of Yezud, runs his corrupt bureaucracy with a confusing multitude of toadies and scribes. His personal guard has taken up a permanent residence here, what the locals derisively call "The Governor's Palace".

There are rumors of hidden tunnels connecting to other buildings and institutions in Yezud — a spider web-like underground network originally intended for defense of the city and now used for far more nefarious purposes.

This well-built, impressive fort is nigh-impregnable, and that's just the way the governor likes it. His personal guard, the High Yezudi, live and train in the keep and watch over the governor at all times. Between keeping Yezud on the take and avoiding the constant requests from the Spider-God cult for an audience, the governor is exceptionally busy and never leaves the keep. Instead, he brings people he needs to see to him. This includes at least one former relic hunter from the Church of Mitra to help him seek out the secret passages under the city.

The National Library Kauul

This hexagonal domed building is carved out of the same black veined rock as the keep. Its outer walls slope inward at a slight angle, and the upper corners are adorned with strange, squatting forms. This is the Library of Zhem, and it houses all of the dark secrets of the Zamorian people and culture.

Getting into the library is not easy. A scholar has to petition the king, though this is usually accomplished through bribing an underling or similar bureaucrat. Bribes speed up the process considerably. Otherwise, the wait takes from one to six months before the scholar receives an answer. This comes in the form of a letter bearing a color-coded wax seal which grants access to the library for a set number of days — usually three, but this can be negotiated up to a fortnight. These letters are valuable, and people have been executed for attempting to forge and use versions of these letters.

Yezud's Temple of the Spider-God

The mysterious Spider-God cult is known more by rumor and reputation than actual fact. The members are extremely secretive about their arachnid deity, and converts are not allowed into the cult's inner mysteries and rituals until they are well and truly indoctrinated. Followers of the Spider-God wear gray robes with silver adornments in a spider motif: rings, bracelets, and necklaces are common amongst the converted. Upper-class converts have small gemstones affixed to their heads, representing the all-seeing eyes of the Spider-God.

The cult completely subverted the local government in Yezud and currently attempts to make inroads in both Shadizar and Zamora. Acolytes carry messages back and forth in a never-ending stream of information, and the leader of the cult, a Zamorian named Kyus Garda, is busy relaying instructions to the faithful and constantly attempting to insert his followers into positions of power. The people of Yezud are resigned to this. Shadizar's population is largely unaware, and Zamora's population likewise has little interest in the backwater religion from the northern hills. Only Zamora's king suspects anything, and he stays well out of sight, surrounded only by people he trusts implicitly.

CORINTHIA

Considered one of the great Western powers, thanks to its considerable trade influence and affluence, Corinthia shares a border with Nemedia and Brythunia in the north, Zamora in the east, and Koth and Ophir in the south and west. Warfare and tension keep the borders of Corinthia shifting. Only the well-paid mercenary armies operating out of the three major city-states keep more aggressive invaders at bay.

The city-states of Corinthia seldom agree on anything save the defense of their territory and the pursuit of commerce, legal and otherwise, as a bargaining chip with their larger neighbors. Stregos, in the east, is close to the Zamorian border. The Red City is centrally located and boasts the largest economy and army. Krotoa lies in the south, near the mountains that divide Ophir and Koth, and is the smallest of the three city-states. Trade is vigorous between the three kingdoms, and political machinations run rampant.

CORINTHIAN HISTORY AND BACKGROUND

Corinthia has the misfortune to be positioned between no less than five strong, ambitious kingdoms. Often in the path of encroaching armies, Corinthia has been sacked and rebuilt several times. Each time it was rebuilt, it became the haven for the political refugees and outcasts removed from their homelands by war.

These exiles came together with the Hyborians to establish trading centers which became towns. These eventually grew into semi-autonomous city-states, each with a distinct tone and outlook. These city-states are vital to trade between the various countries and, with coin flowing into the region, Corinthia employs vast armies of mercenaries to safeguard their holdings. Corinthia has strong ties to Nemedia and Ophir, neutral relations with Zamora and Brythunia, and a tenuous peace treaty with Koth that both nations expect the other to break at any moment.

As both a contested area and an adopted culture, Corinthia's identity is somewhat confusing. Corinthians are short and broad-shouldered, with pale complexions and dark to medium brown hair. Some blonde-haired and blue-eyed Corinthians betray their Hyborian lineage, but they are infrequent.

MAJOR CITIES OF CORINTHIA

The city-states of Corinthia are large, cosmopolitan cities with complicated politics borrowed from Nemedian scholars, religious fervor gleaned from Zamorian heretics, large markets full of travelers from all of the known kingdoms, and a constant state of civil unrest. For many, Corinthia is a place to reinvent oneself and shake off the past, or forge a new future. All of the city-states have established black markets fed by the appetites of the neighboring countries and aided by the Road of Kings, which cuts across the heart of Corinthia. Because of this brisk economy, the roads in Corinthia are well kept, out of necessity. Smaller, less manageable byways lead to the villages and farms that in turn lead to green valleys with ample vegetation. Some areas of Corinthia are dense forest, and there are places close to the southern mountains where the sunlight never strays. Most travelers avoid these areas, though there are persistent tales of merchants encountering half-man horrors along these lonely trails.

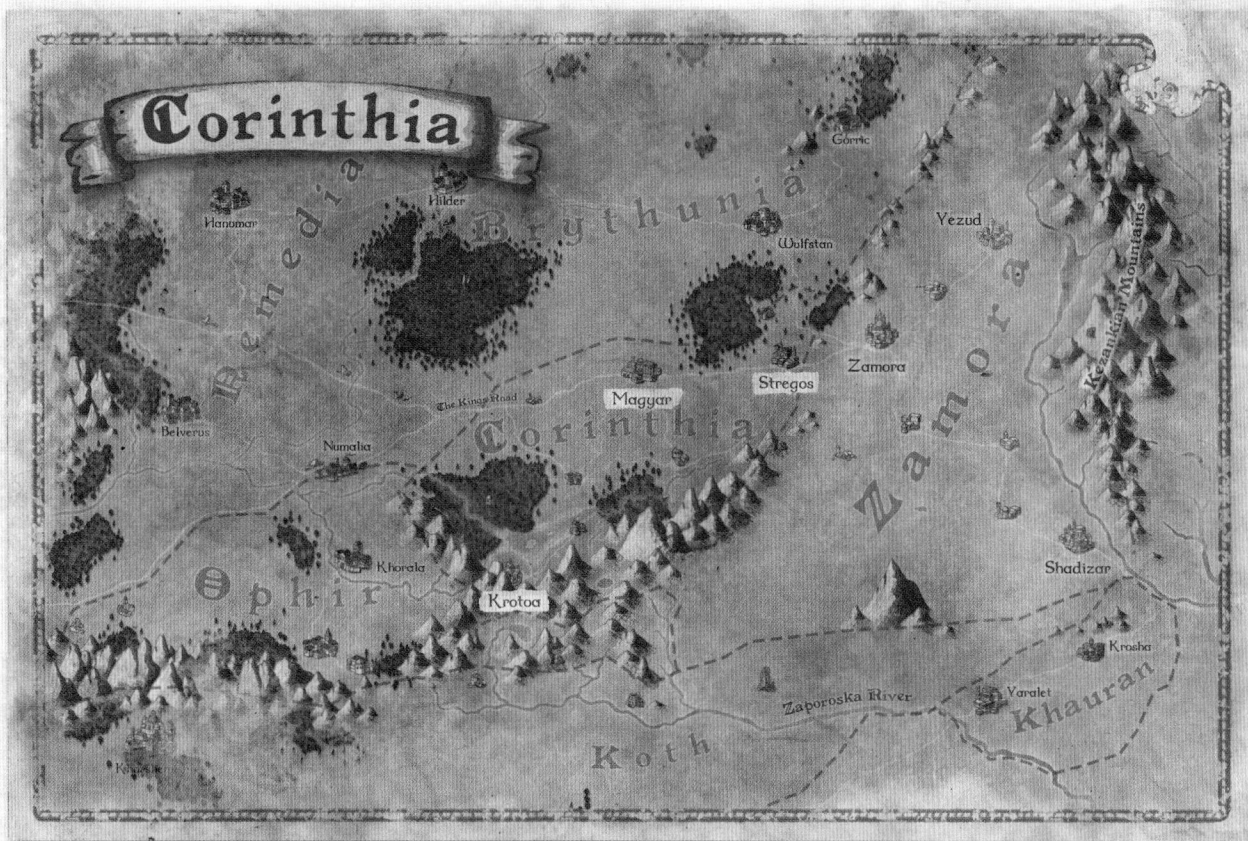

A number of small villages and farms surround the city-states for several miles in all directions and fall under each city's protection, thus earning the allegiance of those nearby. This is useful whenever a fighting force is conscripted or supplies run low. All commerce flows to the city-states like the inexorable current of a river.

MAGYAR
THE RED CITY

This is the largest of the Corinthian city-states, made fat and prosperous by unchecked economic growth and secretly run by a small cadre of moneyed interests, bureaucrats, priests, and merchants. Through the judicious use of coin, they can manipulate the infrastructure of the city to meet their needs. This air of casual corruption is present throughout the Red City; every transaction feels like an illegal one.

All of the usual conveniences and amenities are available to visitors in Magyar. The city boasts several markets in its heart, catering to the locals and traders alike. The economy is more stable than Stregos and the citizens in a more genial mood. But there is an undercurrent in the city, a resistance to the rampant corruption that crept into the latent bureaucracy, and visitors who are insensitive with their comments may find themselves in a fight they didn't know they were starting.

The Maze

The thieves' quarter of the Red City is almost as infamous as the Maul in Zamora. This area of the southern district used to be people's homes before the last invasion from the east left most of the buildings a smoking ruin. The rebuilding effort was abandoned after two years when investors expanded the walls to the east and made a new housing district.

The criminal element moved in and more or less finished the work the honest laborers started. The result is a ramshackle cluster of one-way streets, dead ends, twisting alleys, and small buildings on their last legs. Trade is brisk in the Maze, and it is a favored spot to carouse and spend ill-gotten gains.

Inside the Maze are a number of cantinas and hovels where a thirsty reveler can obtain a drink. But only serious thieves and their ilk frequent The Rat's Den. It's not as desolate a place as the name would suggest. Rather, the bar got its name because of the numerous trap door escapes, hatches, and bolt holes that the building offers, no less than five distinct points of exit that don't include the front and back doors. No guards have ever been able to catch a fugitive from inside The Rat's Den, an achievement for which the thieves who call this place home are proud.

The Red City has a thriving black market focused on the Maze. Anyone wishing to move illicit goods from one

place to the other need only visit Smuggler's Alley. This blind alley terminates at the back of the Temple of Anu and, for the brave or desperate, there are plenty of people sitting in unlit courtyards and leaning on lampposts who can find, deliver, and transport anything from golden lotus to Stygian princesses, if the price is right.

Player characters may find work here, along with competition from any of the local talent who feel that foreign interlopers are taking their clients away. Sometimes the best way to remove the competition is to send them on a job far away or give them an assignment so dangerous that no one in their right mind would take it.

The Agora

In this open-air market, the locals buy, sell, and trade for goods and services. Food, drink, and more can be purchased here, though the prices fluctuate wildly from day to day depending on the commodity and the availability. The Agora is a wide crossroads, with small clusters of booths and stalls and wagons grouped together for ease. The city guard is present in both quantity and frequency, enough to deter casual thievery.

A small gang of urchins roams the Agora, subsisting on scraps, found coins, and the accidental jostle, cut purse strings, and other such tactics. They are incredibly well trained and it's nearly impossible to catch them at their

MAGYAR
THE RED CITY

1 - Palace
2 - House of Nabonidus
3 - Main Sewer Exit
4 - The Park
5 - North Side District
6 - Armory District
7 - The City Jail
8 - Temple of Anu
9 - The Maze
10 - Nationalist's Headquarter
11 - The Agora
12 - Exit from the Maze
13 - East Gate

THE TEMPLE OF ANU

Located at the edge of the Maze, the Temple of Anu abuts the Agora and announces its presence with the massive bronze statue of a bull, head aloft, horns pointing to the stars above. Its base is routinely draped and adorned with garlands of flowers and other offerings. Anu is not native to Corinthia, but its priest was removed forcibly from Zamora hundreds of years ago, and so the church settled in the Red City where it flourished thanks to steady trade routes bringing worshipers to the city.

The priest of Anu, an unctuous man named Branimere Gru, operates out of the back of the church as a fence, dealing in stolen merchandise, and also informing for the city guard on the side, when it suits him. He is only too happy to buy items from player characters, and ask probing questions, if he can.

For campaigns set after the events in Howard's story, "Rogues in the House", Gru will be murdered and the church will be in some disarray until it settles on a new priest. Whether or not this man continues what Gru started or bends his will to the task of restoring the honor of the Temple of Anu is one of the many questions that may be decided by the preference of the gamemaster, or the actions of the player characters.

business. The gang steers clear of the guards, and the guards make no effort to hunt them, even when a cry goes up over some merchant's missing wallet.

The Nationalists' Headquarters

This boxy and unassuming building that used to be an auction house on the edge of the Agora has been closed for a long time, its windows boarded up from the inside. However, if you know who to ask for a key, you can enter through the front door and find the auction block replaced with a podium and the staggered benches on risers repaired and full of earnest young politicos and malcontents, eager to make a change for the city, one way or another. Gaining access to the building in the form of a key should be a minor adventure for anyone seeking this faction out. It is difficult, but not impossible, since the group is an open secret; that is, everyone knows about the nationalists, but not a lot of people know who they are or what they want.

The nationalists meet every fortnight during the dark of the moon and the full moon to discuss the best way to get the corruption out of their city. They are not dangerous to players unless the players side with the government or claim to represent the entrenched bureaucracy. For information on joining the nationalists, see *The Nationalists* sidebar.

The Armory

Located next to the western gate, the armory is actually a small, walled district of public houses and barracks, with stables, blacksmiths, armor and weapon smiths, and leatherworkers — all servicing the needs of the mercenary groups that are paid to protect the city-state and its related holdings. There is a pass-through, an inner gate via the city jail that allows access to the rest of the city. There are always guards and soldiers hanging around in this enclosed area. They live, eat, drink, and fight within the walls, and typically handle their own affairs before things get out of hand. Non-military characters will stand out and be questioned incessantly as to their business in a polite but firm matter. Locals with business to conduct do so quickly and efficiently, which is exactly how both citizen and soldier like it. Needless to say, with so many armed guards around, a thief would have to be crazy to try to pull a job in this area.

City Jail

The city jail exists within the converted gatehouse that separates the armory from the rest of the city. The portcullis that once raised and lowered to restrict access is long gone, its chain and winch removed and the gate itself repurposed a hundred years ago. Two doors face outwards toward the Agora, and they lead to a processing area and the spiral staircase beyond leads down into the converted dungeon or up to the still-functioning guard

THE NATIONALISTS

The nationalists have two goals: uniting the three city-states under a central government and ousting the criminal element from the local (and national) infrastructure. They are idealists all, and devoted in their endeavors, which include, but are not limited to, spying on known criminals, thwarting criminal enterprises, exposing corruption in the church and state — bringing it to light with songs, poems, and occasionally printed matter — and constantly pressuring the law to crack down on all of the above. To say many despise them is a gross understatement.

Joining the nationalists is easy; all one has to do is show up to one of the meetings and profess the intention to help the cause. Player characters so doing are asked to complete a task or two and, if they are thieves of any kind, that task will assuredly involve breaking and entering and obtaining proof of criminal corruption — for the greater good, of course.

As a faction, the nationalists have scant resources to offer the characters. But they are always ready to act as accomplices for larger plans and provide safe harbor for fugitives in need of a place to rest and recuperate.

The nationalists are allowed to operate because they keep their heads down and are, at best, minor nuisances. If that should change for any reason, or if the deeds of a few new recruits should become well known and place the entrenched corrupt players in the spotlight, the nationalists would find themselves with large targets upon their backs.

stand, where members of the city watch working off an infraction or a temporary punishment keep a bored eye on the city market. In the event of a large-scale disturbance, a bell is rung and the rest of the garrison can be summoned.

The City Park

An open space full of trees and flowers not native to the region, this park boasts cobblestone walkways and manicured lawns. The locals consider the park to be vainglorious excess, but the politicians and the visitors consider it a feature, and so the park is always full of visiting travelers, often in the company of a retinue of guards and dignitaries. Around the edges of the city park, a number of ambitious merchants and hustlers are always on hand, selling overpriced food and drink, or trying to get gullible newcomers to purchase the deed to the park for pennies on the dollar.

The North Side

Only the wealthiest and most influential people live on the north side, in the neighborhood surrounding the king's palace. As the homes run from the city park to the king's palace, the ground slopes gently upward, meeting the walls of the palace at the edge of a sharply defined hill.

It's impossible not to look up to the residents of the north side. Mansions, two and three stories tall, break the symmetry of the rooftops, allowing for some of the wealthier citizens to look down upon their less-affluent upper crust neighbors. Politicians, priests, and many merchants call the north side their home.

THE HOUSE OF NABONIDUS

Located closer to the city park than the palace in a semblance of modesty, the House of Nabonidus, the Red Priest, is actually one of the most feared places in the Red City. Known colloquially as "the Murder Castle", this three-story mansion has been heavily modified to suit Nabonidus' more sanguinary tastes.

No member of the upper class is as influential, as powerful, or as thoroughly corrupt as Nabonidus, the Red Priest (an honorific, rather than an actual title). His ruthlessness, coupled with his vast connections and deep pockets, virtually guarantees that his side business of influencing economic trends and policies, arranging for thefts and seizures of whatever he desired, and his amassing of exotic antiques and tomes for his bizarre devices are always successful.

This estate has high stone wall as tall as two men, and the inner and outer edges are rimmed with shrubbery and tall trees that cast deep shadows across the walled garden.

Inside the house, in addition to Nabonidus, are two servants: a cook and the majordomo, Joka. A third inhabitant, Thak, is never seen, but often heard in the upstairs apartments.

Nearly every room in the house features some form of fatal encounter. The estate is a giant mechanical death trap that only Nabonidus can operate and navigate with ease — and possibly Joka, as well. What these traps and devices are is left up to the gamemaster to decide, but some things are known about the house.

Nabonidus and Thak are described in detail on pages 86 and 94, respectively.

Ground Floor

An entrance hall which leads in three directions, as well as stairs leading to the second floor. To the left is a sitting room, followed by a study. To the right is a meeting room, followed by a conservatory. In the center is a circular dining room. Going up the stairs leads to a circular gallery around the dining room and the stairs continue up to the third floor.

Possible hazards Nabonidus might have readied could include poisoned food, a floor opening that deposits victims in the dungeon below, or even hidden blowgun darts that fire when books are pulled from a shelf.

Second Floor

In addition to the large gallery, there is a balcony overlooking the garden in the back. Five bedrooms are here, including Nabonidus' room at the end of the long, broad hall.

Possible hazards include blade traps over bed, poisonous animals released through a hatch in the wall, and chutes that deposit victims in the dungeon below. There are no traps in Nabonidus' bedroom.

Third Floor

Storage space, servant's quarters, and a small observatory.

Possible hazards are that both of the servant's quarters are airtight and the air can be sucked out of the room, creating a vacuum that suffocates the inhabitants.

There is a control room with mirrors for spying into the various rooms of the dungeon, as well as operating mechanisms for many of the traps. The mirrors can be adjusted to peer into several different basement rooms by opening and closing valves and adjusting levers on the copper tubing. Stairs in this room lead down into the dungeon in the basement.

Dungeon Level

Copper tubing runs across the ceiling in a confusing array. There is a long, wide corridor in the center and several rooms on each side. Two of the rooms are actually sunken chambers ten feet deep. One of the rooms seals with thick glass and can be flooded with gas. The other room can be flooded with water.

The greatest danger in the dungeon level are the pits: one of the pits' walls slowly comes together to crush victims, and another pit can be filled with corrosive acid to quickly dissolve bodies, leaving only metal behind.

The central corridor feeds into the sewer, and the entire basement can be flooded so that the corpses and remnants of Nabonidus' victims are easily washed away into the river. The entrance to this sewer under the house has a spear trap over the mouth of the pipe.

The King's Palace

The loftiest and most expensive land in the city lies on the hill upon which the king's palace rests. This castle is actually a small keep with defendable walls and a well-maintained, if not opulent, inner tower. For infrequent entertaining, the gates are thrown open and parties are held all around the small tower on the grounds. Inside the tower, on the ground floor, a small phalanx of royal guards lives and works.

The second floor is dedicated to the affairs of state. Stairs leading up to the second floor flank the left and right side of the hall on the ground floor. Up here, the king holds court with the politicians and priests and merchants and citizenry, depending on how one interprets his bizarre and complicated schedule.

The king, Koval Cedomir, resides at the top of the tower with personal guards and council at his beck and call. Smaller, mostly empty chambers are found up and down the hallway leading to his bedroom. No guests stay overnight at the king's palace.

The Sewers

Part of what makes the Red City so desirable as a destination is its ancient sewer system which takes the muck and filth of civilization and deposits it in the swamps southeast of the city. There are several entrances to the sewers within the city, but few people venture down there for fear of getting lost in the twisting and turning corridors and, of course, the persistent rumors of foul creatures dwelling just below the pavement, waiting to snatch anyone foolish enough to go blundering around in the dark.

STREGOS, THE SLEEPING CITY

Closest in proximity and attitude to Zamora, Stregos is the oldest Corinthian city-state, razed to ruin and rebuilt at least once in its long history. Thieves and outlaws are regularly seen parading up and down Mornaget Street. Many of the smaller, more vocal, and more extreme religions that were displaced from other countries made their way to Stregos to practice freely, if not openly. Those not seeking a more stringent lifestyle should avoid anyone wearing acolyte's robes. The governor of Stregos dictates much of the city's attitudes, customs, and traditions. Currently, the temples enjoy a free hand to convince others to worship, sometimes by force.

The Great Market

Commerce is wide open in Stregos, and the Great Market is where everything is bought and sold. This large, open square is rimmed with small shops with storefronts below and single room apartments above. A few of the newer buildings have a root cellar carved out of the packed earth foundations, allowing for more storage of things

---

AFTER "ROGUES IN THE HOUSE"

This sourcebook is set near the beginning of Conan's career, allowing player characters to potentially run afoul of Nabonidus, or face Thak on their own. For campaigns set after the events in "Rogues in the House", the gamemaster should feel free to use the following conditions or simply create others as required.

■ The house is currently owned by the Temple of Anu, but it is locked and under constant guard after the death of several looters. Nabonidus is said to have perished in one of his own death trap chambers below the earth, and his body was never recovered due to the dangers of navigating the house.

■ Strange lights are seen in the windows at odd hours of the night, leading to rumors that the ghost Red Priest haunts the house. The temple guards do not venture onto the grounds or into the house, preferring instead to keep their distance, stationed at the chained gate, and mutter prayers when something moving in the house catches their eye.

like potables and vegetables. Equipment can be purchased here, though the prices fluctuate wildly from day to day, depending on availability.

Mornaget Street

Crossing the northwestern edge of the Great Market at a diagonal is a short, narrow lane that is home to the thieves of Stregos. Only three blocks long, this is where enterprising player characters can pick up work, replace a broken grappling hook, or Carouse. All of the locals know what Mornaget Street is and avoid it unless they have business there.

The Sow's Ear

Located on the odd, triangular block that forms from Mornaget Street cutting through the northwest corner of the Great Market, The Sow's Ear has a reputation for being dark, dangerous, and unpredictable. There are back exits that open up on either side of Mornaget Street, which makes the Sow's Ear ideal for a dark, drunken rendezvous.

The Philosopher's Quarter

Stregos had aspirations of culture at one point, and the city planners set aside a small neighborhood for temples, monasteries, schools, and libraries. Very little of that original plan remains, but the area is still known as "The Philosopher's Quarter", albeit with a hint of mockery. As Stregos opened its arms to accept the refugees, political and otherwise, many of the more extreme personalities settled in the Philosopher's Quarter, where they could quarrel and bicker with other like-minded zealots until they were blue in the face. Many of these small, stately buildings have courtyards flanked with low stone walls where the devoted hold court and orate at length.

The zealots took over this portion of the city but the governor, Durian Wol, believes that a dose of religion keeps the population in line, and so he lets the priests and reformers have their way, provided they keep their murder and skulduggery in the temple and not out on the streets. Patrols through the Philosopher's Quarter do little to curb the regular disappearances that take place there.

Smoke Street

In the heart of the Philosopher's Quarter is Smoke Street, a wide and well-kept thoroughfare with an array of temples and churches on both sides of the street. Smoke Street is so named because of the acolytes who regularly burn incense, offerings, and sometimes worse in the name of their strange, foreign religions. Their constant ministrations put a blue-black haze over the street that sometimes blows into one end of the Philosopher's Quarter or the other, with appropriate blasphemous remarks from the unbelievers.

Due to the volatile and sometimes predatory nature of some of these lesser cults, most citizens avoid Smoke Street

after sundown. There is a reason why some of these cults and religions were kicked out of the flourishing nations in the dreaming west. If any player characters appear weak, confused, or frightened while traversing Smoke Street, especially after dark, they are set upon by opportunistic zealots looking for an offering of flesh and blood to one of their heathen gods or goddesses.

The Merchant's Quarter

Located between the Great Market and the north gate that leads to the Road of Kings, this neighborhood caters specifically to the needs of the caravans and their retinues. Here wagons can be mended, pack animals bought, sold, or merely stabled, mercenaries hired, and coopers and smiths sell merchants empty barrels, crates, jugs, strong boxes, and anything else needed to survive the long and perilous trip.

The Public Square

At the end of Smoke Street, before it widens to become the Great Market, there is an open pavilion with a fountain in the center, adorned with three women of different ages, each carrying jugs that empty endlessly into the basin. The young girl, the mature woman, and the old crone have no names that the people of Stregos can recall, but people gather under them to debate and discuss politics, religion, and the fates. For many people, this is as far up Smoke Street as they will venture.

Rabble-rousers and politicos can always be found in this crowd, along with minor politicians and their entourages, all operating under the watchful eye of the city guards. Thanks to the guards, the Public Square is sometimes used as a neutral meeting site. There are always at least two city guards on hand, and during festivals or religious holidays that number doubles or triples. Anyone creating a ruckus will be arrested and fined.

The women in the fountain are the Sister Nyrns, and they were placed at this site by the Hybori long ago, but the purpose has been lost to time and conquerors. Though cracked and weather-beaten, this is a popular spot for young lovers and visitors to the city to spend time listening to the speakers.

The Flats

The south end of Stregos sits next to the low land valley, and part of the city runs along those low slopes. This neighborhood is where the working families and the destitute live and work and beg. The neighborhood is uncharitably called "The Flats" because of the low flat-roofed buildings that make up so much of the area. These roofs do not drain water and so the area has a moldy stink about it. The smell of human waste and the humidity make this neighborhood unbearable to people unused to such conditions.

KROTOA

The smallest of the city-states, and also the newest in terms of development, Krotoa is situated in the valley of the southern mountain range that separates Koth and Ophir. Krotoa established itself as a gateway to both countries.

What Krotoa lacks in corrupt bureaucracy and ill-gotten gains, it makes up for in fighting spirit. Krotoa has a small standing army that it pays, and it buys mercenary companies to keep their retinue sharp and their skills polished and also to bolster the ranks in the event of a campaign. Because of Krotoa's military strength and lack of graft, they have made great strides serving as a national jail for the criminal element. Nervous thieves from Zingara to Brythunia speak in hushed whispers of the gaol of Krotoa.

Krotoa is not without its weaknesses, however, and the strength of its morality regarding the law is certainly susceptible to an abuse of power. For the right price, a political adversary can disappear in the Grand Gaol, interred forever, never to be heard from again. In an age of political instability, Krotoa's favor is heavily courted by regimes both foreign and domestic.

The Walls of Krotoa

One of the things that makes Krotoa so unique is its origins as first a fortification, then a keep, a walled village and, finally, a thriving city-state. Rather than remove the old walls, the inhabitants of Krotoa simply knocked down sections of walls as needed and built up new structures over and around the walls that remained. This gives the streets of Krotoa a labyrinthine quality that makes it particularly hard to navigate for newcomers.

The Grand Bazaar

At the intersection of the old fortress wall, the old keep fortification, and the remnants of the walled village lies the Grand Bazaar, a twisting and turning set of streets literally lined with merchants selling goods and services from all over Corinthia and its neighbors. Luxury items and lifestyle items for Carousing can be purchased here.

The Devil's Tail

This small, unassuming side street needs to be pointed out to newcomers who are looking for it. It's also known as Apothecary's Row, and it's a narrow alley that is full of reagents and ingredients necessary for sorcery, alchemy, or other mischief-making. The street and its merchants are kept well stocked by the black-market trade from the southern kingdoms.

The Frayed Rope

Located near the back of the Garrison District, the Frayed Rope shares a common wall with the city's Punishment Square. Here is where the reprobates and ne'er-do-wells that make up Krotoa's small but dedicated underworld meet, drink, and plot, often in elaborate language and jargon-riddled doublespeak, to better confuse the uninitiated. Any thieves not from Krotoa attempting to talk to thieves from Krotoa must make communications tests at one difficulty level higher unless the conversation takes place in private and the fellow thief is sure they are alone.

The bar is usually crowded during executions. Every time the noose drops on a poor soul, the assembled raise a glass in silent tribute.

The City Courts

This impressive structure stands beside the old keep, now known as the Grand Gaol. It's the newest structure built in Krotoa, a temple dedicated to the law and its enforcement. The magistrates gather, along with the public defenders, on the tiered steps to debate the finer points of law on a daily basis.

Once a week, court is convened and the judge hears all matters civil and otherwise. Criminal acts are usually swiftly decided and dealt with. Complicated cases, involving state law or foreign agents, are scheduled for the High Court, a rare occurrence.

It's nearly impossible to win a case without an advocate to argue for the person. Public defenders are fairly easy to obtain, but you get what you pay for. Other rich men have the luxury of buying or retaining private advocates who know the inner workings of the City Courts intimately. They cost much more gold to retain.

The Garrison District

The old Keep is still intact in Krotoa, thanks to its close proximity to the mountains and a set of well-kept high and wide walls. Inside these walls the mercenaries and city guard live and train and fight and gamble and carouse. The remnants of the old fort hold a half-dozen useful businesses, such as the city armorer, the city blacksmith, and the city weaponsmith, and they are kept busy with the soldiers' constant needs. The Keep's original gate is closed at sundown and reopened at dawn. Only official business bearing a court seal can open or close the gate at other times.

The Grand Gaol

Towering above the Garrison District is a five-story round tower with battlements atop it. Each floor above the first has a circular hallway that follows the staircase up to the next floor. Six rooms on each floor serve as jail cells for the absolute worst of the worst — political prisoners, murderers and brigands awaiting trial, enemies of the state, and other miscreants are installed in the twenty-four cells.

Getting in or out of the Grand Gaol is said to be impossible. Guards are installed at the top as well as the bottom, and patrols walk the halls at night. Furthermore, there are rumors of cells for special prisoners that exist underground, guarded by monsters and fiends. It's hard to know what's speculation, what's an outright lie, and what's factual, as no one has successfully made it out of the Grand Gaol alive.

The Commons

The massive sprawl that separates the main gates from the Grand Bazaar is called the Commons, and it's where most of the residents of Krotoa live. Despite the harsh penalties for crime, the citizens in the Commons are not above taking the law into their own hands if they catch a criminal.

This large sprawling area includes small markets and stands for many basics and staples. The citizens in the Commons don't have a lot, and they are mutually protective of what they do have. Any overt criminal activity generates a squad of concerned citizens who will try and break up the action, or stop the criminal. If they succeed and can recover stolen property or undo the damage done, they beat the thief unconscious and throw him into the nearest cistern.

If the law has to be involved, the citizens will march the thief to the nearest stand of guards as a group, to better demonstrate the force of their complaint and force the guards into action.

Provided no laws are broken or liberties infringed upon, the people in the Commons are stoic and decent and proud of their city and would go out of their way to help a traveler in distress.

The Governor's Mansion

On the other side of the Grand Gaol, upwind from the stink of the Garrison and the wail of the prisoners, the current governor, Orso Almar, resides in a converted temple that was once dedicated to one of the Stygian gods, now long desecrated and removed. The building was chosen, in fact, because of its proximity to the old Keep, and there are persistent rumors that there is an escape tunnel that leads from below the old temple to the dungeons of the old keep. To date, no one has ever found the rumored passage…

The governor himself is a severe, pious man, an ex-campaigner and decorated officer that left Nemedia because their military "lacked proper decorum and discipline".

NEMEDIA

One of the most powerful kingdoms in the west, second only to Aquilonia in military might and ambition, Nemedia is the intellectual and cultural center of the Western world. The church of Mitra is the dominant religion in the land, and the church enjoys a cooperative, if sometimes acrimonious, relationship with the king. Nemedians are obsessed with the remnants of the ancient culture upon which they have built their cities, their military tactics, and the trappings of their civilization.

Tall and treacherous mountains divide Nemedia and Aquilonia in the west. In the north, the Border Kingdoms are little more than a nuisance to the mighty Nemedian army, as the divide is regularly patrolled by bands of knight-errants known as the Harrowers. Mercenaries also provide protection near the border of Corinthia for merchants traveling along the Road of Kings. Healthy trade keeps relations with Ophir and Corinthia civil, if not cordial.

NEMEDIAN HISTORY AND BACKGROUND

When the Hybori descended and conquered the region eons ago, they found the remnants of the ancient culture that preceded them. The history and artifacts and scrolls and tablets fueled a renaissance that accelerated the development of the barbarians dramatically as they modeled their civilization and culture on these old remains. When Mitra was declared the official religion of the kingdom, the Nemedians felt that they had met, and maybe even exceeded, the heights of their adopted ancestors.

Nemedia has become the cultural and scholarly center of the Western world, thanks mainly to their standing army and their legendary defensive capabilities — tactics and techniques gleaned from ancient martial tomes, incidentally.

AQUILONIAN PREJUDICE

The only kingdom in the west that Nemedia fears is Aquilonia — aggressive, brash, and ever expanding their territory. Nemedia knows well that their tenuous alliance could crumble at any time. Any Aquilonian player characters needing to make Society tests against Nemedians find the test to be one step of Difficulty higher. Should the player character fail the test, they are unable to interact with the Nemedian in a peaceful manner.

Many a barbarian horde has shed their life's blood on the immovable Nemedian shield wall.

In matters of diplomacy, the Nemedians are quick-tempered, easy to offend, and slow to forgive. This makes dealing with them politically a challenge, to say the least. Trade caravans, diplomats, and envoys from other regions with an accompanying military escort are regular sights along the roads into and out of Nemedia — all the better to curry favor with both church and state.

Nemedians on the whole are tall and strong, with square features and light to dark brown hair and blue eyes.

MAJOR CITIES OF NEMEDIA

The largest cities in Nemedia weren't built upon chosen sites by the Hybori invaders; rather, they stumbled across standing ruins and moved in, the better to study the former culture. Belverus, the capital of Nemedia, has the largest and most complete set of ancient structures, repurposed for the Nemedians' fair use. Numalia, some distance south, holds one of the finest Temples of Mitra. The Road of Kings bisects

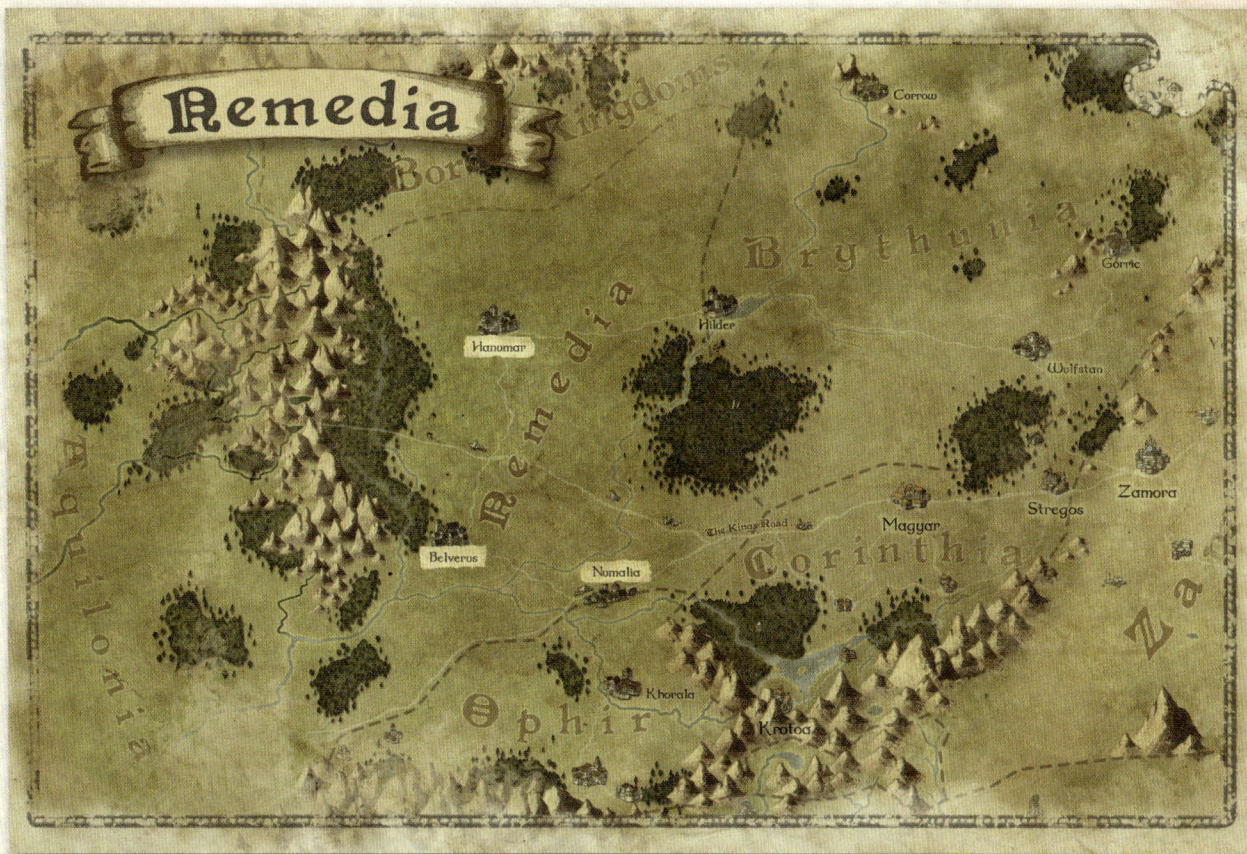

the road connecting these cities on its way to Aquilonia, and both cities enjoy the benefits of regular trade from the east. Hanumar lies to the north, more centrally located, and is the home of the Harrowers as well as the Church of Ibis, which struggles for attention under the Church of Mitra's benevolent gaze and unshakeable political influence.

Nemedia is rich in fertile ground and many farms, villages, and temples lie on the roads or in the hills that roll westward toward the mountains. Every village across the kingdom has a temple dedicated to Mitra, full of acolytes and priests ever watchful for artifacts and trinkets from before the last Ice Age.

BELVERUS

Even from a distance, Belverus is an impressive site; built on an ascending hillside, with massive buildings, temples, and other impressive structures breaking the skyline of the walled city, it's impossible not to look upon it and think of the ancient culture that built the site eons ago. As the capital of Nemedia, its inhabitants are well aware of their role in the culture of the West, and their piety — some would say arrogance — is well known.

Despite the fierce national pride of most Nemedians, they also recognize their role as keepers of knowledge, both modern and ancient. Many of the old buildings in Belverus have been repurposed; temples are now museums, grand estates are now libraries, and partially ruined and razed structures form the cornerstone of public parks. New buildings are made with an eye towards emulating ancient designs and patterns, but not copying or duplicating the motifs outright. This has gradually given Nemedia its own identity and culture, a sometimes-discordant mix of Hybori pragmatism and Acheronian opulence.

Nemedian culture emphasizes strength and knowledge and, in this regard, they have aligned themselves with the Church of Mitra to aid their progress in both areas. Edicts from the church carry nearly the same weight as proclamations from the Royal Palace. Cynics and non-believers whisper that the Church of Mitra actually holds the reins of power in Nemedia but, in truth, the King and the Church enjoy a mutually acrimonious relationship and vie for the public's heart at every turn.

For scholars and anyone interested in studying the remnants of Acheronian culture, Belverus is the best place to start. There are active digs and delvings, most of them orchestrated by the Church of Mitra, and no end of texts to translate, artifacts to puzzle over, and discoveries to make, provided you wish to share your findings with the state. Removal of antiquities from Nemedian borders carries stiff penalties. Naturally, there is a thriving black market for those very items.

The City Gates

These grand columns are fifty feet high with a buttressed arch across the top. Walls on either side of these columns run directly into the hillside that gives rise to the upper-class neighborhoods of Belverus. There are other walls up on the hills with walkways carved into the rocks. Guards camp at the gates at all hours of the day or night, and everyone undergoes cursory questioning if they appear to be law-abiding citizens and pointed questioning if they appear to be otherwise. Of course, some of the more foolhardy simply climb the adjacent hillside and leap over the walls to gain entrance to the city. And that's why the city watch is so vigilant. The city watch is always here, using the shade of the pillars to escape the oppressive heat. They keep an eye on the incoming traffic, but also scan for large parties on the road and off. Should any raiding party be foolish enough to approach the city, the watch has an elaborate system of bells and banners to summon reinforcements well before an attack can begin.

The City Market

Belverus plays host to a number of small open-air markets, but the city market, in the center of town, is something to behold. This large, sunken square has a raised circular dais in the center where speeches are delivered, news is announced, and occasionally musicians and poets perform. Around this stone stage is a broad avenue with stalls and tents on either side. Here the citizens may shop and bargain and trade. Stairs lead down into this sunken area from the street above, and the edges are lined with a small stone wall allowing people to see the speaker on the dais. Lining the wall, facing outward, are an encampment of beggars, infirm, and hustlers, all vying for spare coin. The only time the cacophony of sound is silenced is during royal proclamations.

The Merchant's District

The eastern side of the Central Market is known as the Merchant's District. This is the heart of interstate commerce. Here farmers sell their surplus, and lumberjacks fill orders for ash and fir. Anyone looking to buy or sell commodities finds any number of businesses, legitimate and otherwise, to help them in this district. Commodities are sold in large quantities to brokers, who store them in the large empty buildings and set the price for other merchants. This is part of the empire building going on in the Western kingdoms,

and a lot of money changes hands so that the Aquilonian court can have the finest dresses made of Stygian silk. Getting these commodities to market is sometimes an epic undertaking. The Merchant's District is literally crawling with guards, both personal and state-appointed.

Cork Street

The street that separates the rest of the Merchant's District from the Central Market is called Cork Street, and it's where all of the glass blowers, cask makers, bottlers, and vintners sell their wares from the wine merchants and the grape growers. Nemedian wine is legendary and the artisans on this street are busy all year.

NEMEDIAN WINE

The grapes that grow in the southern hills of Nemedia are legendary for the wine they produce. Nemedian Wine is considered a delicacy in the west, and Nemedians trade shrewdly for it. In the east, they have their own spirits, but Nemedian wine is still considered a mark of wealth. Nemedians do not trade with anyone in the south for it, and this is where it becomes contraband in places like Corinthia. Moving more than a bottle or two can turn quite a profit or bring the law down on a player character's head.

Scholar's District

The street that marks the southern side of the Central Market is the edge of the Scholar's District. Here the ground begins to climb up the hill and, of course, that is where the temples, schools, and public meditation and debate spaces are located. The smaller temples and churches include a smattering of the other Western gods, but these churches are very poor and cater mostly to visitors and merchants passing through. It's obvious to all where the population turns to when they seek divine guidance.

The Temple of Mitra

This is the largest building in Belverus, though not the tallest. It's completely intact, one of the few structures that required no repair. Its gleaming white and gold walls shine across the city, catching reflected sunlight that makes it difficult to stare at during certain times of the day.

This is the central home of the Church of Mitra for all of the Western world. As the heart of the faith, there are constant scribes, advisors, emissaries, priests, dignitaries, and acolytes coming in and out of the building on church business at all hours. There are even armed guards to keep watch over the temple at night, though they are lightly armored, enrobed, and carrying maces that look a lot like holy water sprinklers.

There is a small cadre of acolytes of Mitra known colloquially as "relic hunters". These are sometimes, but not always, reformed criminals and scoundrels who have seen the error of their ways, accepted the wisdom of Mitra, and have gone back to the life that their skills are uniquely suited for. The church provides them with their necessities, and they obtain rare antiquities, plunder historic sites, and even re-acquire the church's stolen property. The church and its dealings should make it difficult to do any mischief in Belverus. Agents of the church are everywhere and many of the citizens are pious, as are the government officials. That's not to say that corruption doesn't exist, but it makes it harder to know who to trust and also who to bribe.

The Royal District

Carved into the largest portion of the hillside, above all other neighborhoods, is where the politicians and the wealthy call home. The intact structure here is a massive estate, three stories tall, cut partially into the hillside and surrounded by large strong walls. King Codrin Saldius lives here.

The Church of Mitra also owns several large houses in this district and the leader of the church, Grigor Flavius, lives in one of these palatial estates.

All of the other villas and estates in the Royal District look like smaller, more modest versions of the two buildings. Family crests are seen on many of the banners at the front gates — less a sign of personal pride and more a system to navigate the winding streets and distinguish one house from another.

The Ruins of Belverus

High in the hills that flank the city, and across the shallow valleys and adjacent hilltops, there are ruins, tombs, and other ancient sites that honeycomb the area around Belverus and go deep into the hills themselves. Teams of excavators, both state and church sponsored, are hard at work digging down into the ground for these buried structures. Everything closest to the city within several miles has been thoroughly excavated and unearthed. Some of these sites are cordoned off as having historical value. Others have been left fallow. All have been emptied of their contents.

Yet there are many treasure hunters, ambitious scholars, and less upstanding citizens who have followed scraps of paper and strange clues and pieces of maps in the hopes of uncovering rare Acheronian artifacts, eldritch magic, or some other quick fortune. On the side of the road, a few enterprising souls each carry a basket full of genuine Acheronian jewelry, plundered just yesterday out of their sainted mother's family crypt, and available to such wealthy and learned travelers for one-tenth their real value.

There may well be some ancient and untouched site left to be discovered by intrepid thrill-seekers, but what strange secrets that lie in the rocks beneath Belverus may be best left undisturbed.

NUMALIA

Smaller in size than Belverus, but in some ways larger in stature, thanks to the ruins upon which it was founded. While not as large and impressive, the ruins run deep in Numalia, and some have theorized that the Acheronians lived partially underground at some point in their development. This is unfounded, of course, but there are a number of impressive treasures and antiquities in the public record (as well as in private collections) to allow Numalia to call itself the cultural center of Nemedia.

Furthermore, the crushing influence of the Church of Mitra is lessened, being somewhat removed from the church's headquarters. Consequently, the population is more cosmopolitan, and certainly more corruptible, but no less haughty and imperious when dealing with strangers, foreigners, or anyone considered beneath their station.

The Palian Way Gates

These gates are a major landmark for travelers on the Road of Kings, as they represent Nemedian culture and security. This set of ornate pillars has no roof attached to them, but the road leading into the city runs directly through them. Few caravans pass by Numalia in their haste to reach Aquilonia, as the city is only a half-day's journey from the Road of Kings, clearly visible from the mountain pass into Corinthia.

As in Belverus, the city watch is always on duty here, asking questions and giving directions and occasionally taking innocent bribes. Likewise, the Road of Kings is visible from the gates, giving the watch plenty of time to assess problems, call for reinforcements, or send a party out to intercept anyone trying to enter Numalia from the flank, rather than through the Palian Way Gates.

The Historical District

The road into Numalia widens past the gate and becomes Palian Way, a street with plants and trees in the median and a two-sided thoroughfare, the better to allow access to the chariots the wealthy ride through town. All incoming and outgoing traffic uses this road, and it is at times brought to a standstill by merchant caravans and the retinues of visiting dignitaries attempting to navigate the streets at the same time. When this happens, the city watch will resignedly intervene and slap horse's bottoms and direct traffic until the blockage is cleared.

Flanking either side of this thoroughfare are most of the intact ruins and structures: old temples, repurposed, one and two story shops that now house a family business, and even the odd villa offset from the road by a stone wall and gates made of iron.

Kallian Publico's Temple

This converted temple is now full of relics and antiques collected by Kallian Publico. There is little of rarity he does not covet and have the means to possess. Relic hunters find frequent employment with Publico both above and below board. Surely such sights dazzle, but who can say what strange histories and sorcery such artifacts may bring with them? Kallian Publico is described fully on page 83.

The Public Forum

This impressive collection of old buildings is arranged around a common square lined with brick streets and regularly painted in the colors of the Nemedian flag. These buildings oversee the city government, where laws are debated, criminals tried, and citizens' concerns are voiced. These discussions and arguments frequently start in the square, and also continue in the square long after the senate has adjourned. The Temple of Mitra and the Court of Justice sit opposite one another across the square, in eternal opposition.

Temple of Mitra

This building bears a strong resemblance to the building in Belverus, albeit half the size. Still, it is impressive enough to draw huge crowds, plan elaborate festivals that clog the streets, and take collections of offerings from the more wealthy church patrons.

This particular Temple of Mitra is more politically aggressive, and the current high priest of the church, Galarian Doulerus, is well known as both a devout priest and a social climber. He's not above administering a more liberal interpretation of Mitra's Blessing if it helps him stay above the huddled masses.

This temple is the second largest in Nemedia, and enjoys a close relationship with the headquarters in Belverus, even if that relationship is occasionally overlooked or ignored to achieve a goal. Several relic hunters operate here, and they are quite aggressive with their acquisitions policy. Some of the artifacts acquired by the church are donated to wealthy patrons and politicians to ensure that a vote or policy is upheld.

The Court of Justice

This low, wide building sits on a raised tier of stairs and faces the Temple of Mitra. This is the court of the land, where criminals are tried and sentenced. Nemedian justice was once considered the highest and wisest in the Western kingdoms, but there is now a ribbon of graft and the smell of corruption in this august body. For example, prominent citizens and the wealthy are not as encumbered by the law as commoners and foreigners, and are likely to be let off with a stern warning instead of a fine or imprisonment.

The Mercadium

In the center of the city is the wide, open space for the market. Not many of the original structures are standing, but the Nemedians have rebuilt around the ruins and travelers may buy and trade for most goods and services here.

The Barracks

The barracks is another walled courtyard, with long, low buildings flanking on three sides and an iron gate to restrict entrance. Here the city watch trains, sleeps, receives assignments, and wastes time when off duty.

The Stockades

In front of the iron gate, in another open area, is the city stockades, a raised platform with wood and stone framed stockades designed to hold criminals for quick punishments, like lashes, or extended punishments in the form of daily humiliations such as rocks and eggs thrown by brazen children and old people.

At night, prisoners are moved to the prison which faces east and shares a wall with the barracks. These small, cramped cells are where the prisoners sleep. Anyone on work detail in the mines or performing community service also sleeps and takes meals here. The cells are barely ten feet square and have no amenities to speak of.

The stocks are a reminder that public beatings and even executions can still take place, though it has been some time since this was needed.

The Pits

Considered by many a barbaric tradition pulled forward in time from Acheronians, it remains a popular pastime to allow certain slaves and criminals to fight in the arena for the pleasure of a bloodthirsty crowd. "The Pits", as they are commonly known, are a complex of four small arenas, surrounding a larger area where men fight to the death. The smaller pits are designed for one-on-one contests, hand-to-hand combat, and the occasional grudge match for the sake of discipline. The large arena in the center is for small groups, skirmishes, and the occasional man-versus-animal match. The smaller pits see action on a weekly basis. The larger pit is only active once or twice a month unless the government orders a match or there is a festival that would culminate in a blood sport.

The Church of Mitra has tried, unsuccessfully, to abolish these games. Some of the priests are still found in the upper boxes, the guest of a politician or a wealthy patron during the monthly matches.

The Arcadium

For those who want to be a part of the crowd, but dislike the blood sports associated with the Pits, there is a large, open forum on the westernmost side of the Pits called the Arcadium that caters to sporting types and gamblers. Of course, visitors can bet on the outcomes of the fights in the pits, but there are a number of sports ranging from cards and dice to scarab races and feats of strength that a gambling man would find very interesting.

Not surprisingly, this is where many of the criminal class can be found in Numalia. However, a fear of the draconian laws of the land keeps their infractions small and their escape routes open.

HANUMAR

Located in the north central portion of the kingdom, Hanumar does not benefit from a close proximity to the Road of Kings, but it does benefit greatly in being the largest city in the territory with a standing mercenary force. Built on the ruins of an older site than the ones found in Belverus and Numalia, these structures and crypts hearken back to a time when Stygia controlled most of the known lands. Hanumar was thought to be an outpost for the then-vast kingdom.

THE ADVENTURERS

Nemedia's famed Adventurers are a band of mercenaries, a loose alliance of mercenaries, former knights, soldiers, penniless nobles, and others who have taken up the trade of steel. Theirs is an informal organization, electing no captains or commanders, holding no rank and drawing no pay. Any two Adventurers can allow a worthy candidate into their fraternity, and an informal oath is all the requirement they need.

The Adventurers have no central base, and their members often join other military groups, fighting alongside Amalric's Free Companions, or as valued members of standing armies. Though there is no official uniform or insignia, Adventurers commonly garb themselves in unburnished chain mail, without surcoats or decorative motifs, an affectation that symbolizes their lack of leadership and their allegiance only to themselves and to each other. This loyalty, though, is not absolute, and Adventurers have been known to slay one another over grievances, though it is frowned upon by the others.

Joining the Adventurers is an easy enough task, requiring the presence and consent of two active Adventurers. The applicant must make successful Challenging (D2) Society and Persuade tests to convince these Adventurers,

though the difficulty may be adjusted by one or more steps based on circumstances, such as assisting them in battle or a past history of military excellence. Once an Adventurer, there is no further commitment to the group, though dishonorable or evil behavior might cause someone to be cast from their ranks. Similarly, an Adventurer can choose to leave the order at any time, and renounce membership without rancor.

The Adventurers lived by their swords.
— The Hour of the Dragon

The primary advantage to being an Adventurer is the respect given them by Nemedians, usually decreasing the difficulty of any Persuade or Society tests by one step, and their tendency to support one another, readily aiding their fellow Adventurers in battle and times of need. Adventurers within the same military company tend to gravitate towards one another, and they are quick to offer assistance when an Adventurer is down on their luck. Additionally, Adventurers generally find it easier to gain employ for mercenary work wherever they go, such is their reputation.

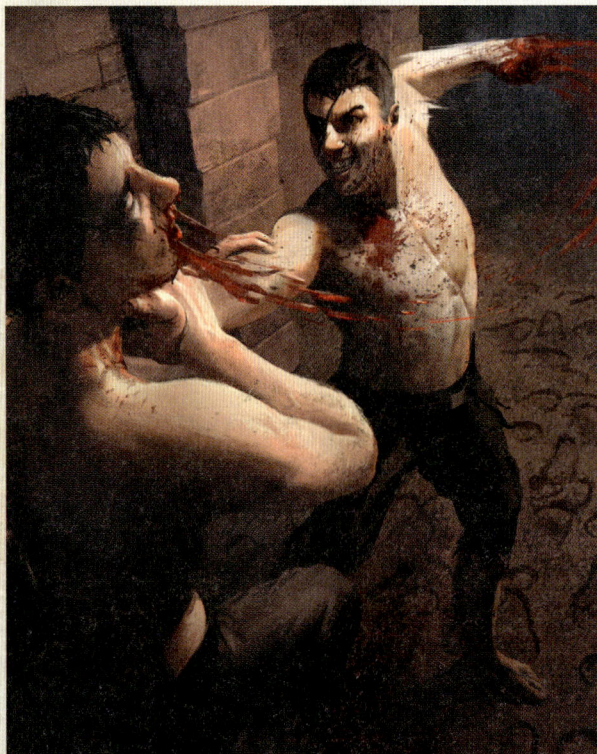

It's because of these incongruities that Hanumar is populated largely with Nemedians for whom the vast bureaucracy of the state and the overarching religion of Mitra is a poor fit. These rule-breakers and iconoclasts are not so great in number that the culture of Nemedia is swept aside, but the city itself and its inhabitants are much more colorful, more varied in nationalities, and the strictures of government are somewhat more relaxed. Belverus continues to try and exert its influence on the politicians in Hanumar, but these dissidents keep the capital at arm's length.

Hanumar is considered a major city (albeit the smallest of the three cities in Nemedia), but unlike its cousins in the south, has no walls around it. There are mounted patrols in all four cardinal directions, mostly from the Harrowers (see page 53) and the city guard takes over the watch within the city limits.

The Arena

The centerpiece of the city is the Arena, a massive coliseum built to hold gladiatorial games. It is the largest such place in all of Nemedia, and it flourishes because the location of the city is so remote compared to the more pious Numalia and the disapproving Belverus. But it draws contestants, willing and otherwise, from as far away as Ophir and Zingara. The matches are held every fortnight, and there is no shortage of fighters to wager upon.

This is the largest active arena hosting blood sports in the Western kingdoms. As such, many visitors from as far west as Zingara and as far east as Zamora have made the trek to watch or to participate in the arena matches.

There are a multitude of lodgings as well as taverns to eat and drink in and to place a friendly wager. These businesses exist to service the crowds during the sports. They are quite jaded when it comes to strangers, and the thieves don't rob from anyone that looks like they can handle themselves.

> *A dully glinting, mail-clad figure moved out of the shadows into the starlight. This was no plumed and burnished palace guardsman. It was a tall man in morion and gray chain mail — one of the Adventurers, a class of warriors peculiar to Nemedia; men who had not attained to the wealth and position of knighthood, or had fallen from that estate; hard-bitten fighters, dedicating their lives to war and adventure. They constituted a class of their own, sometimes commanding troops, but themselves accountable to no man but the king. Conan knew that he could have been discovered by no more dangerous a foeman.*
>
> — The Hour of the Dragon

The Temple of Ibis

This pyramid-shaped building is the dominant structure in the west quadrant of the city, a stunning example of ancient architecture. The top of the building is flat across, only accessible from within. The chambers under the church are rumored to contain the lost wealth of Stygia, but are also rumored to be heavily booby-trapped against intruders. No one has ever braved the catacombs, despite the local toughs always bragging in the local grog-shops.

Ibis is the celestial enemy of Set, and these churches oppose one another to this day. Ibis is the god of knowledge, and it is thought that the earliest attempts to study the ancients' culture came from these initial worshipers of Ibis. The temple has not halted its investigations, and actively competes with the Temple of Mitra in this endeavor. Very recently, Ibis decided to conscript its own relic hunters to compete against the rogues in Mitra's retinue to the prize. This program is too new to determine if it's a success or not.

The Temple of Ibis actively recruits relic hunters, and the process for joining this faction is similar to the Temple of Mitra. The high priest, Kalanthes, is old and wise and crafty, as well. He's fighting a spiritual war on several fronts: a hearts and minds campaign among the people of Hanumar, a race to grab resources from the Church of Mitra, and he must fend off the occasional attempt on his life from Stygian followers of Set. It is rumored that Kalanthes set up the church in Hanumar with a selection of texts and artifacts he borrowed from another priest long ago. Kalanthes is described more fully in the *Nameless Cults* sourcebook.

THE HARROWERS

Nemedian-trained, but not Nemedian-born, these freemen are composed of former gladiators, soldiers of fortune, formally freed slaves and servants, and disenfranchised mercenaries from a dozen lands and cultures. They are fierce fighters and draw a regular pay from the city, supplemented in part by funds from the Arena.

Harrowers patrol on horseback, a light, mobile cavalry force that also specializes in group defense and coordinated attacks with shield and spear, shield and sword, and crossbow. They are respected, if not feared, within the kingdom and revered in Hanumar. Most of the Harrowers have similar hard luck stories. But the steady pay and the awestruck servitude of the masses keep them happy and content to bolster the local army.

They clash regularly with barbarians from the north, and every patrol is outfitted with one or more lightly armored scouts who can cut and run so as to bring news of the fighting force to the regular army. They are an integral part of the country's vaunted defense strategy.

Joining the Harrowers requires little more than expressing your interest to do so, provided you have campaign experience or soldiering credentials you can present. New recruits work the first month without pay, and are given the most dangerous assignments. This separates the wheat from the chaff, and ensures the new recruits know what they signed on for. If they are still alive and interested at the end of the month, they can stay, though they may spend a few more months doing the grunt work until they can prove themselves in battle.

Harrowers receive a modest wage (a few Gold per month), food and shelter, and access to arms and equipment.

The Royal Vineyards

One of the most significant features is located in the south quadrant of town, visible from the road. Its walls are low, and are the only walls around Hanumar, but inside the cordon are rows upon rows of small green grapes that are tended to year-round. These are the Royal Vineyards, and the king visits the farm annually to pronounce them ready to pick. This event has become a minor festival, and the wine flows freely during his visit.

A division of the King's Guard is stationed at the farm and also serves as his eyes and ears in the city.

The Nemedian Crypts

The ground at Hanumar is excellent for growing grapes, and also for carving tombs into the earth. There is, in the east quadrant, a large field of burial sites, all from wealthy Nemedians who fell out of favor with the Church of Mitra, some going back several hundred years. There are many sinners, evil men, corrupt merchants, and feckless politicians buried in these august fields.

Some of the tombs and plots have been cleaned out and sit vacant, having been sold to wealthy Nemedian rogues wishing to be interred with the Acheronians. Other tombs have been marked as unsuitable for re-interment or dangerous. No one from Hanumar comes here after dark.

The Site of the Battle of Hanumar

In the north quadrant, on the outskirts of town, lays the remnant of a standing wall, and on the other side of the wall is a vast killing field. This was the site of the Battle of Hanumar, believed to be the first campaign the Hybori waged against the ancient Stygians. The site has been mostly excavated and has little to no artifacts of any kind, but it does serve as a meeting place for severe conversations, business negotiations, and political dealings. It's not uncommon to see mortal enemies seated upon the various cairns and markers, nose to nose, arguing to high heaven.

There is, however, an unspoken rule here: the site is neutral ground. The citizens of Hanumar agree that enough blood was spilled there already. Anyone fighting or attacking another physically in the boundaries of the site is arrested, fined, and shunned. It's considered bad luck to even draw a weapon on the battle site.

BRYTHUNIA

Northeastern-most country among the countries of the dreaming west, Brythunia is still young compared to its more established neighbors in the south and west. In this remote corner of the civilized world, the wheel of progress turns at a slower pace than to the west — and, in fact, it appears that the Brythunians sometimes drag their feet to halt the forward march of progress.

From a political perspective, Brythunia is broken into four major territories, with generous overlap between each border. These territories — kingdoms, more accurately — are held together by a ruling clan or family backed by the peasantry to secure their sovereignty, and with cooperating families and clans to enforce the rule, collect taxes, and so forth.

These alliances are fluid and shift freely, as often as the wind changes direction. The kingdoms are named after their ruling family. Each house has a fortified keep and land holdings in a defensible area, usually near favorable land for farming and raising livestock. The rest of the kingdom's holdings consist of rugged farmland, stark plains, rock-strewn hills, and a rawboned, healthy people who live in villages and try to eke out a life for themselves.

Brythunians are tall, rangy people, with fair to ruddy skin color. They are built for the cold climate and harsh living conditions. Hair color is blonde to light brown, with eyes of hazel, green, and blue.

BRYTHUNIAN HISTORY AND BACKGROUND

Brythunians can trace their lineage back to the Hybori in the north, themselves the descendants of Hyperborea, who moved north and east through the steppes and came to the cradle of the mountain range. There they planted their flag, encountering no resistance in this dim country.

For many generations, Brythunians became their own worst enemy as greed, ambition, lust, and worse sent the giant clans scurrying to secure property and hold onto it. For hundreds of years, the clans stole and murdered and ravaged indiscriminately.

Eventually, attrition and commerce conspired to do what morality and scruples could not, and the four kingdoms eased into a kind of peaceful truce. This allowed the Brythunians to establish roads, trade routes, agriculture, and other bartering necessities.

Now the country of Brythunia is healthy, but that has not stopped the clan leaders from plotting and scheming to better their political situation. No one wants to go to war and so diplomacy, arranged marriages, and the occasional political bribe do much of the work.

There are rumors of dire plots, as is always the case, but the Brythunian clans have their own agendas, some of which may be considered hostile to their neighbors. The country is awash in spies, both within the families and without, to feed information back and try to keep things under control, lest a costly war break out.

Almost all farmers in Brythunia are also fighters. The entire kingdom is one massive army waiting for a battle, making villages and townships while it waits. This make the average Brythunian more dangerous in a chance encounter. Only in the halls of the kings and queens does the influence of civilization bring about corruption of mind, body, and spirit, as the leaders vie for political control and engineer elaborate plans to avoid having to go to war over farming rights. The leaders themselves may have been battlefield generals in their youth, but their sons and daughters are already used to a life of relative comfort and never wanting for food or drink.

These family members, then, are the most vulnerable political targets, and they tend to spend their time well out of sight, or far behind the walls of their sanctuary. Women are married off as soon as possible to avoid becoming a political liability, and the sons are sent away to school in neighboring countries under false names. Those sons and daughters who end up staying are taught to fight and trained to lead armies and command forces from a battlefield camp.

The population is well spread out; instead of clusters of cultured cities, a multitude of hamlets and towns litter the countryside, connected by crisscrossing roads and buttressed against acres of farmland. There are four major kingdoms in Brythunia — although by the standards of most other nations of the Hyborian Age, these "kingdoms" are scarcely worth the name.

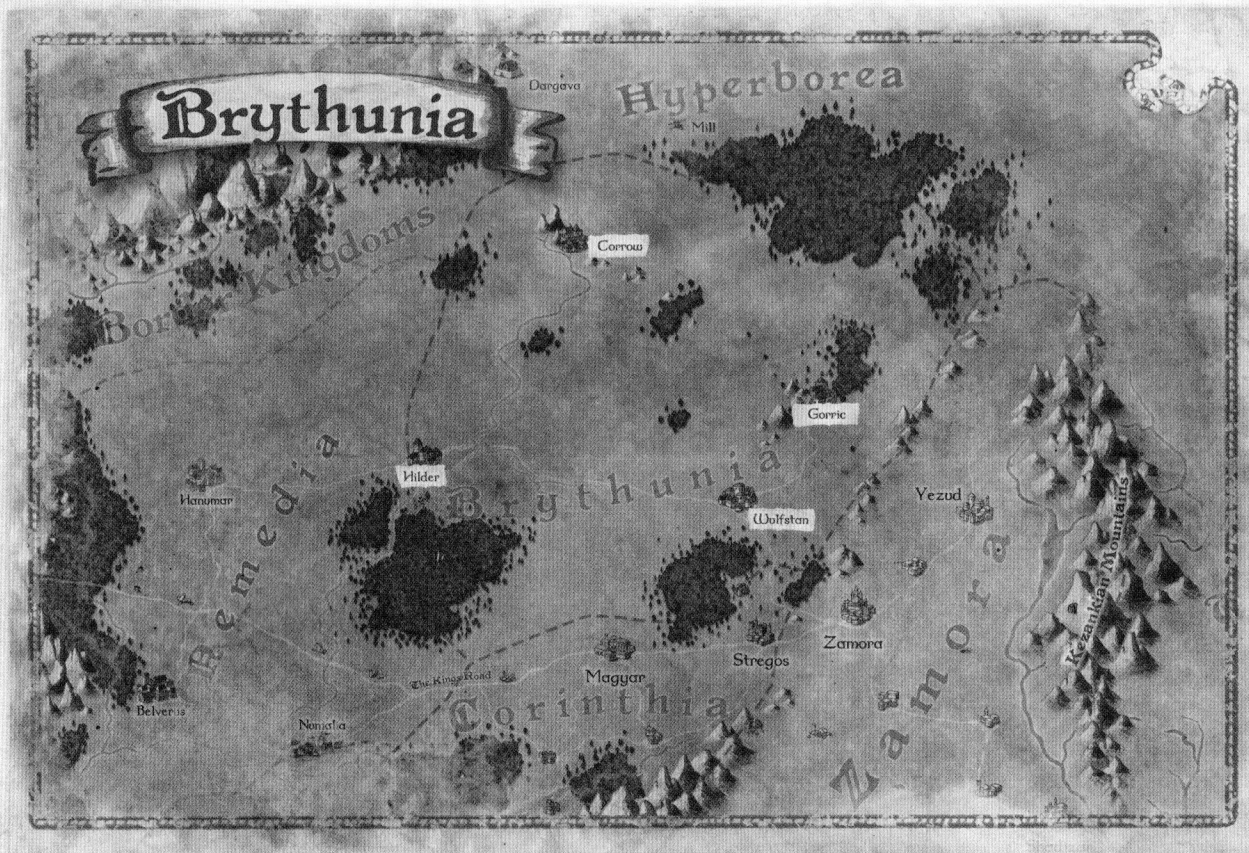

ZAMORIAN PREJUDICE

Zamora is the gateway to the decadent east and, despite the mountains that separate Brythunia and its most exotic neighbor in the east, the people of Brythunia have had many dealings with Zamorians and consider them a criminal culture. As a result, any Zamorian attempting a Society test against a Brythunian will find that test one step of Difficulty higher. Should the Zamorian fail the test, they are unable to interact with the Brythunian citizen in a peaceful manner.

"Let a Zamorian dog wander the steppes with no food or water...," a Brythunian is apt to say, *"if they don't first meet their end upon a sword."*

MAJOR KINGDOMS OF BRYTHUNIA

The four major kingdoms include trading posts, villages, farms, and forts, all loyal to the ruling family or one of the extended clans of families that pledge fealty. These peasants are taxed in goods and gold in exchange for protection, security, and sometimes advancement.

Despite their uneasy political alliances, the four kingdoms would rally under a single banner against a foreign threat, the leader the one whose border was threatened. In this manner, Brythunia maintains its sovereign status despite refusing to conform to the more progressive advances of Nemedia and the ancient, corrupt wisdom of Zamora.

- **Corrow:** The northern king is Dreuvis Corrow, latest in an unbroken line several hundred years old. Land and king see Corrow as protector of the realm, ready to halt the barbarian horde across the mountains. The folk of Corrow are proud and honorable in their dealings, sometimes to their detriment.

- **Gorric:** Prince Valcuss is the young leader in the east, a hot-tempered, impulsive, and charismatic man. Gorric raises fierce fighting clans, hungry for battle, who bicker and fight constantly.

- **Wulfstan:** King Pendrys is the leader of the prevailing power in the south. Wulfstan is a cautious kingdom, its people sullen and untrusting of strangers. They value intelligence and knowledge and are known for their cunning in battle.

- **Hilder:** The most progressive kingdom is steered by Queen Rainnic, leader of the richest and most powerful family in the west. They have profited from many lucrative business arrangements with Corinthia and Zamora. Their political ambition is as deep as their coffers.

Their alliances constantly shift, as business dealings fail, treaties are broken, and borders are crossed. Brythunia is more concerned with foreign neighbors, and accords with Corinthia and Zamora are reached and maintained with deliberate care.

CORROW

Corrow is cold, stark, and rocky. Farms are in short supply, but there are plenty of animals to raise for meat and resources, including goats, which fetch a premium as food and pack animals. The capital is located at the edge of a bluff, overlooking the plains in the north. It is an ideally defensible position, with high walls and ramparts and battlements, and siege engines ready to deploy. Only a fool would attack Corrow from the south.

King Dreuvis and his court have scant political ambition. They are content with their lot and seek only the advancement of Brythunia as a unified country. Personal honor is important to the people of Corrow, and they insist on honoring agreements, treating people fairly, and following the law.

Corrow's Relationships with the Other Kingdoms

Corrow's insistence on all dealings being above-board is perceived as a weakness by the other Brythunian kingdoms. In truth, Corrow employs spies in the form of emissaries, vassals, political strategists, and diplomats, all the better to listen openly rather than covertly. These agents use bribery, threats, and other forms of persuasion, but King Dreusian draws the line at assassination, for now.

- **Gorric:** Corrow spends a lot of time calming Prince Valcuss. The two kingdoms are most alike in philosophy, if not temperament, and Gorric would be the first to assemble with Corrow if war was inevitable.

- **Wulfstan:** King Pendrys and King Dreuvis are openly opposed to one another. Pendrys embraces all the tactics of Zamora, including assassins to achieve his political ends, despite his open hostility and contempt for Zamorians. All the kingdoms are a chessboard, its people the pawns. If Wulfstan could make a move against Corrow, it would.

- **Hilder:** Queen Rainnic and King Dreuvis are cordial to one another, but Corrow doesn't trust Hilder. Hilder tries to better relations with Corrow, because Hilder needs Corrow's famed Iron Brigade as part of their defense against the other kingdoms. The Queen sees Corrow as naive and trusting to a fault, especially where Gorric is concerned.

GORRIC

The harsh mountains in the west give way to hills and canyons, and eventually a vast grassy plain. The hill-bred folk of Gorric are proud, fierce, and live for battle. They hunt along the divide where the streams from the mountains feed into the plains. Situated in the middle of a high steppe, the capital of Gorric overlooks the sparse forests that flank the hills between the plains. From their lookout perches, Gorric's watch can see for miles in every direction.

Prince Valcuss is new to rule, having lost his father in a hunting accident. What he lacks in wisdom, he makes up for in magnetism. As such, his political ambitions have yet to fully develop. His is the wild card in the Brythunian game of kings.

Gorric's Relationships with the Other Kingdoms

Gorric's famous fiery temperament makes it unwise political allies and worse political adversaries. Prince Valcuss knows he has much to prove to himself and his people, and is acting as a young man would act — beating his chest and daring others to fight him. But he is quickly realizing that there are more weapons at his disposal than just his lancers.

- **Corrow:** King Dreuvis was friends with Valcuss' father, and has taken an interest in Valcuss' development as a leader. He hopes to teach Valcuss the folly of war before he gets a taste of it. The two kingdoms are close allies.

- **Wulfstan:** Valcuss doesn't trust King Pendrys because he doesn't understand the machinations Wulfstan employs to survive. That doesn't keep Wulfstan from its peaceful overtures towards Gorric, in hopes of swaying their considerable military might over to their cause.

- **Hilder:** Queen Rainnic and Valcuss openly despise one another. Their forces skirmish constantly, moving their borders forward or backwards a few yards at a time. Rainnic thinks Valcuss too young to rule, uncontrollable, and he thinks she's duplicitous and cunning to a fault. He suspects Rainnic had something to do with his father's death.

WULFSTAN

The dry, arid plains that run south and east into the mountains are harsh and unforgiving, a perfect match for the kingdom of Wulfstan. They are a careful people, taking every advantage, farming where they can, and hunting when they can't. This adaptability makes them cautious and cunning, in both life and politics.

Wulfstan's capital is nestled into a desert canyon with only one entry. The canyon and the arroyo it feeds into is honeycombed with tunnels, trap doors, and bolt holes. Death can strike from every direction before an army can make it to the walls of the city. King Pendrys is an older man, no stranger to complex political games, especially with his old rival, Queen Rainnic, with whom he shares a complicated history. His strategy is to let the other kingdoms destroy themselves so he can claim Brythunia without a fight.

Wulfstan's Relationships with the Other Kingdoms

Wulfstan's watchword is patience. They wait for the opportune moment to act. King Pendrys keeps a steady eye on the other kingdoms, looking for exploitable signs of weakness.

- **Corrow:** There is no love lost between King Pendrys and King Dreuvis. Their acrimony goes back hundreds of years in their lineage. Corrow can't overlook Wulfstan's lies, and Wulfstan can't understand why Corrow does not lie.

- **Gorric:** Prince Valcuss keeps his distance from Wulfstan, recognizing he is out of his depth. King Pendrys, though, extends the olive branch, trying to drive Corrow and Gorric apart.

- **Hilder:** Rumors and a couple of bawdy songs tease about happened between King Pendrys and Queen Rainnic in their younger days, an event that drove a wedge between the kingdoms that has yet to be mended.

HILDER

The western fields, wide open save for the rolling hills, are home to Hilder. The smallest, but richest, kingdom, Hilder attempts to do what the other kingdoms won't: compromise for peace. Without massive military resources, the soldiers of Hilder must outthink their opponents, or better, never engage the enemy. Hilder's capital sits at the mouth of a major river, ensuring abundant farmland and room to raise livestock. This is the garden spot of Brythunia, making Hilder a target for the rest of the kingdoms.

Queen Rainnic is aware of her precarious position, and has cultivated relationships with nobles in Corinthia and Zamora who would ride to her banner, if the need arose. She is not above using her access to foreign powers to completely overthrow Brythunia, if she thought she could reclaim it after the dust settled.

Hilder's Relationships with the Other Kingdoms

Hilder wants to rule Brythunia. They have made inroads with their neighbors, and have a progressive outlook on the future. The country's strength is in its deep purse. Mercenaries, assassins, and other tools of empire-building are readily purchased and ferried in and out of Brythunia on its eastern trade routes.

- **Corrow:** Queen Rainnic thinks King Dreuvis to be charmingly naive in matters political. She has tried several approaches to make peace with him and quickly run out of patience. But she recognizes his strength as an ally, especially against Wulfstan.

- **Gorric:** Hilder was first to acknowledge the sovereignty of Prince Valcuss. She considers Gorric dangerous because of his unpredictability, and tries to manage her expectations of what the Mad Prince may do.

- **Wulfstan:** Queen Rainnic hates Wulfstan and spits to the south whenever the name is mentioned. Their mutual hatred is legendary and keeps either side from advancing politically.

BRYTHUNIAN VILLAGE DESIGN

Most of the political intrigue in and around Brythunia is likely concentrated in the small villages which comprise the kingdom; while this may seem dull, it shouldn't. Instead, the player characters should see this as an opportunity to truly affect the nation they find themselves in. Things can go very wrong, very quickly in a small village, but build enough of a following and one might just find themselves with a chance of taking over with political influence and the beginnings of an army.

These places are rife with adventure and opportunity. Murder, magic, mayhem — it can reside in a village as readily as a city… it just hides itself better. Should the gamemaster need a village during the player characters' travels, the following system can be used to quickly generate a small settlement for the purpose of setting a scene.

BRYTHUNIAN SETTLEMENTS

Roll	Building Type	Unique Feature	Personality Trait	Person
1	Farm	Cairn	Affable	Villager
2	Farm	Cairn	Cantankerous	Villager
3	Farm	Public Well	Cautious	Homesteader
4	Dwelling	Public Well	Curious	Homesteader
5	Dwelling	Standing Stones	Emotional	Laborer
6	Dwelling	Standing Stones	Fatalistic	Laborer
7	Trading Post	Fountain	Gloomy	Ex-Soldier
8	Blacksmith	Fountain	Hostile	Ex-Soldier
9	Inn	Hanging Tree	Humorless	Criminal
10	Tavern	Hanging Tree	Kind	Trader
11	Stables	Pigeon Coop	Mean	Pilgrim
12	Meeting Hall	Pigeon Coop	Narrow-Minded	Merchant
13	Church	Deserted House	Overbearing	Widow/Widower
14	Butcher	Deserted House	Prejudiced	Village Elder
15	Tanner	Old Ruins	Proselytizing	Mother
16	Carpenter	Old Ruins	Secretive	Father
17	Herbalist	Bridge	Stern	Youth
18	Healer	Bridge	Surly	Spy
19	Brewer	Stockade	Unfriendly	Thief
20	Unique Feature	Stockade	Weary	Fugitive

Generate the Road

The gamemaster should roll 3⚔. The number rolled is the number of roads in the village. You can map this out on paper or remember it. The larger the number, the larger the village. A result of 1 means that the road the players are on is the only road — literally a stop along the way. A result of 6 means that there is a crossroad and other streets that branch off from the main roads. No roads means that the village is barely on the map, and is merely a small cluster of buildings with no rhyme or reason, and only faint trails leading in and out.

Once the number of roads in the village is determined, the gamemaster can assign or randomly roll on the *Brythunian Settlements* table (above). Not every village has every business or building listed. A good rule of thumb is to take the number of roads rolled and

Continued on next page…

...continued from previous page.

multiply it by three. Roll up to that many times for the settlement, or choose as desired from the list.

If necessary, the gamemaster can also roll for the person or people of note in the village — either running a business, passing through, or involved in some other way as required.

Building Type

- **FARM:** This can be a farm that grows crops or raises livestock, or both, if it's small.

- **DWELLING:** This is a small house, made of sod and wood, with a thatched roof that shelters a single family.

- **TRADING POST:** A general store, relying on merchants and peddlers to stock and restock its shelves. Barter is accepted if gold is not available. Each trading post is different and is not guaranteed to carry what a player character might need.

- **BLACKSMITH:** This person can re-shoe a horse, make or repair iron tools, and, if the player characters are lucky, can mend armor or make and repair weapons.

- **INN:** Smaller, less opulent than the common houses in cities, these inns offer indoor sleeping in the common room, and food and drink for people on the road.

- **TAVERN:** Similar to an inn, only without the sleeping privileges.

- **STABLES:** Player characters can board their horses here and feed them, as well. Some stables have a horse or two for sale.

- **MEETING HALL:** If the settlement is large enough, the meeting hall is where the villagers gather to discuss community-wide problems, enact laws, and dispense justice.

- **CHURCH:** This small church belongs to a pious wanderer spreading the gospel of Mitra, Ibis, or one of the other friendly religions in the Western kingdoms.

- **BUTCHER:** This person guts and processes game and livestock for those unwilling to do so themselves or for traveling caravans.

- **TANNER:** Usually found right next door to the butcher, this person tans, treats, and cures animal skins.

- **CARPENTER:** This person makes and repairs items from wood.

- **HERBALIST:** A country version of an apothecary.

- **HEALER:** This person may also be the village soothsayer, delivering prophecy and curing the sick.

- **BREWER:** This person makes beer or mead from the local farmers' crops.

- **UNIQUE FEATURE:** Roll or pick from the Unique Feature column.

Unique Feature

- **CAIRN:** An old burial mound near the settlement, and one that the villagers wisely steer clear of. It may be a more recent Brythunian mound or something more ancient and awful.

- **PUBLIC WELL:** A watering hole with a bucket and maybe even signposts for travelers to take a cool drink and water their horses. There may be other people present at the public well.

- **STANDING STONES:** An ancient configuration of stones, currently in use by the local villagers. These stones may be Hyperborean, or even older.

- **FOUNTAIN:** A carved fountain, small and simple but tapped into fresh well water. It serves as a gathering spot for the local villagers.

- **HANGING TREE:** There may or may not be corpses hanging from the boughs of this ancient tree, usually at a crossroads, and a reminder that Brythunian justice is swift and merciless.

- **PIGEON COOP:** These coops of pigeons are trained to fly to their masters' keep in whichever kingdom they are found. Commonly used to pass on time-sensitive information.

- **DESERTED HOUSE:** There are any number of reasons why this house is deserted. It's up to the gamemaster to decide if this is an advantage or a disadvantage for players.

Continued on next page...

...continued from previous page.

- **OLD RUINS:** The remnants of a stone edifice of some kind are present in or near the village. They may be cursed, off-limits, forbidden, sacred, or in use as another dwelling for travelers or merchants.

- **BRIDGE:** This wood or stone bridge crosses a creek or small river. It may be guarded, decrepit, washed away entirely, under construction, or very rickety.

- **STOCKADE:** Here is a set of stocks and maybe even a sign, so that everyone riding by will know what the person in the stocks is guilty of.

Persons

- **VILLAGER:** A native Brythunian peasant, inevitably from the Brythunian kingdom in which they are encountered.

- **HOMESTEADER:** Farmers or settlers from elsewhere, trying to eke out a living for themselves.

- **LABORER:** Hard-working, strong-backed person, most likely from somewhere outside of Brythunia and working off a debt in manual labor or indentured servitude.

- **EX-SOLDIER:** Brythunian campaigner, not necessarily old, possibly injured and unable to serve in the army. There's a small chance the soldier is from somewhere else, like Nemedia or Corinthia.

- **CRIMINAL:** This person is wanted for crimes he may or may not have committed. This is not something he will readily admit to, of course, and should the truth come out, he would do anything to keep it from spreading.

- **TRADER:** This person barters for a living, and the business he operates is an outgrowth of that.

- **PILGRIM:** Someone from another country, living a pious and simple life, spreading the word of his faith to all of the heathens and savages in Brythunia.

- **MERCHANT:** This person spends time on the road buying and selling commodities, but his home and base of operations is in this Brythunian village.

- **WIDOW/WIDOWER:** Brythunian citizen who has lost a loved one to war or disease.

- **VILLAGE ELDER:** This person need not be ancient and wizened, merely the oldest or one of the oldest people around.

- **MOTHER:** Roll 1+1🐦. That's the number of children this person has in her care.

- **FATHER:** Roll 1+1🐦. That's the number of children this person has in his care.

- **YOUTH:** A teenager or young adult. Presumably an orphan, but not necessarily.

- **SPY:** Roll again on the *Person* column on the *Brythunian Settlements* table (page 59). That result is his assumed identity. His mission is entirely up to the gamemaster. A spy will never reveal his true nature unless the player characters are somehow involved in his mission, and it's necessary to bring them into the spy's confidence.

- **THIEF:** This person has set themselves up to fleece the population. Roll again on the *Person* column on the *Brythunian Settlements* table (page 59). That is his assumed identity, and the thief will have a business or a cart or an operation in keeping with his rolled persona. A thief pretending to be an ex-soldier, offering protection for a small settlement, may be stringing them along until he can learn where the family treasures are hidden. Once the thief has stolen or acquired the desired target, he leaves as fast as his feet or his horse can take them.

- **FUGITIVE:** Roll twice more. The first roll is who they really are and the second roll is what they pretend to be. This kingdom wants them for a crime they may or may not have committed. Uncovering a fugitive's secret can be very dangerous to everyone.

CHAPTER 3

EVENTS

> *He needed no meditation for decision; what he needed was a tool. And Fate furnished that tool, working among the dives and brothels of the squalid quarters even while the young nobleman shivered and pondered in the part of the city occupied by the purple-towered marble and ivory palaces of the aristocracy.*
>
> — "Rogues in the House"

The status quo is enemy of the thief. Crime flourishes when the eyes of the crown look outside their own domains. A thief works in the shadows of the larger world, but if those shadows do not move, he is a stationary target. The underworld is not a calm, placid sea. Like the world it reflects, the underground is volatile, dangerous, and ever shifting.

As events in a town, city, or kingdom change, so must the underworld move to accommodate and exploit these new positions. Old thieves are rare, and those who reach advanced years in this business do not do so by remaining predictable. Just as the history of the earth is a cycle of rising and falling civilizations, barbaric savagery and grand monuments, so too the career of any thief shall see its highs and lows. Some are purely personal, while others are beset upon him by the wider world. The streets are ridden with filth, torch-grime, and bloody knives — in this world one thrives or perishes. Simply "making due" is an expedient route to an unmarked grave.

PERSONAL EVENTS

You may have compatriots, fellow knives and cutters, but they are temporary, of an evening or a fortnight. Loyalties move with the wind as shadows move with the light. The greater bulk of humanity is a target, an obstacle, or a threat — they are not friends.

Thieves are solitary, loners out to line their purses, not make friends and lovers. He or she may have both in their seasons, but no lover or friend is as loyal or lustrous as gold. The world acts more upon the thief than he upon the world — for such is life in the gutters — but personal events are common, motivating, and often lead to the greatest, or most disastrous, of adventures.

RIVALRIES

It should first be said that all thieves are rivals to some degree. Jewels split in two are not as grand as those shared with no one. Yet a thief can take such temporary betrayals in stride. It is, after all, what the thief himself would do. Sometimes, though, a particular thief meets his equal, and the two never get along. They become rivals.

One may seek ever to outdo the other — to have the best tale, steal the best score, or join the most prestigious guild. Such rivalry is friendly or, when it is not, it is unlikely to inspire true hate. These rivals are enemies, true, but they are respected enemies. They have bested you and you them in your time. You would not cry if their corpses were found in the river, but you would unlikely be the one to put them there... at least not cheaply.

Having a rival raises the stakes and the skills of the parties involved. It is often our enemies which push us the hardest, which make us rise greater to heights. *"A good enemy is more valuable than a good friend,"* Shevatas once said, *"for you expect the former to betray you, and if you are wise you will see it coming!"*

> The Cimmerian made no attempt to match wits and intrigue with Thutmekri and his Shemitish partner, Zargheba. He knew that if Thutmekri won his point, he would insist on the instant banishment of his rival.
>
> — "Servants of Bit-Yakin"

GRANT ME REVENGE

Rivals are enemies who live to one-up each other, but there are some enemies who are bitter, bound by blood spilled and promises broken. Often, they began as friends. In Yezud, they say, "There is little profit in revenge, but there is even less in being seen to have been beaten." Revenge is not strictly a means to riches, but thieves aren't always after gold alone. Like anyone, they have times when their blood boils and murder flares in their eyes like falling stars in the night. If someone wronged you, you are likely going to take revenge out of anger or necessity. Of course, if you wrong others, they are likely to do the same to you.

The event causing this need to avenge oneself is rarely trivial. There are enmities which begin with but a slight, though they escalate if one reaches this point. Revenge is a bloody business and some cultures have rules to guide it. Vendhyans, for example, have a codified system for exacting what they call "blood justice". Other cultures have no such rules, but there is yet to be found a human culture where revenge wasn't present. Whether considered sacred or simply part of business, vendettas are common in the underworld from the Western Ocean to far Khitai.

The gamemaster should decide how far the opponent is willing to go to gain — or avoid — vengeance. An entire campaign might center on a wronged crew of thieves tracking their betrayers one by one until each is dead or driven mad. Conan, after all, was not one to easily forgive a slight.

TARGET FOR MURDER

While some want to kill you for personal reasons — bedding their mates, killing their relatives, stealing their prized gems — others do it merely as the simplest, cleanest course of action. It is not personal... to them. To the throat-slitter so targeted, it is personal in the extreme. There is a bounty on one's head or an assassin following one's step.

For whatever reason, one or more of the player characters have become liabilities to someone with the means to dispose of such problems. While it could be some equal who seeks their death, it is usually more interesting if the death mark comes from a powerful individual or organization. Such resources employed toward killing the player characters can make any town, city, or even kingdom dangerous territory.

There are usually three ways to respond to a death threat — run, fight back, or resolve the issue between the targets and the killers.

Running is by far the most common course of action, and the gamemaster can use it to move the player characters out of one area and into another with a reasonably smooth narrative transition. Left to their own devices, player characters are often able to make powerful enemies that chase them out of town. Should they seek to resolve the situation, the player characters must fix whatever situation has required their death. If they know too much about a certain job, they have to make the consequences of that job disappear. If they stole something the guild wanted, perhaps they have to give it back. Neither option brings coin, but it does buy them their necks.

The alternative to those options is fighting back. This is perilous given that the person or organization who set killers upon them likely has significant resources. But think what a legend a group of lowly thieves would become if the top gang in Shadizar put a death mark on their heads and, instead of running, they sought out and killed those who wanted them dead. Well, the player characters might wind up dead in this case, but what a storied way to become (posthumous) legends. By the House of Shades, they might even win!

FRAMED OR SET UP

There is no reason to take the blame for something you did if someone else is there to bear the burden of your guilt. There is always more than one thief, or fool, to frame or set up. If you cannot spot who that fool or thief is, chances are it's you.

As we've said, thieves have few friends and many more alliances of convenience. Turning on one another is common to the point of being expected, and even the absence of betrayal breeds further suspicion. The larger the job — a score, a murder, a kidnapping — the more effort goes into catching the perpetrators. An excellent means of buying time, or getting away entirely, is to set someone else up for the crime. It wouldn't do to frame a royal for pilfering his own treasury, but a fellow thief? Well, the authorities make little distinction between one rat and another. Feeding a rival or hapless cur to the city guard is respectable practice. Yet, despite what novice cut-purses claim, guards are not fools as a rule. They may lack motivation and a desire to delve deep into a crime but, when they are so prodded, they can become quite tenacious. Better then to have set up another group of thieves prior to the crime.

Player characters might be the ones doing the setting up or the ones framed by others. They plan the former and try to find a way out of the latter. Like making an enemy, this could run them out of town or another locale. It could also land them in prison, where someone may believe they owe a debt if their name is to be cleared.

DEBT

Some debts are earned, others are foisted upon the rogue. Life is not fair, especially for those who steal from, rather than reside inside, the great spires of civilization. You may have gambled your way to a flophouse, and your marker has just been called in. Perhaps a powerful princess once did you a favor and now demands payment in kind.

The player characters may have landed in jail — by their own actions or the plotting of others. If escape is impossible, someone might come to them with a deal. After all, a group of killers and pickpockets on hard times is not only useful but disposable.

> *"He is due ten years at hard labor for housebreaking, but if you say the word, we'll arrange for him to escape and none but us will ever know anything about it. I understand — you wouldn't be the first young nobleman who had to resort to such things to pay gambling debts and the like. You can rely on our discretion."*
>
> **— The Inquisitor, "The God in the Bowl"**

What the debt is should come either from the course of the campaign itself or agreed upon character background. It is rarely fair to impose a debt on a player character that they have no say in. Some Howard tales begin with Conan so indebted, and the gamemaster may well do the same, but having players agree beforehand is generally considered good form.

The nature of the debt likely determines the difficulty, danger, or expense of the debt's resolution. That having been said, the leverage which the person owed can apply to the debtor may exceed the original nature of the debt. If you owe more money than you'll ever be worth, and the gang you owe wants someone killed, then that debt is suddenly worth someone's life.

As the campaign progresses, the player characters may find they are in the position of being the ones owed. Non-player characters or even fellow player characters might cow under their will as they once cowed under the will of others. Of course, one is only the toughest person in the Maul until someone tougher comes along. Too few thieves remember that when the time comes.

THE JEWELS CEASE TO SPARKLE

A life of poverty is where most thieves began. To return to the gutter is ever in their minds and, while by no means desirable, is not the worst fate. No, worse still is when the gold loses its luster, when the gems no longer sparkle, and when thrill of the score no longer slakes one's thirst. Thieves burn out.

Now, not all do, but it does happen to some. A life of stealing, of being so close to the rude razor of civilization can, on occasion, cause one to reflect. Thieves who reflect have probably already lost their edge. The world has little utility for a thief without avarice or an addiction to danger. The cautious thief, it is said, is soon dead.

You may have gotten old, acquired a paunch whilst not looking, or merely begun to believe — Bel forbid — that there is more to this life than ill-gotten wealth. When and if this happens, you need to reignite the larcenous flame which drove you in the seasons of your youth. As old soldiers sometimes lose their bloodlust, old or accomplished thieves lose their greed. There's always a young comer ready to take their place.

That comer may be a non-player character or group thereof who seek to usurp the well-appointed player characters. This reinvigorates a campaign in which the player characters have reaped the rewards of the thieving life. Likewise, putting the player characters in the position of would-be usurpers can start a campaign. Nothing is stable in the underworld. Nothing is certain. Like the untamed wild, the urban centers of this earth also have survival mechanisms baked in. The strong rule until they become weak. The old dictate until the young eat them. Such is the commonality between savagery and civilization. Such is the truth that men are never so different as their surroundings may allow them to pretend.

CITY AND TOWN EVENTS

The countryside is a place for chicken-killers and cattle thieves. True men of the night make their way to towns and cities if they hope to increase the size of their purse and reach of their name. While the odd village may possess a rare treasure, or be bilked of their coin, stealing it proves but a trickle for an enterprising rogue.

Instead, the minarets and spires, the foul sewers and bloating river corpses call. Home is the Maul, the ghetto, the bad side of town. Here, where populaces are dense and accustomed to a harsh world of lies and backstabbing, fortunes are won and lost — sometimes both in a single night. Like rats, the greater host of larcenous hearts flock to where man and woman warren under the stone arches of so-called "civilization".

GANG WAR

Any location with significant crime sees an organized version thereof. Some flourish, while others sink beneath the scummy surface of whatever pond they attempted to control. The most common cause of such demise is a gang war, a battle between thieves, gangs, guilds, crews, and the like.

There are towns, and even some cities, controlled by single gangs but most are split among two or more entities perpetually vying for control. Territory staked out one day

is contested the next, and Bel help any burglar who steals from the wrong side of some imaginary border between gangs. Treaties exist, both written and unspoken, which bind gangs to certain conditions, but only fools trust a thief to keep his word. In Zamora the Accursed, an entire year saw bloodshed, kidnapping, murder, extortion, and economic upheaval in what was known as "The Year of the Thief".

Player characters can be members of any side in such a war or caught in the middle. Perhaps, if they are independents, both sides seek to hire them or use them as mediators. If the campaign is set in a single locale, the player characters could be well-established gang members whose friends have died or been "vanished" in the war. Such "rat's wars" — for such are they commonly known — spill over into the daily life of otherwise honest folk. The tavern owner, paying protection to the neighborhood gang, finds rivals are now leaning on him, as well. The supply of certain goods is reduced to a trickle as one gang cuts off the supply of the other. All of this creates economic consequences and, when the coin of the wealthy is threatened, soon the town guard step in.

WATCH CRACKDOWN

A certain amount of larceny, murder, smuggling, and the like is expected — even encouraged — by those who rule over the hoi polloi. No large town or city functions without its underbelly. The world of the thieves is at once an outlet to vent the psychic frustration of the populace, a source of hard-to-find items, a vital part of the economy, and a useful tool when one powerful noble plays against another. In dire times, though, a clever prince may blame those who live in the shadows for the ills the ruler himself has brought upon his subjects. "There!" he says, "Those are the degenerates to blame!"

The reason for a watch crackdown could also be legitimate. As seen above, gang wars get out of hand and threaten more than those rogues who wage them. Whatever the cause, thieves generally dread those days when the watchmen are extra sharp, nigh impervious to bribes, and beset with quotas to haul in a goodly number of their lot.

While prices for illicit good can rise in these times — thus increasing profit — penalties for every crime go up, and the likelihood of being found out is far greater. Any crime, no matter how petty, might become "an example" which the guard uses to deter further crime. Scaring up jobs in such a clime becomes a hustle in itself, and those thieves who are not the most clever, sharpest knives in the drawer often do not make it through. This does weed out the curds, but even a great thief can get caught in a run of bad luck. If they are lucky, penury or mere imprisonment in the king's dungeons are their penalties. If unlucky, they die of starvation in a gibbet, pelted by rotten food and worse.

SIEGE!

Every city-dweller fears a siege… well, almost every one. When the king's army or companies of mercenaries camp outside the walls of Khorshemish, smart citizens pray to whatever gods they worship or those the soon-to-be-conquering enemy venerate.

Sieges are hard on cities; prolonged sieges are nightmares. No city has an infinite supply of food, and some even find access to fresh water cut off. People die of infection, of battle wounds, of plague that festers, and starvation and thirst. Look closely into the scrolls of the Nemedians if you can read — the great sieges nearly all speak of cannibalism. One would be forgiven for thinking hell, or the Outer Dark, had visited the earth during such times.

Yet some see profit in it. At first, goods are cut off and those who still have them, or can filch them, get a premium price. Once such goods run out, people get desperate, nerves fray, and citizens turn on each other. A skilled, practiced thief knows this a gainful opportunity. A throat-slitter knows he can trade his familiarity with murder for coin and food.

Gangs thrive at times like these but know their position of fortune is temporary. In the end, whether it be the butcher or wainwright, spaewife or thief, all inside the city walls suffer if the siege is not lifted. One cheat a thief might keep to herself is the greatest treasure of all in such times — a way out. Holes in old walls, an under city, aquifers, and sewers are all potential ways out of a besieged city. Thieves and other lowly folk are the most likely to have maps of such places burned behind their eyes. Yet the army outside may have already collapsed the tunnels, set guards where the sewers spill out, and have sappers working the under city. What then?

Sell out your fellow citizenry, if you can. The difference between a thief and a spy during siege is the difference between a dead man and a living one.

THE PRINCE OF THIEVES IS DEAD!

Let us be uncharacteristically honest — many claim the title "Prince of Thieves". One can go all the way from Shadizar the Wicked to mighty Tarantia and in every tavern between hear that someone claims that title. Yet true thieves know only the very few are heir to such storied monikers — Shevatas and Taurus among them.

What happens when one of them dies?

First, every thief worth his own petty name wants to take their place. A rush of wild, daring heists occur in the wake of the death of great robber. Some are expertly executed. Those who survive tell others of the event in seedy rookeries.

Yet, far more tempting is not merely taking the name of dead but his treasure. Any thief who has earned legendary status must have something put away. It stands to reason that your fellow skulkers in the dark will come to the same conclusion. Where did the dead individual store his accumulated loot? Is it buried, locked behind ingenious traps, stored in a cursed crypt, or, even worse to the world of thieves, completely illusory? Having a name does not always mean having the coin to back it up. There are more stories of legends dying without an Aquilonian Luna in their pocket than a treasure hoard of them. Of course, if a fellow thief discovered the body, there is no reason any coin should be found on the corpse!

Stories surround these hoards, and maps and guides; even samples of the treasure are like to be on offer in dark taverns and whore houses throughout any major city once word gets out. Nearly none of these are legitimate, but what if the player characters find the one that is? Or, what if they pursue a false lead only to run into a rival group of cutthroats who have the real location in mind?

> *"So I have," grunted the ruffian. "And I owe more than gold to you, king; I owe you a debt of gratitude. Even thieves can be grateful."*
>
> **— The Hour of the Dragon**

FLEECING THE SHEEP

Outright theft is not the sole means of support for every magsman. A good portion of one's shadowy income may come from confidence tricks and swindling. Thieves can quickly find themselves on the operating or receiving end of such chicanery. Whether the player characters pull the strings on a long con, or become entangled in the scheme of another, deceit is part and parcel of their world. Liars should always expect to be lied to, after all.

First, let us assume the player character thieves propose to run a scam. This scam might take place in a city, town, or village. There are varying benefits to each. The further away from a city one travels, the more gullible the populace usually is. Astreas writes of an entire Corinthian village that paid a charlatan to "proof their souls against demons" after her partner came through pretending to communicate with the foul beings of the Outer Dark. An entire season's profits from harvest were given over to the duo.

Thieves plotting the scheme must have a good idea and gird their loins against the consequences. The two thieves written of by Astreas got away; not all are so lucky. A village of friendly "marks" can quickly turn into a riotous mob out for blood if the thief overplays her hand. A quick escape from a village is often more difficult than disappearing into the teeming masses of a city's Maul. One risks exposure in smaller populations, and wiser populations in crowded urban tenements. One might be inclined to advise the thief to choose wisely, but wisdom and larceny are not commonly coincident.

KINGDOM EVENTS

Personal and local events are like to visit the thief's life sooner than those of the wider world, but all things come to all men in time save riches. War, plague, usurpation, and a host of other upheavals eventually trickle down to the world of the bottom-feeders, the highwaymen, and their disreputable ilk.

Such events may provide the means for profit or the means for escape. A city whose streets fill with the newly dead, as a plague scythes the population like a reaper manifest, makes ample cover for a wanted man or woman to slip away. Likewise, while the royals and well-off lock themselves deeper inside their towers, their guards are no doubt depleted from the same illness that rides the air and poisons humors outside. Any tragedy or calamity might be turned to the advantage of a clever and enterprising individual of proper disposition.

WARS AND RUMORS OF WAR

Few people fail to see war in their life. The days of man are marked by bloodshed and only the elite or quickly dead miss the spectacle that is warfare. Whether local or between kingdoms, even the rumor of war in the air can change the very disposition of a town, city, or nation.

You can feel your fellow man tense when the winds of war presage the stench of teeming dead. Everyone becomes on edge, and economies shift. Prices usually inflate for most goods, but others are dumped at cost or less; even gold changes in value given the situation.

Outright war can bring refugees or armies. Both can destroy the land after their fashion. If the kingdom in which the player characters are located goes to war, conscripts may be pressed into service. This often clears out those who first look after their own hide, but remaining player characters find much less harsh competition for jobs.

Moreover, a thief has similar skills to a spy and can gain employment from the very crown he previously robbed. Or, the thieves can skip serving the crown entirely and take to banditry with other highwaymen as the situation destabilizes. If the king's troops march to the front, they do not police the roads. Times are ripe for picking. By the same token, if the war requires massive amounts of troops, city guard often return to their previous jobs as soldiers. One need not strain the mind to imagine who steps in to fill that power void.

Anyone who says war isn't good for business is likely operating an honest enterprise. No respectable thief wants any part of that foolishness.

STEAL THE HEIR

Nobles play games, and those games often have living pieces. Among the varying machinations of the wealthy and those who rule, kidnapping of heirs, or even kings and queens, is common. A city-state can stave off war with a neighbor if they hold the royal heir as hostage. A rival kingdom can leverage ransom to fund a future war. Or, by simply taking a member of the royal family, someone seeks to gain advantage and intelligence.

Conversely, those heirs kidnapped are in need of rescuing. If a king does not trust his rival to keep to the terms of ransom, what course is left but to steal his child back? Earls and dukes, barons and marquises alike experience these same dilemmas. What better person to steal another than a thief, what better one to steal someone back than a kidnapper?

The politics may well be of little interest to the player characters, but there is gold where there is ransoming — on either side. They might be paid to sneak into the capital of Nemedia and abscond with the princess, then spirit her back to Koth. Perhaps, some other rogues already took her, and the player characters are instead hired to get her back. Methods of breaking into and out of varying fortifications are the same, oft times.

Such deeds demand great payment but can quickly spiral beyond the ken of lowborn folk. The princess may be but a pawn in a larger gambit, and the player characters find themselves sought by both sides. Perhaps the princess in question is being "kidnapped" of her own accord, for she loves a rival prince who promised the player characters gold he cannot now pay as he has been found out and exiled. The kings and queens of either side care not about the specifics. The player characters are collateral damage now. Few thieves will ever wear a crown or sit upon a throne, but rogues play their role in grander affairs just as do dog-brothers of the sword. While it is those who rule that are more often recorded for posterity, it is those who earn their coin that do the real business of the world.

> Over shadowy spires and gleaming towers lay the ghostly darkness and silence that runs before dawn. Into a dim alley, one of a veritable labyrinth of mysterious winding ways, four masked figures came hurriedly from a door which a dusky hand furtively opened. They spoke not but went swiftly into the gloom, cloaks wrapped closely about them; as silently as the ghosts of murdered men they disappeared in the darkness.
>
> — "The Phoenix on the Sword"

ASSASSINATION AND REBELLION

Plotting an assassination often requires passing secret messages, obtaining hard to come by information, and vetting conspirators. All these jobs are perfect for a thief. Moreover, as conspirators turn on one another, thieves are in a position to make the best of it. A successful assassination, or even an unsuccessful one, creates far-reaching consequences.

Usurpation is also not uncommon in the Hyborian Age. Rebel princes and rival queens seek to overturn the current ruler and take the throne. Spies, informants, and thieves are routinely employed in events leading up to a revolt. A city-state about to turn against the crown must of necessity learn everything they can about the situation in the capital — number of troops, the availability and price of mercenaries, the loyalty of varying lesser nobles. Spies are needed, but one cannot always trust a spy who works

for the crown or even one groomed by the upstart — they have ambitions of their own, don't they?

Assassins and slayers are a strong alternative. They work only for money and often care nothing of who sits on the throne. They are a convenient solution to the plotting within, and between, kingdoms.

If the player characters are sufficiently renowned, they may even be hired to assassinate a ruler. An entire campaign might involve gathering the necessary information, finding the allies, and determining the means of escape, leading up to the killing. Even if offstage characters are responsible, a dead king means change. The new ruler may have to quell riots, consolidate power, and root out those still loyal to the old crown. This leaves little time for catching gangs and thieves. Crime is rampant in the wake of such upheaval.

Yet a king or queen who survives an assassination oft times looks to punish anyone they suspect is responsible. Hanging groups of known scoundrels goes some way toward reminding the populace who truly wields power.

PLAGUE AND OTHER SUCH CHAOS

Larceny thrives best in two places — darkness and chaos. Plagues, and any other of a host of possible calamities, bring both. Pestilence sweeps the land and rulers are as powerless as lowly peasants to halt its march. The dead mount; people lock themselves inside their homes or are quarantined. A town or city suddenly depopulated is ripe for picking.

Guards are suddenly repurposed toward enforcing so-called "plague law", and charlatan plague doctors wander from town to town peddling fake cures and remedies. People are suspicious at these times, but not of having their tangible property stolen. No, in these dark times they are afraid dark demons will make off with their souls.

Like war, plagues and epidemics divert resources. Troops move in response. Trade may dry up, but necessary supplies still move. Highwaymen grow in number just as warehouses become fat with goods that might otherwise have been moved. Superstition runs wild at these times, and clever women and men play that to their advantage. A crime committed in the midst of chaos is harder to notice and even harder to solve. Calamity draws the eye better than any planned diversion.

UNNATURAL EVENTS

The lives of simple people may not be touched by the unnatural with any regularity, if at all, but they recognize it when they see such things… and they fear them. Thieves do not necessarily truck with demons, but their business sometimes brings them in proximity to the Outer Dark.

Sorcerers have use for thieves, and the unnatural powers that work beyond the usually visible world influence not only the penumbra of the unknowable void but that void in the heart of every sizable human population.

JUST ANOTHER SNAKE CULT

Religion is a force that gives the world meaning and terror. The gods watch, priests say, they may even intervene. Behind them, though, lurk other things, things which are not gods, things which perhaps even gods fear. To this darkness strange cults are enthralled.

Set's cults are well known, and a thief can find rare treasures in his temples. The same can be said for those who seek to spread Mitra's counsel or Ishtar's wisdom — priests and churches are rarely known for vows of poverty in the Hyborian Age. A sect, a cult, a church — all are targets where gold, gems, and other rarities and valuables are found.

But darker cults to nameless horrors have even stranger and more valuable things still, and a thief does not always know for whom, or what, she is working. Another snake cult to Yig may quickly turn out to be in service to Nyarlathotep, whose many masks appear in forms that suit him. Such a thief may well wish she'd stolen from Set's favored, for being fed to the Children of Khemi is preferable to the madness now awaiting her.

THE POWER BEHIND THE THRONE

In Koth, people say the wizard Tsotha-lanti holds real power. The sorcerer Yara's dominance is well known in Zamora. Nabonidus' own influence is as well-known as it is feared. Those who tap the Outer Dark for power still have need of mortal agents. It is not surprising they tend to employ those men and women whose hearts are already partially corrupt.

Whilst these sorcerers may scry upon opponents via unnatural means, they might also employ a thief to do so. A thief could, unwittingly, also stumble into their skein of plotting only to realize how very much out of his depth he is. Sorcerers are not like other men — some say they are not men at all. That is not to say some of their aims are unfamiliar.

Just as kings, queens, and other rulers might kidnap an heir or have one killed, the sorcerer who wields power behind the throne, or wants to, also kidnaps and kills. Rarely does such a person do so directly, for that could well mean exposure. Spies and rogues are hired to do the lowly dirty work that wizards have no time for. They often pay well, very well, but can a thief deal with the powers behind such men and women as they can with crude humanity?

> *Murilo felt his blood turn to ice again. He could see in this twist of fate only the sinister hand of Nabonidus, and an eery obsession began to grow on him that the Red Priest was more than human — a sorcerer who read the minds of his victims and pulled strings on which they danced like puppets.*
>
> — "Rogues in the House"

OBTAINER OF RARE ANTIQUITIES

Thieves are routinely hired to steal things for patrons. Not every job, or even most, is self-motivated. The best scores are often found because someone else needs, or wants, what lies on the end of that job. Middlemen are used to distance employer from contracted thief, so a burglar may never know for whom she works. In the best cases, this is preferable.

There are scores that defy human ken and quickly point to employers who do likewise. A thief is accustomed to stealing maps and documents, gems and golden chalices. Other, rarer items and even animals are also targets of theft. Though items might be unusual, they are rarely of themselves dangerous.

Such is not the case with certain things sorcerers desire. Gems and gold have nothing compared to the value of rare texts, puissant artifacts, and things crafted by inhuman means long before what man considers history began.

A thief may be employed to steal such a thing, or she may seek it out on her own. In either case, a sinister surprise awaits those who do not have access to proper knowledge. For the most part, sorcerous knowledge and ancient history lies beyond the grasp of robbers and thieves.

What the object of desire appears to be, and what it truly is, are rarely the same in these jobs. A golden bowl might contain a god, a gem might be the heart of a long dead wizard, and a curious luminescent stone may be a piece of unfathomable technology from a planet far, far away. These objects are corrosive. They erode both will and sanity and can unleash horrors man should never see. Thieves may count themselves lucky to obtain such a thing and pass it on for payment received — even then, that job is like to haunt them later, for even the quickest brush with Outer Horrors lasts some while and pervades the life of a mere human being.

COMBINING EVENTS

Many more events than those above are possible, and a good many still lie in Howard's own stories. A gamemaster can create seemingly new adventures from the events above merely by combining them. There is no reason a war cannot be instigated by a sorcerer pressing a thief to obtain an artifact because that thief owes the sorcerer a debt.

Entire campaigns are created around thieves, and mashing disparate ideas is what narrative "originality" is most often about. We have told the same stories since the Hyborian Age, the Thurian Age, and other ages unnamed. What differs are the way elements are combined, the people (and other beings) involved, as well as the outcomes.

A group may begin having been set up, imprisoned by an enemy upon who they now seek revenge. Later, as the story progresses, it becomes clear that their adversary acted in the interest of her child, kidnapped by even more ruthless scum who now demand ransom. Someone engineered the entire plot who is more powerful than that individual they sought to kill. Certainly, they can call it a day, dispatch their foe, and move on, but why did the real antagonist insist it be this group, these characters who were framed? What does he, she, or it have against them?

Like blocks, one idea builds on another until a precarious tower erects from a flat plain and blank page. Knocking that tower down makes for sword and sorcery campaigns true to the spirit of the Conan stories.

"It was hidden in a cavern below the temple of Mitra, in Tarantia," said Orastes. "By devious ways I discovered this, after I had located your remains in Set's subterranean temple in Stygia.

"Zamorian thieves, partly protected by spells I learned from sources better left unmentioned, stole your mummy-case from under the very talons of those which guarded it in the dark, and by camel-caravan and galley and ox-wagon it came at last to this city.

"Those same thieves — or rather those of them who still lived after their frightful quest — stole the Heart of Ahriman from its haunted cavern below the temple of Mitra, and all the skill of men and the spells of sorcerers nearly failed. One man of them lived long enough to reach me and give the jewel into my hands, before he died slavering and gibbering of what he had seen in that accursed crypt. The thieves of Zamora are the most faithful of men to their trust. Even with my conjurements, none but them could have stolen the Heart from where it has lain in demon-guarded darkness since the fall of Acheron, three thousand years ago."

— The Hour of the Dragon

MYTH & MAGIC

"But he was not satisfied with what I taught him, for it was white magic, and he wished evil lore, to enslave kings and glut a fiendish ambition. I would teach him none of the black secrets I had gained, through no wish of mine, through the eons."

— Yag-kosha, "The Tower of the Elephant"

Every thief lives by his or her own private, personal myth. It's the myth which explains why their actions, the purloining of other's wealth is acceptable, justifiable, righteous. Heroic, even. It is perhaps for this reason that thieves are so attracted to the temples and ritual sites of the world; it is not simply the wealth which such places of worship accrue, not simply the lure of danger, but to test the truth of their own personal convictions against those older gods which linger in the darkness, waiting.

HONOR AMONG THIEVES

The greatest myth which thieves cleave to, in spite of all evidence to the contrary, is that known as "honor among thieves". The notion that those bound by the fraternity of crime remain steadfastly loyal to one another has existed, so it would seem, since the first men and women stole from the second men and women. In some cities, this idea is so potent that codes of conduct have been etched into the stone walls of thieves' favored haunts and are pointed to and venerated as proof of the true value of the thieves' way of life over and above that of the law-abiding.

Of course, even most thieves know this is nonsense. Really, honor amongst thieves? Friendship, yes; loyalty, occasionally. But a codified set of laws which prohibit one thief from throwing over another if it suits them? Unrealistic at best. After all, why be a thief if this is the case? Why not work on a market stall or drive a cart for a farmer? They don't steal anything at all. They calmly go about their business, day in and day out; there's honor there. Just like every thief believes themselves, deep down, to be in the right when they steal — yes, they might not be hungry now but they were once, right? — so too does every thief believe that he is more important than those others who share in their profession. Why give *that* thief his full share? He was useless, almost betrayed you to the police, and you're fairly certain he tried to stab you in the alleyway a few weeks ago.

No, the thief's instinct states: only trust those who you know. It will keep you alive longer and it's a whole lot more sensible. There is comradeship and tight bonds between certain thieves, that much is undisputed. There may even be honest thieves plying their trade. That is, men and women willing to steal but only from those who can spare it and never simply for the thrill of purloining something valuable. And yet, though each thief knows that no such honor exists amongst them, the myth becomes more potent with every year that passes.

Some speculate its worth as a legend lies in its very untruthfulness. That it is the one consistent thing which all thieves share — the worthless aphorism that each thief is loyal to another. It has perhaps allowed thieves in dire situations to find common cause with those near to them, irrespective of factional infighting and general antipathy. It likely led to the forming of the first thieves' guilds and, while no guild would ever attempt to prohibit its members from stealing from one another if they can get away with it (how else would they practice?), the idea that thieves might have something in common beyond simply a taste for stolen goods has proven stubbornly resistant to exposure for the noble lie that it truly is.

GODS OF THIEVERY AND DARKNESS

For the most part, thieves of different kingdoms worship the gods of their people, whether Mitra, Ishtar, Anu, Set, or others. There is no reason thieves should worship a thief god — surely, they are just as welcome in the temple of Erlik as is a tradesman or mercenary. It is for the god to gauge the hearts of the worshipers and determine if they are devout — not their fellow worshipers. That said, there are two gods whose cults are almost synonymous with thievery and the underworld: Bel, claimed by many countries, and the nameless Spider-God of Yezud. Functioning much like a cult is the Council of the Hidden, a far-reaching organization known to the thieves of every civilized land.

BEL, GOD OF THIEVES

In every nation in the civilized world — and, from what scholars have been able to learn, the uncivilized world, too — there is only one god to whom thieves offer prayer. His name is Bel, although he has other appellations, secret titles which are whispered by those who have learned his mysteries and been chosen to speak the words sacred to the god. Bel is rarely depicted in art — what kind of thief knowingly records his appearance for those who would hunt him? — and even those few temples which have been erected in his honor are carefully concealed, often behind the façade of a brothel or well-attended tavern.

Bel is not simply the God of Thieves, he is also a Thief God. The dreams and desires of his worshipers are always at risk from his felonious hands, or so it is said. *Do not dream of a heist too big or too spectacular,* old thieves murmur to young apprentices, *or Bel himself will steal it from your head and you will awake with the hangman's noose about your throat."* There are some who claim that Bel stole life from the jaws of the Outer Dark and created humankind and the world from the raw stuff of chaos.

> *"Bel, too, is Shemitish, for he was born in ancient Shumir, long, long ago, and went forth laughing, with curled beard and impish wise eyes, to steal the gems of the kings of old times."*
>
> — Bêlit, "Queen of the Black Coast"

Bel's worship is an intensely individual belief. Unlike the solemn ceremonies carried out in the name of Mitra, or the bloody rituals enacted in worship of Set, Bel's devotees dedicate a heist to him in the smallest of ways, usually invisible to all save themselves. And their god, of course. Sometimes, before a heist begins, a thief might scratch Bel's sign into the stone of a wall they are about to ascend. For others, a valedictory mark might be carved into the wooden panel of a room recently ransacked. There are few dogmas proscribed within the worship of Bel.

Bel the Unknowable

Fittingly, the gender of Bel is, for instance, far from fixed. While most seem to believe the god male, there is little to confirm this either way. Indeed, older traditions seem to depict the god as being wholly fluid in gender. True thieves should be able to conceal themselves and change themselves utterly in order to avoid detection. This is, so some believe, the case for Bel, who is male or female as it suits the god to be. There are some stories in which Bel seduces the great demon Nyarkan and deprives him of the jewel which grants invisibility to the owner. In some of these tales, Bel performs this feat as a woman. In others, he remains a man. None of this matters. None have gone to war over the correct theological interpretation of these myths; to do so would be to misunderstand the very nature of the Thief God. Bel is as changeable as the circumstances of his worshipers. Just as their riches may disappear in moments, and be reclaimed in a few moments more, so too will Bel's nature.

The Temple of Bel

There is a temple to Bel hidden in Zamora, somewhere within the Maul. It is not often visited, as there is too much real thieving to be done and too many slights to be avenged in that teeming pit of humanity. However, what can be found there is nevertheless instructive with regards to the means by which thieves worship their god. The shrine — the only part of the temple which might truly be so described, as the rest is a distillery for a particularly unstable form of spirits — is wreathed with small scraps of paper covered with names. Each of these names is that of a thief who chose Bel as their patron god. These little wrinkled rolls are left here by believers so that Bel will steal their souls from Hell when they die. Of course, as every thief knows, they must make themselves worthy of stealing. Bel is a thief, after all; the god won't take a risk for a prize not worth the having. No thief needs to be told this, even those who choose not to listen to the stories told by elder thieves or whispered by those who steep themselves in the mysteries of Bel. It is, of course, nothing less than what they would do.

Bel as a Patron

Thieves who truly dedicate themselves to the service of Bel gain certain advantages for their loyalty — of course, this loyalty is to thieving itself and not to the god they worship, however closely these two might intertwine. The relationship between a dedicated thief of Bel and the god itself is similar to that forged between a sorcerer and their patron — it draws on the strength and spirit of both participants and the gains which the thieves might achieve are done so at the cost of some part of themselves.

If thieves wish, they may choose to make Bel their patron. This requires them to take the *Patron* talent — as though they were attempting to learn sorcery. In place of the usual *Master of Formulae* talent, the thieves may choose one of the special thief talents (found on page 16 of this book) or an appropriate talent from the main list (see page 170 of the **Conan** corebook). The thieves must, as a result of this benefit, pay a tithe to Bel. This requires the thieves to take 5 ⚷ Gold or its worth in treasure most recently acquired and leave it in a place from which it can be easily stolen. This must be done at each Upkeep period. Failure to do so results in the talent earned from their patron being forfeited. Thieves may only do this once, in contrast to a sorcerer.

> *Zamora with its dark-haired women and towers of spider-haunted mystery…*
>
> — The Nemedian Chronicles,
> "The Phoenix on the Sword"

THE CULT OF THE SPIDER-GOD

The great tarantula, the spinner of the black web, the holy arachnid — there are many names for the creature whose worship has become so entrenched in the city of Yezud and already begun to spread to neighboring locales. The creep is slow and insidious, but it is happening. The cult grows from its birthplace in Zamora and will soon infect neighboring cities and kingdoms. In fact, anywhere a populace is beset by poverty and exhaustion — and all the other afflictions which the world reserves for those least able to bear them — the cult might begin to take root. To the Spider-God, all are welcome to shelter beneath his eight vast legs. Perhaps these new worshipers will prove to be new spiders — hunters who can be sent into the world to fulfill the whims of their new god. Or perhaps they are flies, to be consumed and remade as the holy web of the Great Spider, the fabric of the universe itself. It doesn't matter — both roles have value in this life.

The cosmology of the spider cult is, in truth, this easy to understand: there are spiders and there are flies. The flies become the food of the spiders. Strength makes a spider, fear creates a fly; memorize this and you have swallowed the entire theology and doctrine of the cult. There are rituals, of course, other means of demonstrating devotion to the Weaver of Nighted Silk, but in essence the cult of the Spider-God prizes strength and ferocity and agility. This is not, it should be understood, the same belief as the gods of the frozen north who give those inhabiting their lands enough strength to prove their worth. For the Spider-God, strength is the means to take that which belongs to others, to make the weak obey or become food.

The Cult of the Spider-God

Unsurprisingly, the holy number of the Spider-God cult is eight. Their temples are all built to reflect this perfect symmetry — eight walls, eight windows, eight doors. An octagonal altar occupies the center of each temple from which a true priest of the god can watch all eight doors. The Spider priests are extremely scarce, and the means by which they are inducted into the true worship of their god is a horrifying process. The devotee is, so the rumors insist, led to a secret chamber. Far below the Temple of the Spider in Yezud, it is said, there is a cave hewn from the rock by inhuman hands. Certainly, it precedes that cataclysm which sank Atlantis, perhaps it predates even that fabled epoch. There is no light in this chamber; all torches are extinguished long before the potential initiate reaches the cavern.

The priests who lead them have no need of the light — they have already made this journey. Once within the cavern, the initiates are left alone. No one returns for them; a handful stagger into the light, half blinded, three or four days later. They are marked, ever after, for the Spider-God's service; their flesh is mottled as though flakes of it have simply died. Their eyes are curiously distended, protruding from their sockets and with pupils which are much too large and much too black. Their limbs move differently, the joints no longer obeying the limitations which once constrained them. The muscles beneath the piebald flesh writhe with unnatural strength, even at rest. No one who has returned from the Chamber of the Web speaks of what transpired there but those who worship in the temple, those many miles above the chamber, call it "the Spider's kiss".

The Cult of the Spider-God achieved its ascendancy through other means than the simplicity of its message and the strange, potent preaching of its priests. It also brings its own currency with it, wherever it travels. The Cult of the Spider-God deals in information, and it makes procuring this information — and the means of its dissemination — an integral part of the faith it would seek to promulgate. The network which the cult carefully constructed, thread by thread, stretches across the continent — the Cultists of the Spider-God will secure the knowledge they require by any means: there are many spies and information brokers who have no idea of precisely who, or what, it is they traffic with but welcome the gold or the favors it secures for them. Sometimes the information is secured through torture, threats, and the assassins' knife. This is the cult's purpose; it exists to collect and collate knowledge and to return it to the temple in Yezud and to do so with as much secrecy as can be managed. This is how the Spider-God's highest ranking followers wish it — the extent of their influence must never be known, for the Spider-God hunts in the shadows, spinning its web gradually, unfurling silken threads which connect it to the wealthiest and most powerful in the land. This is how the cult made itself so wealthy and so formidable — it cultivated the favor and friendship of those in a position to help it. It collects the obligations of politician and noblemen, the lowly pickpocket and the Master Thief, the knight and the squire. It will help any who require help, but the price, of course, is obedience when required. The Spider-God's cult lures in those flies it wishes to feast on, and it does so gradually.

The Spider Lurks

Whether or not it truly is the Spider-God itself lurking in the subterranean chambers of the temple in Yezud is difficult to know — certainly something obscene and dangerous waits in those caverns. Where the god's worship sprang from is likewise an impossible question to answer. Stories abound of a crazed prophet emerging one day in Yezud's great market square and preaching the Laws of the Spider. In some tales, he is wreathed in thick webbing and each of his eyes had four pupils, each shifting and swarming with chitinous life.

Hunting down the god might offer a worthy adventure for those whose lives have grown somewhat stale — after all, who knows what treasures might wait in the chambers of a god? Do monstrous, pale-eyed hybrid spider-creatures lurk in the darkness — those who sought to be priests and instead became the devoted, maddened slaves of the spider, maws slavering, limbs broken and flopping in insect parody of the thing they worshiped and now merely imitate — who can say? Only those daring or mad enough to risk the wrath of the cult and its god will find out. Whether they survive long enough to tell anyone else is its own matter.

The Nightmare Web

What cannot be disputed is that the Spider-God, the god itself, exists in truth. Too many of the cult have seen the vast, chitinous bulk of the eight-legged deity moving through their dreams. Too many have heard the spider's chittering song or have seen the vast webs which drape the entrance to the cavern which the priests must peel back before they can enter. So sticky is this web that it often removes layers of skin from those supplicants who would make their way into the darkness. On rare occasions, the web has adhered so tightly to the flesh of the potential priest that it was ripped away to reveal the pale white of bone. It is said that these are the true chosen of the Spider-God, that this bond formed between flesh and thread is the mark of the Spider-God's blessing. Although, what this blessing might be has never been explained, as those who receive the blessing never return from the chamber beneath.

The followers of the Spider-God continue to grow in strength and in faith; more and more people in Yezud have dreams of the Spider-God, and see the way in which the web it spins binds the world together, trapping the weak within so that the strong may prey upon them as they wish. It is said that some of the greatest lords and ladies of the continent have heard the message of the Spider-God's cult and are intrigued by it. It is also said that the priests of the Spider-God grow more powerful, their miracles more brazen and more impressive. There are whispers that the Spider-God will soon reveal itself, or that the priests will announce the true name of the god so that all may sing that name in praise and all will be enfolded within the great web it weaves around its worshipers. Who can say what the truth of these things are, or what the Spider-God may truly be, but, as more bow before the eight-sided altar in the Temple of the Spider-God, the world may soon be shown forcibly what it has thus far failed to find out for itself.

THE COUNCIL OF THE HIDDEN

In certain legends, which thieves whisper to one another when the torches in the tavern are nearly extinguished, when the wine and ale has run out, when the tales of daring feats and impossible heists are concluded, darker things emerge. Sometimes, these are stories of those thieves whose ambition outstripped their grasp and became involved with those who draw their power from the Outer Black. At other times, when those who remain awake and sufficiently sober are quite sure that no one is conscious enough to mock them, they talk of the Council of the Hidden. They take care, of course, to claim that they themselves do not believe in the council. They may even try and smile when saying as much. But the smile will be forced. The fear in the eyes and the slight tremor in the voice will not be.

YEZUD'S GIFTS — EGGS OF THE SPIDER

Unlike Bel's strength, the power of Yezud is not bestowed upon his devotees in the form of sorcerous enhancements to strength and speed, nor in the hidden teachings of the great darkness behind this world. Instead, Yezud's blessing manifests itself as small tokens that may take many shapes, but are in truth all of a piece. Through what warped sorcery and twisted logic, it is impossible to tell; these tokens are the eggs of the Spider-God itself. Each token, each egg, is unique, though most are spherical and may appear to be composed of any substance — onyx, obsidian, granite, marble, steel, bronze, or jade. Only those who have been cleansed, through the administration of the eightfold rite of the Spider-God, may touch the egg without inflicting the deadly secret contained in each token upon themselves. For, upon the hand of an unsanctified person coming into contact with the thin skein which surrounds the egg, the shell will break and a fragment of Yezud will inject the unsuspecting holder of the egg with a poison more potent than any conceived of by even the most skilled assassins. This splinter, this sliver of a god, will then vanish — a tiny scuttling spider which will flee, secreting itself in the shadows and withering, quickly, to nothingness.

Getting hold of a Token of Yezud is incredibly difficult; indeed, they are so rare as to constitute a myth cycle in themselves. Player characters are unlikely to ever encounter one, let alone acquire one; even then, they would require a properly sanctified worshiper of the Spider-God willing to carry it for them. However, should an enemy they have been seeking attempt to assassinate a well-protected monarch, or they are asked to intervene in an inter-faith war between the cult of the Spider-God and that of Ibis, then they may witness such dreadful weaponry in use.

Token of Yezud

AVAILABILITY: Incredibly Rare

COST: —

A fragment from the body of the living Spider-God of Yezud. These tokens cannot be bought; they can only be gifted to the true devotees of the Spider-God and to receive such an honor requires a full and deep initiation into the deranged truths of the god's sinister cult. Such weapons are used for the most secretive and essential of assassinations and the suddenness with which death visits those who come into contact with the Token is terrifying to behold.

TOKEN OF YEZUD				
Range	Damage	Enc	Size	Qualities
C	8🗡	—	1H	Intense, Vicious 1

- **THE PRESERVE OF THE BLESSED:** The weapon can only be carried by those who have undergone the special preparatory rites of the Spider-God cult; to touch the Token without having undergone these steps is to trigger the full and immediate effects of the Token.

- **CERTAIN DEATH:** The Token of Yezud automatically causes one Wound, before any damage is rolled normally. The Token also ignores all Soak provided by armor.

- **THE MANY EYES OF GOD:** To witness the deadly effects of the Token is to be in awe of the lethality of a living god, suddenly aware of one's insignificance in the face of such power. Witnessing the Token's effects firsthand causes 5🗡 mental damage.

The Council of the Hidden is a dark legend amongst the thieves of the Hyborian Age. Some form of it exists in every corner of the continent, in every city where thieves congregate, its existence whispered about and speculated upon. The greatest lords and ladies of the age, it is said, formed the council. Tired of their wealth being preyed upon by contemptible thieves and frustrated by the ineffectuality of the watch in their cities, they formed a secret order dedicated to the extermination of all who made their living by purloining the wealth of others.

"It was like a big black jade bead, such as the temple girls of Yezud wear when they dance before the black stone spider which is their god. Yar Afzal held it in his hand, and he didn't pick up anything else. Yet when he fell dead, a spider, like the god at Yezud, only smaller, ran out of his fingers."

— Conan, "The People of the Black Circle"

Judgment of the Seven

Of course, the Council of the Hidden could not carry out this work themselves, and so each appointed a champion — a warrior and assassin of unmatched skill, speed, and lethality. Now, thieves whisper, the council hunts those who would call themselves thieves. Each time a thief is found dead, there are some who claim it is the council's doing. In some cities, graffiti is found, smeared in thick red paint, claiming that the council's justice is nigh at hand. Those who spend too many nights inhaling the smoke of the black lotus believe the process has already, inexorably, begun — that the thieves' guilds have been infiltrated and are the tools of the Council of the Hidden.

Most thieves do not believe in the council; why should they? Thieves are a pragmatic bunch by and large, and such unlikely stories carry little weight. And yet... sometimes the coincidences and impossibilities which mark the lives of all who inhabit crowded cities coalesce in such a way as to imply that perhaps the story is less outlandish than it might appear. The headless corpses of those four thieves found only last week, the mutilated pickpocket pushed into the well-known guild tavern without his eyes, tongue, or hands, and the handwritten notes which the head of the guild claims he has not received — yet which three children all swear blind they delivered — are these things not evidence of the Council of the Hidden? Are these things not proof of that vengeful conspiracy? The answer may never be known. But, in the darkness of a tavern corner, thieves still whisper amongst themselves about hired killers chasing them across rooftops and the Council of the Hidden, always seeking to carry out its savage retribution.

> *"It will bear thrice my own," answered Taurus. "It was woven from the tresses of dead women, which I took from their tombs at midnight, and steeped in the deadly wine of the upas tree, to give it strength. I will go first — then follow me closely."*
>
> — "The Tower of the Elephant"

TOOLS OF THE DEAD

Many who know the lore of thieving have heard of the Hand of Glory. It is a grisly trophy formed from the hand of an executed thief which, when properly ensorcelled and utilized, offers light to the person who holds the Hand, leaving everyone else tightly swaddled in darkness. But, to the cunning sorcerer, the entire corpse of an executed thief can be... converted.

NEW TALENT

Tools of the Dead
PREREQUISITES: *Patron (Bel, God of Thieves)*, *Alchemist*, *Master Thief*, *Sorcery Expertise 1*
EXPERIENCE COST: 400

This talent taught only to devout worshipers of Bel, the god of thieves. When creating a Trick of the Trade and combining it with a suitable offering of a necromantic nature (items from the dead) the tool grants a bonus of 2 Momentum to any Thievery test, in addition to any benefit the item might normally confer. The tool is consumed after use.

It is also well known that Taurus of Nemedia possessed a rope woven from the hair of dead women — it is less well known that these women themselves were skilled thieves, the Sisters of Adlerth, who once stole the King of Aquilonia's throne from beneath him, so the stories say. But this is not the end of such necrotic utility: the belly fat of the hanged thief can produce candles which never smoke. The fingernails of the dead can be used to pick the most challenging of locks. The flesh flayed from the face of a thief killed during a heist can be laid over the features of a second forming a mask which can only be removed by him who put it on. The heart, cut from the chest of an executed thief, can become a hiding place for anything which a thief needs to conceal; once placed inside the pulpy mass, it can never be located except through the speaking of a single word appointed by the sorcerer who creates the heart.

All of these things can be crafted from the remains of a dead thief — it merely requires a pliant sorcerer (although finding one of them is likely to be something of a task in itself) and a sum of Gold sufficient to pay the same.

Why it should be that only thieves' corpses will work for such tasks is not clear. Perhaps it is merely the caprice of some deity of the Outer Black — the kind of creature who delights in such arbitrariness, in such callous whimsy — or perhaps there is some alchemical secret which has yet to be unlocked by the masters of that particular art. Either way, for those thieves who can stomach the dismemberment and recycling of their former comrades, these corpses produce the most exquisitely useful of all thieves tools — some internal magic lingers that needs only the sorcerous touch to bring forth.

CHAPTER 5
ENCOUNTERS

> The whole affair had a distinctly unreal atmosphere. He felt as if he were watching the play of puppets, or as a disembodied ghost himself, impersonally viewing the actions of the living, his presence unseen and unsuspected.
>
> — Murilo, "Rogues in the House"

The great kingdoms of the West are home to the legendary and the larcenous. From the rude beginning of a gutter thief to the noble birth of the aristocrat, no man or woman lays claim to their name without the world pushing back. While wealth buoys the weak, it does not prevent them from being drowned in the great waves created by men of action.

ROGUES GALLERY

Though thieves whisper of supernatural foes, strange and terrible creatures that haunt the night, and other enemies too horrible to describe, the reality is that the greatest threat to any thief is their fellow humans, whether opponents or rivals.

ASSASSIN (TOUGHENED)

A master of murder, the assassin has learned the means to inflict death from any number of possible situations and circumstances, using any means available. Skilled and deadly, studied in the administering of poison, and able to move with the guile of a panther, assassins can take any of these forms. The only thing which unifies them is their capacity for bringing death to even the most highly protected of targets.

ATTRIBUTES			
Awareness	Intelligence	Personality	Willpower
9	8	7	8
Agility		Brawn	Coordination
9		8	9

FIELDS OF EXPERTISE			
Combat	1	Movement	1
Fortitude	1	Senses	1
Knowledge	—	Social	—

STRESS AND SOAK

- **Stress:** Vigor 8, Resolve 8
- **Soak:** Armor 1 (Clothing), Courage 1

ATTACKS

- See Special Ability

SPECIAL ABILITIES

- **Master of Death:** No two assassins are the same or approach their trade in the same way. For this reason, a gamemaster may choose one melee weapon and one ranged weapon for an assassin, depending on the most suitable weaponry for the assassin's targets.

DOOM SPENDS

- **Escape Route:** When the assassin is reduced to a single Wound, the gamemaster may spend 2 Doom to have the assassin steal away, suddenly, perhaps dropping a smoke bomb (or something similar) and making good his escape. This represents an escape plan put into place beforehand. The assassin may use this ability repeatedly in the same encounter.

BACK ALLEY KILLER (MINION)

Professional murderers take two forms. There are the subtle, devious, elegant killers who have trained, exhaustively, in the art and forms of killing. And then there are those who are simply quiet enough and vicious enough to find a moment when the target is vulnerable and take it. Both are skills, but, while a trained assassin is careful to ensure that his target never suspects his approach, back alley killers care nothing for such niceties. Pursuing their quarry into a dark ginnel and delivering a knife to the spine is just as effective as more elegant methods.

ATTRIBUTES

Awareness	Intelligence	Personality	Willpower
8	8	8	8
Agility		Brawn	Coordination
8		7	8

FIELDS OF EXPERTISE

Combat	1	Movement	1
Fortitude	—	Senses	—
Knowledge	—	Social	—

STRESS AND SOAK

- **Stress:** Vigor 4, Resolve 4
- **Soak:** Armor —, Courage —

ATTACKS

- **Dagger (M):** Reach 1, 3 ♦, 1H, Hidden 1, Parrying, Thrown, Unforgiving 1
- **Club (M):** Reach 2, 3 ♦, 1H, Stun, Knockdown

GUILD THIEF (TOUGHENED)

For those lucky and talented enough to become something more than hired muscle or disposable meat to be interposed between a master thief and a crossbow bolt, the next stage is to become a guild thief. This is an esteemed position, and the individuals who attain such a rank are not to be trifled with. Few, of course, will ever be acclaimed as a master thief — there are too few worthy of that name to ever generalize — but they are nevertheless skilled purloiners of things the wealthy (and not so wealthy) forget to guard with sufficient care. Dangerous foes and, in a pinch, loyal companions, guild thieves are the kind of men and women who give the profession a good — which is to say, a bad — name.

ATTRIBUTES

Awareness	Intelligence	Personality	Willpower
9	8	7	7
Agility		Brawn	Coordination
9		8	8

FIELDS OF EXPERTISE

Combat	1	Movement	2
Fortitude	—	Senses	1
Knowledge	—	Social	—

STRESS AND SOAK

- **Stress:** Vigor 8, Resolve 7
- **Soak:** Armor —, Courage 2

ATTACKS

- **Dagger (M):** Reach 1, 3 ♦, 1H, Hidden 1, Parrying, Thrown, Unforgiving 1
- **Sling (R):** Range M, 3 ♦, 1H, Stun, Volley
- **Steely Glare (T):** Range C, 2 ♦ mental, Stun

SPECIAL ABILITIES

- **Nimble as a Mouser:** All guild thieves may reduce the Difficulty of any Movement tests by one step.

DOOM SPENDS

- **Loyal to the Guild:** The gamemaster can spend 1 Doom to have the guild thief summon one street thug (see page 80), loyal to the guild, to assist the guild thief in combat. Alternatively, the gamemaster can spend 2 Doom to summon two street thugs. This Doom spend can only be used once per combat encounter.

INQUISITOR (TOUGHENED)

Just as there are watchmen that do their job from a desire to help and protect the needy and destitute, there are also those who do it from a deep-seated enjoyment of causing pain and anguish. Usually, these sadists become inquisitors — commanding several watchmen and tasked with monitoring the possibility of political dissent, challenges to the status quo, and threats to the flow of gold and goods which their superior officers inevitably have their hands in.

ATTRIBUTES

Awareness	Intelligence	Personality	Willpower
9	8	8	7
Agility		Brawn	Coordination
7		8	8

FIELDS OF EXPERTISE

Combat	1	Movement	—
Fortitude	—	Senses	—
Knowledge	1	Social	1

STRESS AND SOAK

- **Stress:** Vigor 8, Resolve 7
- **Soak:** Armor —, Courage 1

ATTACKS

- **Interrogator's Knife (M):** Reach C, 3 🦅, 1H, Hidden 1, Parrying, Thrown, Unforgiving 1
- **Steely Glare (T):** Range C, 2 🦅 mental, Stun

SPECIAL ABILITIES

- **We Are Asking the Questions!:** The inquisitor automatically generates one success for any Social tests related to intimidation or questioning.

MERCHANT OR TRADER (MINION)

Those who have made the pursuit of coin through the exchange of goods usually share a few traits: ruthlessness and greed. Beyond that, there is little that connects them. Thieves and merchants form a strange sort of symbiotic relationship, with one taking in order to sell and the other selling in order to take. Many merchants have learned to be as unscrupulous as any master criminal. Duplicitous, conniving, and willing to use any means to survive, expand, and become rich, thieves might learn a great deal from men and women like these. Merchants do not travel unaccompanied — or do so only rarely — and usually rely on bodyguards or companions for protection, though they will keep some form of weaponry close by at all times.

ATTRIBUTES

Awareness	Intelligence	Personality	Willpower
8	8	8	8
Agility		Brawn	Coordination
6		6	6

FIELDS OF EXPERTISE

Combat	—	Movement	—
Fortitude	—	Senses	—
Knowledge	1	Social	1

STRESS AND SOAK

- **Stress:** Vigor 3, Resolve 4
- **Soak:** Armor 1, Courage 2

ATTACKS

- **Knife (M):** Reach 1, 3 🦅, 1H, Hidden 1, Improvised, Unforgiving 1
- **Crossbow (R):** Range M, 3 🦅, Unbalanced, Unforgiving 1, Volley

SPECIAL ABILITIES

- **Buying Friendship:** Whenever attempting a Social test, a merchant automatically generates one success.

NATIONALIST (TOUGHENED)

A small but dedicated cadre of men and women, committed to the restoration of their country's reputation and honor, after the sinister machinations of the Red Priest have reduced it to near servility; the nationalists may prove to be both a help and a significant hindrance to those who encounter them. With but a single aim, in truth, as a group and as individuals they are prone to a monomaniacal fixation on their own goals; while they will be loyal and steadfast while their goals align with those of their allies, the celerity with which the nationalists can turn on erstwhile comrades renders them a threat at all times.

ATTRIBUTES

Awareness	Intelligence	Personality	Willpower
8	8	8	9
Agility		Brawn	Coordination
8		9	9

FIELDS OF EXPERTISE

Combat	1	Movement	1
Fortitude	1	Senses	—
Knowledge	—	Social	—

STRESS AND SOAK

- **Stress:** Vigor 9, Resolve 9
- **Soak:** Armor 2 (Leather Coat), Courage 2

ATTACKS

- **Sword (M):** Reach 2, 5 🦌, 1H, Parrying
- **Sling (R):** Range M, 3 🦌, 1H, Stun, Volley
- **Dead Man's Stare (T):** Range C, 3 🦌 mental, Vicious 1

SPECIAL ABILITIES

- **Fanatical:** Nationalists are quite prepared to die for their goal. For this reason, all Threaten attacks inflict 1 🦌 fewer damage when used against them.

STREET THUG (MINION)

The average, workaday man or woman who occupies the underworld can best be summed up by the two words: street thug. They are the backbone of a crime lord's empire, the easily bought companions a master thief uses to bulk out his or her crew, the ones who are caught by the watchmen when it finally becomes necessary to find the perpetrator of one crime or another. Every thief begins as a street thug of some kind and every thief desperately hopes to become something more. Most don't.

ATTRIBUTES

Awareness	Intelligence	Personality	Willpower
7	7	7	7
Agility	Brawn		Coordination
7	7		7

FIELDS OF EXPERTISE

Combat	1	Movement	—
Fortitude	—	Senses	—
Knowledge	—	Social	—

STRESS AND SOAK

- **Stress:** Vigor 4, Resolve 4
- **Soak:** Armor —, Courage 1

ATTACKS

- **Shortsword (M):** Reach 1, 4 🦌, 1H, Parrying
- **Sling (R):** Range M, 3 🦌, 1H, Stun, Volley

WATCHMAN (MINION)

In almost every city, in every nation, there is some equivalent to the watchman. Some might be better trained, some might be less inclined to drunkenness and corruption, others may even have something like a conscience (though this may well be the least likely of the three possibilities), but, roughly speaking, all will be as likely to stab you and take your purse as any thief you meet — the difference is that a watchman might have to think of an excuse for it later.

ATTRIBUTES

Awareness	Intelligence	Personality	Willpower
9	7	7	8

Agility		Brawn		Coordination	
8		9		8	

FIELDS OF EXPERTISE

Combat	1	Movement	—
Fortitude	—	Senses	1
Knowledge	—	Social	—

STRESS AND SOAK

- **Stress:** Vigor 5, Resolve 4
- **Soak:** Armor (Padded Leather) 1, Courage 1

ATTACKS

- **Shortsword (M):** Reach 1, 5 ⚔, 1H, Parrying
- **Bow (R):** Range C, 4 ⚔, 2H, Volley
- **Knife to the Throat (T):** Range C, 4 ⚔ mental, Stun, Vicious 1

NAMES TO FEAR

Herein are a collection of scoundrels and killers, petty tyrants and would-be rulers. These are some few of the people who move the great powers in the west or, perhaps at times, said powers move them. Regardless, their presences shall be felt some while after their deaths. Few who live during the Hyborian Age can say the same.

AZTRIAS PETANIUS (TOUGHENED)

Being wealthy and influential, perhaps more than anything else outside of the Outer Black itself, has the capacity to corrupt. Aztrias Petanius is the spineless, deceitful proof of this. The nephew of a Nemedian governor, Petanius is educated, refined, and civilized. He is also corrupt, greedy, and incapable of countenancing any course of action not of immediate benefit to him and him alone.

Petanius may not always have been this way, but he assumed the role of licentious fool fairly early in his life and nothing was able to dissuade him from the path. His uncle, a man of fairly abstemious habits, never took much

interest in the debauches which his nephew engaged upon. When usurers began to visit his residence, however, asking for him to make good on his nephew's extensive debts, Aztrias Petanius suddenly found his uncle somewhat less disinterested.

Dragged unceremoniously to his uncle's residence and treated with something less than the deference he usually demanded, Petanius was quickly obliged to beg his uncle's forgiveness. Then for his money.

Given Petanius' taste for wine, women, and gambling, along with his penchant for losing money on all three pastimes, it soon became necessary to find a new source of income. He soon hit upon a scheme he thought foolproof. He would persuade a local thief to procure some expensive item from a nearby temple, mansion, or museum. Petanius would pay a small fee for the service and then sell the stolen item on for vastly more money to any wealthy, unscrupulous client he could find. It was the perfect scheme for, if caught, Petanius would simply invoke his uncle's name and watch as the man-at-arms or the captain of the watch ran away.

It seemed, to Petanius that his fortune will soon be made, after all, what can go wrong?

Foppish and effete, with a fashionable lisp which many try to imitate, Aztrias Petanius seems the typical aristocrat. However, in reality he is quite poor, desperate, and only too open to betraying those whose services he retains.

ATTRIBUTES

Awareness	Intelligence	Personality	Willpower
10	9	10	7

Agility		Brawn		Coordination	
9		8		10	

FIELDS OF EXPERTISE

Combat	—	Movement	1
Fortitude	1	Senses	—
Knowledge	1	Social	—

STRESS AND SOAK

- **Stress:** Vigor 8, Resolve 7
- **Soak:** Armor 1 (Padded Doublet), Courage 1

ATTACKS

■ **Guardsman's Sword (M):** Reach 1, 4 🦅, 1H, Vicious 1

SPECIAL ABILITIES

■ **Don't You Know Who I Am?:** The name of Aztrias Petanius, and more importantly, his uncle, are well known. Attacking him requires the assailant to pass a Daunting (D3) Society test or pay 2 Doom. Even if the foe has no idea who Aztrias is, so complete is his sense of entitlement and self-absorption that the attacker cannot fail to notice it. This ability is only used once per encounter.

DEMETRIO (NEMESIS)

It is the greatest regret of Demetrio's life that, as Chief of the Inquisitorial Council of Numalia, much of his intellect is spent restraining the brutish instincts of men like Dionus. Demetrio came to join the Numalian police owing to the absence of any other employment which might allow him to utilize an intelligence which had long exceeded those around him.

Preoccupied with the truth and uninterested in the extraction of untrustworthy confessions through violence, Demetrio's meticulous investigations quickly gained him promotions. The fact that he also caught those guilty of the crimes was merely an attractive bonus. This endeared him to the local populace, however, who soon came to associate his presence with surety of justice and fairness, a quality not often found in the Numalian inquisition.

Committed to his deductions and to the distribution of justice — irrespective of convenience or station — Demetrio is an honest man. There are few who can say that in this epoch of the world without smirking.

While trained in the use of the sword, the halberd, and the bow, Demetrio is far more comfortable employing his remarkable powers of observation and logic. He believes in reason over violence.

ATTRIBUTES

Awareness	Intelligence	Personality	Willpower
11	12	10	11
Agility		**Brawn**	**Coordination**
9		8	9

FIELDS OF EXPERTISE

Combat	1	Movement	—
Fortitude	—	Senses	2
Knowledge	3	Social	2

> *"Fellow, I am chief of the Inquisitorial Council of the city of Numalia. You had best tell me why you are here, and if you are not the murderer, prove it."*
>
> — Demetrio, "The God in the Bowl"

STRESS AND SOAK

■ **Stress:** Vigor 8, Resolve 11
■ **Soak:** Armor 3 (Mail), Courage 1

ATTACKS

■ **Guardsman's Sword (M):** Reach 2, 4 🦅, Vicious 1
■ **Eye of Authority (T):** Range C, 4 🦅 mental, Stun. Demetrio's very look makes the guilty and innocent alike wither.

SPECIAL ABILITIES

■ **Keen Senses:** Sight

DOOM SPENDS

■ **Insight:** For 1 Doom, Demetrio gleans some useful bit of knowledge about any foe. This adds a bonus of 1 Momentum that he can stpend immediately on his next attack. If it is not used, the Momentum is discarded, though the information may still be of use.

DIONUS (TOUGHENED)

A large, strong, highly aggressive man with brains as diminutive as his body is bulky, Dionus is rude, abrasive, and incapable of listening to reason. He is cowardly and unlikely to engage in any fight he feels he cannot win. That said, if there is a chance of issuing a consequence-free beating to a foe, Dionus can move more quickly than would seem possible.

Dionus was confronted with two choices when he came of age. He could join the Nemedian army or he could join the Numalian police. Despite his impressive bulk and not inconsiderable strength, Dionus had always been the type of man who preferred inflicting pain on those who could not fight back to the alternative of equal combat. It should be noted that this is as close to self-awareness that Dionus ever came.

He joined the Numalian watch and found his calling in the intimidation of the poor and the weak and the sadistic thrill he took from beating confessions from those who were found near to the scene of a crime. Dionus soon found that evidence was not required in such cases; throw enough punches into the face and guts of anyone — man or woman

— and chances were they'd confess to make you stop. With this *modus operandi* in place, Dionus was soon, if not liked, at least respected, within the ranks of the police and reached the rank of Prefect — a not inconsiderable achievement.

The ascent of Demetrio to Chief Inquisitor, however, soon made Dionus' life more difficult as the new Inquisitor did not hold with the more physical methods of detection which Dionus relied upon. Soon, Demetrio insisted that Dionus attend crimes only with him by his side in an attempt to keep the brute from doing too much damage — to others or to himself, for Dionus was far too stupid to realize the number of enemies he was earning himself.

ATTRIBUTES

Awareness	Intelligence	Personality	Willpower
8	6	6	8

Agility	Brawn	Coordination
9	12	7

FIELDS OF EXPERTISE

Combat	2	Movement	1
Fortitude	1	Senses	—
Knowledge	—	Social	—

STRESS AND SOAK

- **Stress:** Vigor 12, Resolve 8
- **Soak:** Armor 2 (Boiled Leather Cuirass), Courage 1

ATTACKS

- **Broadsword (M):** Reach 2, 8 🦅, Unbalanced, Parrying
- **Improved Steely Glare (T):** Range C, 3 🦅 mental, Stun

DOOM SPENDS

- **Cower in Fear:** By spending 3 Doom, Dionus makes his opponents halt in terror, an Area attack. They must pass a Challenging (D2) Discipline test or lose their next turn.

"Why go to all this trouble of questions and speculations?" complained the burly prefect. "It's much easier to beat a confession out of a suspect. Here's our man, no doubt about it. Let's take him to the Court of Justice — I'll get a statement if I have to smash his bones to pulp."

— Dionus, "The God in the Bowl"

KALLIAN PUBLICO, ARCHIVIST AND COLLECTOR (TOUGHENED)

A wealthy collector of antiquities and rarities, Kallian Publico is well known throughout Numalia, a distinctive figure in purple finery riding arrogantly throughout the streets upon a golden chariot while sneering contempt for all beneath him. He is a native Nemedian, born to wealth and power, inheritor of a magnificent estate. His father was a merchant prince with a substantial collection of curios and *objets d'art*, assembled out of his own interest in antiquity and culture. Kallian assumed ownership of his family's holdings through a series of occurrences as suspicious as they were fortuitous and, under his hands, established himself as the preeminent dealer of rare and invaluable items.

Kallian Publico's Temple — his gallery and shop's grandiose title — is famed in the city, a landmark for rich patrons such as scholars, princes, nobles, and other wealthy collectors of rarities. Within its halls are found curios, artworks, relics, artifacts, and more, sacred and impossibly rare, coveted across the civilized world. It is not open to the public and is accessible by appointment only, a feat requiring a Challenging (D2) Society test to arrange. The Temple is described more fully on page 50. His villa, in the eastern suburb of town, is equally opulent, filled with less precious treasures but still appointed to a decadence that would shame the most vain of kings.

In the flesh, Kallian is a corpulent man, prone to many vices. He dresses all in purple silks to conceal his girth and travels solely by chariot, necessitated by his poor physical condition. Descending from his broad girdle of black velvet is a golden key, worn prominently, the only key to his Temple. He trusts few, and thus the only servants he allows access to the Temple are his chariot-driver Enaro and his clerk Promero. Each hates Kallian separately and for their own reasons but are equally cowed to submission by their domineering patron.

Utterly ruthless and holding few scruples, Publico is more than willing to bribe, steal, cheat, or defraud others to further his interests. Kallian's obsession with the wealth of antiquity extends particularly to artifacts from Acheron of old, and many are the treasure hunting and expeditions he financed in search of these rare and valuable items.

He acts as an occasional fence for stolen goods, putting him into contact with many disreputable elements, as well as the noble circles he normally cultivates. Player characters might be enlisted as such agents, or cross paths with Kallian's own forces. They might also encounter him within the courts of Numalia, or even — depending on social class — be invited to one of his galas or parties held within the Temple itself.

ATTRIBUTES

Awareness	Intelligence	Personality	Willpower
9	10	10	8

Agility	Brawn	Coordination
7	6	7

FIELDS OF EXPERTISE

Combat	—	Movement	—
Fortitude	—	Senses	1
Knowledge	3	Social	3

STRESS AND SOAK

- **Stress:** Vigor 6, Resolve 8
- **Soak:** Armor —, Courage —

ATTACKS

- **Stiletto (M):** Reach 1, 3🗡, 1H, Hidden 1, Parrying, Thrown, Unforgiving 1
- **Arrogant Sneer (T):** Range C, 4🗡 mental, Non-lethal

SPECIAL ABILITIES

- **Collector's Eye:** Kallian Publico can re-roll one d20 per attempt at assessing the nature or value of any particular item he sees.

DOOM SPENDS

- **Know the Market:** With his extensive network of contacts and sources, Kallian Publico can spend 1 Doom to lower the Difficulty of any test involving the procurement of a rare or valuable item.
- **Hard Bargain:** Kallian Publico can spend Doom to increase the Difficulty by one step per Doom for any player character to acquire an item, if Kallian desires the item for himself.

"MANY EYES", SPYMASTER OF YEZUD (NEMESIS)

The real name of the person known as "Many Eyes" is unknown, and some say it is less a moniker than it is a title, passed from one to another. There may have been previous men or women to hold the title, though the individual called Many Eyes now is said to be a tall, shaven-headed Zamorian of indeterminate age, though even this might be distraction from his (or her) true identity. How Many Eyes came to assume the role of the master of spies is as shrouded in mystery as everything else about the person.

Who Many Eyes really is, and what his past might tell us, is as well guarded as the secrets he and his guild traffic in. Like the spider his name suggests, he sits patiently at the center of a web of spies, assassins, and kidnappers. It is said there is nothing in Yezud and little in Zamora that he does not know or cannot find out. To outsiders, he plays the world like a game. To those inside his sphere of immediate influence, he devotes himself to the Spider-God, mimicking the ways of that great arachnid in all things.

In the gutters of Yezud and the dingy taverns of her Maul, they say that Many Eyes does not think as men, but looks with the eyes of his kind — many faceted and all-seeing. This is, perhaps, an exaggeration, but one Many Eyes gladly encourages. His name alone invokes fear in most Zamorian thieves, from Yezud to Shadizar. His influence does not much extend beyond the borders of Zamora, but he deals in any information that comes his way. King and queens of surrounding nations seek to hire Many Eyes' minions, though they often find those minions come away with more information about the client than they give back.

Should the player characters encounter Many Eyes, they will soon learn that he has a network of informants and agents doing his bidding, directly or otherwise. When necessary, he can send a wave of street toughs or even a select few assassins after his foes. It may even be that the player characters are hired for such tasks, perhaps not even for the first time, though they may have been previously unaware of his role in their past.

ATTRIBUTES

Awareness	Intelligence	Personality	Willpower
11	12	9	10

Agility	Brawn	Coordination
9	8	8

FIELDS OF EXPERTISE

Combat	1	Movement	2
Fortitude	2	Senses	3
Knowledge	3	Social	4

STRESS AND SOAK

- **Stress:** Vigor 10, Resolve 12
- **Soak:** Armor 2 (Alchemically Treated Robes), Courage 4

ATTACKS

- **Longsword (M):** Reach 2, 4🗡, 1H, Parrying
- **Shortsword (M):** Reach 1, 4🗡, 1H, Parrying
- **Secrets Told in an Unnerving Whispery Voice (T):** Range C, 7🗡 mental, Stun
- **Fierce Orator (T):** Range C, 4🗡 mental, Stun

SPECIAL ABILITIES

- Inured to Poison
- **Sorcerer:** Many Eyes has learned the *Placate the Dead*, *Astral Wanderings*, and *Summon a Horror* spells, though he keeps his use of sorcery a closely guarded secret
- **Spymaster:** Many Eyes routinely summons horrors and has them spy on impregnable places, while cultivating a network of informants to provide him with insights that such creatures might not possess.
- **The Ring of Spiders:** A minor petty enchantment, this magic ring allows Many Eyes to summon a single spider horror (see page 94) that will serve him for two encounters, accompanying him to new zones, if required, at no Resolve cost.

DOOM SPENDS

- **Hidden Agents:** Any non-player character from Yezud has the potential to be one of his spies. Once per encounter, Many Eyes can spend 1 Doom to reveal that an otherwise loyal non-player character has been his spy all along. This non-player character is immediately activated and player characters do not count as having Guard against them! For 1 additional Doom, the agent gains the Undead quality, having been near-murdered and revivified through diabolical use of spider venom.
- **Hidden Friends:** At any point, Many Eyes can spend 2 Doom to reveal that he has a mob of spider horrors (see page 94) waiting and ready to pounce.
- **Master Poisoner:** Many Eyes routinely coats his and his agents' weapons with poison. Any agents that don't naturally have poison can spend 1 Doom to give their weapon the Persistent 2 quality.

MURILO (TOUGHENED)

Brave, resourceful, and trustworthy are not words one would commonly associate with the nobility in any nation. Murilo, however, is an exception in these matters. Though a young man and accustomed to the trappings of civilization, Murilo is hardier than he looks. Yes, his hair may be carefully coiffured and laden with spiced oils, his skin artfully painted with the choicest of pigments, and his fingernails carefully maintained, but in spite of the taint of cities and refinement, Murilo is a man of integrity and inner steel.

Born to wealth and raised in the finest houses the city had to offer, Murilo was never allowed to simply become a foppish, thoughtless rake. While Murilo has, of course, indulged in drinking and whoring and fighting, his mother — Lady Castellio — instilled a sense of inner discipline in him as a child which no exposure to the entitlements of his rank has managed to permanently wither.

> *Murilo, for all his scented black curls and foppish apparel was no weakling to bend his neck to the knife without a struggle.*
>
> — "Rogues in the House"

Instead, after the death of his remarkable mother, Murilo began to build himself a modest reputation as a politician with a grand vision and the force of personality to achieve his aims. This brought him into contact with powerful people; amongst whom, somewhat unfortunately for Murilo, was Nabonidus, the Red Priest. Nabonidus, who had the ear of the King and had spent long years establishing his power base, was disconcerted by the ascent of this young man.

The fact is that Murilo seemed reluctant to engage in the usual economics of corruption which made the flow of power in the city so much easier. It was not that such things did not tempt Murilo; he was a man and as intrigued by the promise of gold and the entreaties of his peers as any other, sensing the danger that rejecting these bribes might engender for him. However, his mother's teachings resolved him to honesty and impartiality as far as he was able.

Not accepting the importunities of those who would have his loyalty in exchange for jewels and women in fact proved Murilo's making. He became, in the eyes of all those who negotiated and lobbied for extra power and attention in the court, an honest man. Someone who could be trusted to deliver an urgent letter to a wife or mistress and be guaranteed not to read the contents and use it to secure obedience. In all things, Murilo tried to ensure that he followed the example of Lady Castellio.

A fine swordsman, poet, and orator — talents which his parents bestowed upon him — Murilo is everything one would expect of a decorous, intelligent nobleman. But there is a hardness to him, a willingness to sacrifice his own life in the pursuit of something truer. How rare are such men in a world like this.

A skilled duelist and a staunch ally — if he perceives the player characters as worthy of his trust — Murilo is as likely to support them with sword as with a peroration. His favor may just be worth cultivating.

ATTRIBUTES

Awareness	Intelligence	Personality	Willpower
9	10	11	12

Agility	Brawn		Coordination
11	10		9

FIELDS OF EXPERTISE

Combat	2	Movement	2
Fortitude	1	Senses	1
Knowledge	1	Social	2

STRESS AND SOAK

- **Stress:** Vigor 10, Resolve 12
- **Soak:** Armor 1 (Padded Doublet), Courage 3

ATTACKS

- **Dueling Sword (M):** Reach 2, 3 ♦, 1H, Parrying, Unforgiving 1
- **Duelist (T):** Range C, 4 ♦ mental, Stun. If given time prior to any fight, Murilo may show off his skill, a dazzling array of intimidating swordsmanship.

NABONIDUS, THE RED PRIEST (NEMESIS)

The Red Priest Nabonidus is the true power behind the throne, a plotter and conspirator with schemes ranging far beyond the spiritual and wholly into the political. Nominally a priest of Mitra, Nabonidus is of that strain of the faith that is judgmental and intolerant, consigning sinners to the pits of hell. Long having lost true faith, Nabonidus instead uses his office as a key and a shield — a toll to gain access to power and wealth and to keep his foes at bay by claiming the authority of his holy office. As such, he has accumulated a litany of crimes and vices over the years, ranging from treachery, excessive ambition, exploitation, greed, swindling, and oppressing the common folk of the city.

Nabonidus is rumored to be a sorcerer, able to read minds, curse foes, see the future, and tug at the strings of destiny. His hooded red gown is as distinctive as it is hated, a sign of all that is corrupt and decadent about the city and its ruling class.

He tends to be sardonic and mocking, highly intelligent, and gloats over those he can. There is nothing he enjoys better than being the cause of his enemies' destruction, and Nabonidus has many enemies. He uses his position as the king's spiritual counselor as a means of protecting himself from their reprisals, and flaunts his actions brazenly, trusting that none have the courage to oppose him.

Many have tried to kill him and failed, though most are never able to marshal up the strength to make the attempt. However, a growing number of revolutionaries view Nabonidus as an easy target, more vulnerable than his noble peers.

His estate, described on page 41, is surrounded with walled gardens, with many secrets, ranging from death-traps, spy-tubes, hidden compartments and chambers, secret passages, sliding walls, and acid baths in the cellars by which he can dissolve the corpses of his enemies. A silent man named Joka and a dog are the only apparent guards. Some eyewitnesses report another servant, a hunched figure never seen clearly enough to identify as a man. This mysterious servant is none other than the man-ape Thak (described on page 94), an astonishing creature Nabonidus has trained from a cub, a powerful manservant and bodyguard.

ATTRIBUTES

Awareness	Intelligence	Personality	Willpower
10	11	10	11

Agility	Brawn		Coordination
7	7		7

FIELDS OF EXPERTISE

Combat	—	Movement	—
Fortitude	—	Senses	1
Knowledge	3	Social	3

STRESS AND SOAK

- **Stress:** Vigor 7, Resolve 11
- **Soak:** Armor —, Courage 1

ATTACKS

- **Fist (M):** Reach 1, 2 ♦, 1H, Improvised
- **Stinging Mockery (T):** Range C, 4 ♦ mental, Stun

SPECIAL ABILITIES

- **Power Behind the Throne:** Nabonidus may roll an additional d20 for any tests involving his reputation, local and otherwise.

DOOM SPENDS

- **Nabonidus' Lair:** When in his estate, Nabonidus draws from a pool of 5 Doom (separate from the regular Doom pool) solely used to introduce and trigger environmental effects, additional complications, etc., based on mechanisms and traps built into the construction of his home. He may also use the normal Doom pool for additional actions or traps. Once spent, each Doom cannot be replaced.

NESTOR (NEMESIS)

One of the many Gundermen mercenaries conscripted into Aquilonia's border wars, Nestor fought on the frontier for eight years. In this time, he served as a guard on frontier forts, skirmishing with Picts and Cimmerians, and took part in the regular conflicts along the passes between the Bossonian Marches and the Border Kingdom. After putting in his service, the gray-eyed, tawny-haired Gunderman mustered out, taking with him a small quantity of gold and the gear he carried.

> A squad of Zamorian soldiers, led by the officer Nestor, a Gunderman mercenary, were marching down a narrow gorge, in pursuit of a thief, Conan the Cimmerian, whose thefts from rich merchants and nobles had infuriated the government, of the nearest Zamorian city.
>
> — Untitled Fragment

After some interesting misadventures in Aquilonia and Nemedia, Nestor made his way to Zamora. He enlisted in the standing army there for a time as a mercenary, but grew bored with patrols and skirmishing Turan when it rattled its saber in Zamora's direction. He saw that the city militia was more to his liking, with the ability to sleep in the same place each night and to enjoy the privileges of rank, and so he soon found himself enlisted as a guard captain with a small company of guardsmen at his command.

In person, Nestor is fairly typical for a Gunderman — tenacious, calm, careful, honorable — but he is nonetheless a mercenary to the core. An excellent warrior and tracker, he has a gruff charm and is ultimately pragmatic; on occasion, he is prone to rash action, usually when pushed to desperation. Nestor has come to enjoy his current status, and excels at it, though he can already see how tenuous it is. City officials frequently call upon him to serve the wealthy and influential of the city, the latest example calling upon him to stop a series of outrageous robberies performed by some sneak-thief capable of scaling walls without the use of a rope or climbing gear.

ATTRIBUTES

Awareness	Intelligence	Personality	Willpower
8	8	8	10

Agility	Brawn	Coordination
10	10	10

FIELDS OF EXPERTISE

Combat	3	Movement	2
Fortitude	2	Senses	1
Knowledge	1	Social	1

STRESS AND SOAK

- **Stress:** Vigor 12, Resolve 12
- **Soak:** Armor 4 (Skullcap, Mail, Greaves), Courage 2

ATTACKS

- **Broadsword (M):** Reach 2, 7 🗡, Unbalanced, Parrying
- **Dirk (M):** Reach 1, 5 🗡, 1H, Hidden 1, Parrying, Thrown, Unforgiving 1
- **Hunting Bow (R):** Range C, 3 🗡, 2H, Volley
- **Steely Glare (T):** Range C, 2 🗡 mental, Stun

SPECIAL ABILITIES

- **Gunderman Mercenary:** Gundermen mercenaries are famed throughout the Hyborian kingdoms for their discipline and effectiveness. They may reduce the Difficulty of any Social test while dealing with military, mercenaries, or similar groups.
- **Seasoned Veteran:** Nestor is an experienced mercenary able to draw support from discipline and camaraderie. He and any forces under his immediate command gain an additional 1 🗡 Courage Soak whenever confronted with any test relating to morale or threatening Displays, performed in a military or combat-related context. This is not useful against supernatural or unnatural threats, monsters, or while alone without allies.

DOOM SPENDS

- **Tenacity:** Nestor is a survivor, especially hard to kill. Whenever he suffers one or more Wounds that would reduce him to 0, he can spend 1 Doom per Wound to restore himself to 1 Wound, though he is unconscious. Once per scene, he can attempt a Daunting (D3) Fortitude test to reawaken, and can then spend Doom points to recover otherwise. If Nestor fails this test, he remains unconscious, and a Complication indicates he is somehow additionally incapacitated. If there is not enough Doom for him to use this ability, he dies.

QUINTUS, PRIEST OF ANU (TOUGHENED)

Physically, Quintus is of little threat. He can nevertheless call upon allies from almost any quarter of society and be assured of swift support. He collects favors, knows everyone, and has made himself necessary. He fulfills a narrow function exactly and even those who loathe him see his use. This makes him a dangerous foe, even if he is unlikely to last long in single combat.

Priests of Anu are not, as a rule, renowned for their piety as are the priests of Mitra. Nor are they remarked upon for their fanaticism as the priests of Set. They are men chiefly remarkable for their cynicism and their wiles. And even amongst this mob of cunning delinquents who obscure their lust for money and influence behind the apparent humility of the police, Quintus, who presided over the temple in the Maze, earned a reputation for connivance that few could equal. Acting as a fence enabled him to acquire the wealth he coveted and the names and faces of those criminals he could offer up to the police in exchange for protection from the dangers of the slum district.

Of course, those who dealt with the priest knew of his duplicity; but, so carefully did he balance those who owed him favors and those who depended upon him to sell their illegally obtained goods, he was able to flourish for many years. Unfortunately for Quintus, the subtle architecture of checks and balances he had constructed around himself is not infallible. One day, some foe, perhaps some savage, will be his undoing.

> There was a priest of Anu whose temple, rising at the fringe of the slum district, was the scene of more than devotions. The priest was fat and full-fed, and he was at once a fence for stolen articles and a spy for the police.
>
> — "Rogues in the House"

ATTRIBUTES

Awareness	Intelligence	Personality	Willpower
10	11	11	10

Agility	Brawn	Coordination
7	8	8

FIELDS OF EXPERTISE

Combat	—	Movement	—
Fortitude	1	Senses	2
Knowledge	2	Social	1

STRESS AND SOAK

- **Stress:** Vigor 8, Resolve 10
- **Soak:** Armor —, Courage 2

ATTACKS

- **Dagger (M):** Reach 1, 3🏵, 1H, Hidden, Parrying, Thrown, Unforgiving 1

SERVIUS OF AQUILONIA, INVETERATE ROGUE (NEMESIS)

Though he always embellishes his past, Servius grew up the mere son of a farmer. Pretense was not in the family's nature, but it was in young Servius' own temperament. He lied, he says, before he learned how to speak... and speak he does. Eloquently, in fact, which gets him out of a good deal of trouble his same words get him into. He is quick to insult, but has enough charm and wit to avoid having his head separated from his body — at least thus far.

He spins tales of an orphaned life in the gutters of Tarantia where, left to his own devices, he learned the world was harsh, uncaring, and demanded of mere curs what it demands of men. None of this is true, and Servius did not see Tarantia until he'd also seen ten winters. A passing charlatan that swindled his father (with Servius' help) brought him to Tarantia. The two bonded after that.

Since then, Servius made a small name for himself as a daring thief, a bold rogue, and a man with more lives than a cat. Countless strong, clever, and powerful men have sought to kill him. None have yet succeeded. Servius' nature demands he presses the fates, pushes the cruel ladies as far as they will go. One day, he is certain, such audacity will be revisited upon him tenfold. He tries not to think about that day.

About thirty years of age, Servius sports blond curls, a lithe frame, and the best clothes he can afford. He is handsome and beds only with the finest of professionals. While his name is not unknown in many cities, he has yet to reach the status of notables such as Shevatas or Taurus. Time, though, is on Servius' side — or so he believes.

Servius is an ex-member (not by choice) of several city guilds, and there are thieves from Argos to Agrapur that would pay for his head. He makes friends quickly and loses them even quicker. His charm is balanced by sheer bravado and arrogance. Still, people often find they like him in spite of themselves... that is until he robs, tricks, or otherwise betrays them. It is his nature, he'll tell you, and you cannot blame man for the way the gods forged him. No, blame Bel and Mitra, Anu, and Erlik instead!

ATTRIBUTES

Awareness	Intelligence	Personality	Willpower
11	12	12	9

Agility	Brawn	Coordination
11	8	10

FIELDS OF EXPERTISE

Combat	1	Movement	1
Fortitude	1	Senses	1
Knowledge	1	Social	3

STRESS AND SOAK

- **Stress:** Vigor 9, Resolve 10
- **Soak:** Armor 2 (Brigandine Jacket), Courage 3

ATTACKS

- **Shortsword (M):** Reach 1, 4 🔱, 1H, Parrying
- **My Friends are Just Around the Corner (T):** Range C, 6 ♦ mental, Stun. Servius lies very well. Maybe there are some of his large friends just out of sight?

SPECIAL ABILITIES

- **Nine Lives:** Servius is hard to kill. Fortune is on his side. Any Momentum spent by someone trying to do him harm is doubled. Any Momentum or Doom costs spent by Servius to save his own skin is halved.

DOOM SPENDS

- **If You'd Only See It My Way:** For 2 Doom, the gamemaster requires that any character wanting to harm Servius must attempt a Daunting (D3) Willpower or Discipline test. Failure means that they relent, just shy of killing him. They might tie Servius up, give him over to authorities, or other unfortunate things, but they do not kill him or cause permanent damage.

SHEVATAS THE THIEF (NEMESIS)

Shevatas came of age in the Maul, the most dangerous and ruthless place for any thieves to cut their teeth. Surviving initially through relieving older thieves of coins they had themselves stolen only moments before, Shevatas soon attracted the attention of the local gangs which patrolled the Maul, demanding tribute from those who could not defend themselves — either through force of arms or weight of reputation.

It was as part of this gang that Shevatas encountered his mentor, a grizzled thief whose name has been forgotten, while the name of his pupil becomes legend. Recognizing the inherent talent for larceny in his new student, Shevatas' mentor schooled the young, impetuous thief in the rudiments of the art. From the picking of pockets with the celerity and style which Shevatas' amateurish attempts had lacked, to gaining entry to the most secure of buildings, Shevatas learned quickly and he learned well.

> *Shevatas was wiry and lithe, as became a master-thief of Zamora. His small round head was shaven, his only garment a loin-cloth of scarlet silk. Like all his race, he was very dark, his narrow vulture-like face set off by his keen black eyes. His long, slender and tapering fingers were quick and nervous as the wings of a moth. From a gold-scaled girdle hung a short, narrow, jewel-hilted sword in a sheath of ornamented leather.*
>
> — "Black Colossus"

Soon, he was considered one of the Maul's most talented and effective thieves. And, anyone considered such in the Maul is automatically one of the finest thieves in the whole of Zamora. Whatever happened to lead to Shevatas' mentor being murdered by the gang that had originally taken in the young thief is unknown. Was it a power struggle? Had the old man become greedy in his dotage?

It does not matter. The gang to which Shevatas belonged slaughtered his mentor in cold blood. Shevatas did not take kindly to this particular piece of criminality, or to the suggestion made by the gang's leader that he should return to thieving on the gang's behalf if he did not wish to end up in a similar state to his former teacher. A week later, over half of the gang were dead — most of them executed in their sleep. Shevatas' reputation was secured and the young thief spent considerable time enhancing it.

The pursuit of greatness is likely to be Shevatas' ultimate undoing. While the raids he carries out procure him prestige and enough gold to fulfill his baser instincts, the need to secure his fame forever is an obsession. The speed with which his old master's name was lost began to preoccupy him maddeningly; that a man of so many years and so much experience should be killed and immediately consigned to anonymity obsessed Shevatas.

His plans become more daring and his heists ever more ambitious. His reputation grows, as does his skill, but one can only push the fortunes and vagaries of the gods so far. Shevatas will push those to the edge and beyond. Like any gambler, though, one day, he'll have to pay up.

A thief of guile, wit, and cunning, Shevatas is the most professional and expert of thieves. Specializing in lengthy infiltrations and the planning of heists over many months, he is the kind of thief from whom any aspiring burglar might learn much if not left penniless by the better man.

ATTRIBUTES

Awareness	Intelligence	Personality	Willpower
11	9	9	12
Agility		Brawn	Coordination
12		9	11

FIELDS OF EXPERTISE

Combat	1	Movement	1
Fortitude	1	Senses	1
Knowledge	2	Social	2

STRESS AND SOAK

- **Stress:** Vigor 10, Resolve 13
- **Soak:** Armor —, Courage 4

ATTACKS

- **Dagger (M):** Reach 1, 4 🔥, 1H, Hidden, Parrying, Thrown, Unforgiving 1
- **Toothsome Grin (T):** Range C, 3 🔥 mental, Stun. Shevatas' very smile speaks of skill with both blade and the disposition of bodies.

SPECIAL ABILITIES

- **Keen Sense:** Sight
- **Keen Sense:** Hearing
- **Darkness, My Old Friend:** No one can easily spy Shevatas in the shadows. Any time he attempts to hide, characters attempting to spot him find their Observation test raised by two levels of Difficulty above and beyond any already applicable.

DOOM SPENDS

- **Didn't See It Coming:** For every 2 Doom spent, Shevatas can add 3 🔥 damage to any attack for which the gamemaster decides he has some element of surprise.

TAURUS OF NEMEDIA (NEMESIS)

A thief of enormous proportion and equally enormous reputation, Taurus of Nemedia is the epitome of the master thief — swift, smart, and courageous. The fact that he is enormously fat does not preclude any of these qualities. In fact, it only makes him more deadly.

There are few men whose fame is such that it crosses the borders of nations and is known as readily to the men of Kush as to the women of Argos. There are even fewer men whose fame as a thief is enough to make the bandits, backstabbers, robbers, footpads, cutpurses, pickpockets, burglars, forgers, filchers, and flitters of Zamora intone their name in whispered awe. Such a man is Taurus of Nemedia. The stories which are told of him, in the Maul and the Maze and in all the places where thieves gather to swap information, are scarcely to be believed. Most of them are, in one form or another, true.

The theft of the Eye of Ibis; the procurement of the seven Gems of Night; the raid on the Keep of the White Raven... all of these miraculous escapades are attributed, rightly, to Taurus, and there are hundreds more, each of them as unlikely as the last.

And yet they were carried out. In a few instances, there are comrades who can testify to the skill with which Taurus negotiated the perils placed in his path: the disabled traps, the deftly handled guards, the speed with which a wall could be scaled and a point of entry located. Taurus of Nemedia did not use the stolen wealth to make himself rich; he might have done, of course, might have procured that most expensive of all things, respectability, had he wanted it. But Taurus of Nemedia was a thief from birth — a master thief — and so burglary was not the means to an end but the end in itself.

The planning and execution of the perfect theft was the purpose to which Taurus dedicated his life. Usually the riches he stole were used to procure three things: wine, food, and information. The food made Taurus fat, but even this was part of his legend: his paunch grew but never seemed to slow the speed of his reflexes, the nimbleness of his fingers. It did, however, offer him a security against the guardsmen and watchmen who publicly swore that they would catch Taurus and introduce him to the noose. Who suspects the fat, cheerful man at the table, eating roast meat by the platter and quaffing wine until it seemed he might drown?

And of course, even those who were intelligent enough to see beyond his physical bulk to the calculating mind beneath would have to actually find a dungeon that would hold the wily thief.

> Taurus leaped up, caught the wall and drew himself up. The man's suppleness was amazing, considering his bulk; he seemed almost to glide up over the edge of the coping.
>
> — "The Tower of the Elephant"

ATTRIBUTES

Awareness	Intelligence	Personality	Willpower
12	10	12	11

Agility	Brawn	Coordination
14	11	10

FIELDS OF EXPERTISE

Combat	1	Movement	5
Fortitude	1	Senses	3
Knowledge	3	Social	2

STRESS AND SOAK

- **Stress:** Vigor 12, Resolve 12
- **Soak:** Armor 1 (Extra Bulk), Courage 1

ATTACKS

- **Dagger (M):** Reach 1, 5⚔, 1H, Hidden, Parrying, Thrown, Unforgiving 1
- **Rope and Grapple (R):** Range L, 1⚔, 1H, Grappling
- **Legendary Reputation (T):** Range C, 5⚔ mental, Stun

SPECIAL ABILITIES

- **More Agile Than He Looks:** Any attack which Taurus could conceivably dodge is made at one step of Difficulty level higher. He seems immovable and slow. He is not.

DOOM SPENDS

- **Pressing His Luck:** Taurus has no special Doom spends as such, but he can spend Doom at 2 for 1. Any Doom spent by the gamemaster by Taurus counts as double. Like all thieves, though, one day his luck will run out.

YARA (NEMESIS)

How Yara came to know of Yag-kosha, the sage who was driven out from his home planet of Yag, is in itself a tale more of legend than of truth. How Yara learned the deep, terrible secrets of ancient Atlantis and steeped himself in the dark magic which man may call upon — if he is willing to lose his mind and the essence of himself in doing so — is a tale of bloody deeds and grim betrayals.

Yara's journey into the secrets of the earth began when he was only a young man; preoccupied with thoughts of power and unable to attain it as a slave in the house of a lord of Zamora, the slave slaughtered his master in his bed and fled into the wilderness, clutching the item he had long coveted — a volume which his former owner claimed had been the journal of an Atlantean wizard.

> *Yara came not often from his tower of magic, and always to work evil on some man or some nation. The king of Zamora feared him more than he feared death, and kept himself drunk all the time because that fear was more than he could endure sober. Yara was very old — centuries old, men said, and added that he would live for ever because of the magic of his gem, which men called the Heart of the Elephant, for no better reason than they named his hold the Elephant's Tower.*
>
> **— "The Tower of the Elephant"**

Hunted by those seeking vengeance for the fallen lord, Yara followed the strange hints and maps in the journal deep into the wilderness. A precocious intellect, even those aspects of the Atlantean language which had not been debased into forming the modern languages of the Hyborian epoch became known to him in long hours of study. Finally, this study, undertaken even as he fled from his pursuers, led Yara to a remnant of old Atlantis — thought lost millennia ago.

A network of caves on an island in the south seas was in fact the twisted corridors of an Atlantean fortress rent apart by the cataclysm which dragged the continent beneath the waves but left this behind: a tumor of a bygone age, blemishing the skin of the new. As he explored these water-filled caverns, Yara stumbled upon a carefully maintained library of Atlantean lore. And, beyond this, something he had always desired: knowledge of things beyond this world. In Atlantean texts, he found them.

It was via these arcane recordings that Yara learned of the existence of Yag-kosha, the elephant-headed creature who had descended to the Earth even before Atlantis was young. Resolving to learn what he could from this strange creature, Yara set out to the distant east in search of the alien being that had made its home on these continents. Yag-kosha was generous when Yara first appeared to him, but unsuspecting of the human's savage guile, was unprepared when Yara's final and greatest treachery overwhelmed him and left him a blind, broken slave. Such is the mind and morality of Yara and, perhaps, of many such men.

Yara presents a formidable foe to any who fight him. Whether with magic or with a blade in his hand, there is a cold glint in Yara's eyes, revealing a man whose life will not be ended by natural means.

ATTRIBUTES

Awareness	Intelligence	Personality	Willpower
12	14	9	12

Agility		Brawn		Coordination
8		8		8

FIELDS OF EXPERTISE

Combat	1	Movement	—
Fortitude	2	Senses	2
Knowledge	3	Social	2

STRESS AND SOAK

- **Stress:** Vigor 10, Resolve 14
- **Soak:** Armor 3 (Alchemically Strengthened Robes), Courage 4

ATTACKS

- **Dagger (M):** Reach 1, 3 ⚔, 1H, Hidden, Parrying, Thrown, Unforgiving 1

SPECIAL ABILITIES

- **Student of the Planet Yag:** The planet, and its surviving citizen, is steeped in more spells than men can know. As such, Yara knows all spells contained in the **Conan** corebook, and others besides, at the gamemaster's discretion.
- **Fear 1**

DOOM SPENDS

- **Cruel Master of Fortune:** Complications only cost half the usual amount when bought by Yara. He has not survived and outplayed alien beings without learning something of turning the misfortune of others to his advantage.

FEARSOME CREATURES

Night conceals more than the knives and glittering eyes of thieves and their ilk: it is also home and host to a variety of darksome monsters and uncouth beasts, beings that thirst for life as much as thieves crave gold and jewels. These beings are an ever-present hazard to thieves, either set to ward over treasure hordes, defending their shadowy homes, or summoned by dreadful sorcery and pitted against the dishonest as well as the honest.

RAT, GIANT (MINION)

A loathsome creature the size of a smallish dog, a giant rat on its own is no threat to a healthy adult, but they rarely challenge anyone singly and instead come at their intended prey in vast swarms, racing alongside vast numbers of their lesser brethren. In such groups, they can overbear the most powerful of warriors, dragging them to the ground, gnawing through leather and cloth in moments, and tearing deep into any unexposed flesh.

These vermin can be found anywhere — from the filthiest sewers to the densest jungles, gnawing bones in catacombs, scavenging trash and refuse in back city alleys, and even working alongside sorcerers or witches as familiars, providing eyes and ears where humans cannot. Giant rats live alongside ghouls (described on page 338 of the **Conan** corebook), though sometimes ghouls prey upon them when other food is not available. Rats turn on one another in the same circumstances, so it is not particularly noteworthy.

Giant rats typically hunt at night and rule over swarms of lesser rats, guiding these lesser vermin into ravenous boldness.

ATTRIBUTES

Awareness	Intelligence	Personality	Willpower
8	4	5	6

Agility		Brawn		Coordination
10		8		8

FIELDS OF EXPERTISE

Combat	1	Movement	2
Fortitude	2	Senses	1
Knowledge	—	Social	—

STRESS AND SOAK

- **Stress:** Vigor 3, Resolve 3
- **Soak:** Armor —, Courage —

ATTACKS

- **Bite (M):** Reach 1, 2 ⚔, Persistent 2

SPECIAL ABILITIES

- **Overwhelm:** A giant rat's attack inflicts an additional +2 ⚔ damage against any creature that has already been attacked this round.
- **Keen Senses (Scent)**

SKELETON WARRIOR, GIANT (TOUGHENED, HORROR)

These mighty sentinels were the honor-guard of a king of bygone times, either of the race of the giant-kings or of the Zhemri themselves, perhaps even older still. Bound to their lord through bonds arcane, they were charged with an eternal vigilance, their sole command to see that the eternal slumber of their liege was undisturbed and his tomb unpillaged. Such is the nature of this cursed enchantment that their bodies remain upright and seemingly at watch, while their skeleton remains for a time beyond the natural process of decay.

A group of such wardens sat in an eons-old vigil in a ruined city outside Zamora, sitting at the ready upon carven stone thrones in a tomb-chamber in the midst of a great palace built into a monstrous hill. Still others likely inhabit other ruins in other places, waiting for the unwise to signal their awakening. The magic to transform mortal warriors into eternal watchmen is likely a combination of the spells *Favor of the Gods* (to set the conditions for awakening) and *Rise Up the Dead*, an enchantment not solely confined to guards and wardens. Some past kings or queens may have had the spell performed upon their own selves, enabling them to rise from death and defend their barrows from the pilfering hands of thieves and scavengers.

Despite their prowess, these guardians have a great weakness in that they are highly vulnerable to the touch of sunlight, and walking into bright daylight destroys them rapidly, causing them to molder and collapse into dust almost at once. For this reason, in combat they strive to keep foes engaged and out of the sunlight, trusting in teamwork and might to confine their enemies until they are slain.

ATTRIBUTES

Awareness	Intelligence	Personality	Willpower
8	6	6	8
Agility		Brawn	Coordination
8		14	9

FIELDS OF EXPERTISE

Combat	3	Movement	1
Fortitude	3	Senses	1
Knowledge	—	Social	—

STRESS AND SOAK

- **Stress:** Vigor 14, Resolve 8
- **Soak:** Armor 2 (Moldering Chainmail and Bone), Courage 2 👁 (Loyalty)

ATTACKS

- **Great Broadsword (M):** Reach 2, 9 👁, Unbalanced, Parrying
- **Ancient Shield (M):** Reach 2, 6 👁, 1H, Knockdown, Shield 2

SPECIAL ABILITIES

- **Fear 1**
- **Inured to Pain:** The giant skeleton suffers no penalties from Wounds.
- **Night Vision**
- **Undead:** The giant skeleton can be summoned by the *Raise Up the Dead* spell, though doing so requires the bones of a giant. If no bones are present, the spell has a base difficulty of Daunting (D3) instead of the usual Average (D1). It can be subdued by the *Placate the Dead* spell.
- **Unflinching:** The giant skeleton is immune to Threaten Actions.
- **Unliving**
- **Vulnerable 5 (Sunlight):** The giant skeleton suffers 5 👁 physical damage per round when exposed to direct sunlight.

SPIDER HORROR (MINION)

A many-eyed horror, this spider lurks in the dark corners of the world — in caves and tunnels, the tops of haunted towers, and in the depth of nameless ruins. The venom dripping from its oversized fangs burns on contact and kills once injected.

Roughly the size of a wild boar, spiders like these are surprisingly fast and agile, spinning webs as they scurry around their prey, ensnaring them with webs. Sorcerers keep them as guards, for they are long-lived and only grow more dangerous as they mature. Man has an atavistic fear of even the smallest arachnid, and a spider the size of a pig causes the mind to reel. For, if a spider the size of one's thumb can kill, what might of beast of this size do?

ATTRIBUTES

Awareness	Intelligence	Personality	Willpower
9	7	7	8

Agility	Brawn	Coordination
11	7	7

FIELDS OF EXPERTISE

Combat	1	Movement	2
Fortitude	—	Senses	2
Knowledge	—	Social	1

STRESS AND SOAK

- **Stress:** Vigor 4, Resolve 4
- **Soak:** Armor 2 (Horror), Courage 4 (Horror)

ATTACKS

- **Tiny Poisoned Fangs (M):** Reach 1, 2 �, 1H, Persistent 3
- **Alien intelligence (T):** Range C, 2 � mental, Stun

SPECIAL ABILITIES

- **Flight:** Spider horrors dangle from hidden invisible webs. These webs afford them great maneuverability
- **Invisible Webs:** When facing spider horrors, all physical actions increase by one step of Difficulty as the thousands of strands of invisible web materialize around them. This Difficulty increase lasts until the player character takes a Standard Action to attempt a Simple (Do) Athletics test to break free.
- **Inured to Poison**
- **Minuscule Target:** All observation tests to discover or attacks made against the spider horror are increased by two steps of Difficulty.

DOOM SPENDS

- **Strange Alien Poisons:** The spider horror can spend 3 Doom to perform any of the following effects on a player character it has bitten: it can grant its perception to him (causing 3 � mental damage); it can wrap his soul in ethereal silk (granting the Undead quality until the end of the encounter); or can wrack the victim with fever (inflicting 2 � Fatigue).

> *That monstrous body housed a brain and soul that were just budding awfully into something vaguely human. Murilo stood aghast as he recognized a faint and hideous kinship between his kind and that squatting monstrosity, and he was nauseated by a fleeting realization of the abysses of bellowing bestiality up through which humanity had painfully toiled.*
>
> — "Rogues in the House"

THAK (NEMESIS, HORROR)

In the uppermost craggy peaks of the mountain range that runs along Zamora's eastern border lives a tribe of creatures — half-ape and half-human — caught in the midst of the climb from beast to humanity, a process that may take another hundred thousand years. They are tribal, with rude customs and a rough and rudimentary language of grunts and clicks, but have not yet mastered the use of tools or the building of shelter.

Years ago, the Red Priest Nabonidus came to those mountains and captured one of these creatures. He named the cub Thak and trained it as a bodyguard, manservant, and assistant. The beast learned quickly — far faster than a mere animal — and was able to serve him well. Thak pays close attention to Nabonidus, and now knows many, but not all, of Nabonidus' secrets. Thak knows the inner workings of his estate, including most of its death traps, hidden rooms, concealed passages, and defensive mechanisms.

As his bodyguard, Thak is without peer, spawning rumors of a fierce captive beast capable of tearing a man into pieces, a situation close enough to truth. Unfortunately for Nabonidus, the creature is no mere shadow of a man, no vessel to be filled with its master's will, and he has an independence and thoughts that the Red Priest cannot guess at. Thak harbors resentments at every slight, and in his savage breast swells a growing ambition to strike down his master and take his place. Currently, Thak bides his time, waiting for a moment to strike, though the brute buried within his seemingly obedient demeanor cries out for blood and violence.

ATTRIBUTES

Awareness	Intelligence	Personality	Willpower
9	6	7	10

Agility	Brawn	Coordination
10	14	10

FIELDS OF EXPERTISE

Combat	2	Movement	2
Fortitude	3	Senses	2
Knowledge	—	Social	—

STRESS AND SOAK

- **Stress:** Vigor 17, Resolve 13
- **Soak:** Armor 1, Courage 2

ATTACKS

- **Grapple (M):** Reach 1, 6 ⚔, 1H, Grappling
- **Bite (M):** Reach 1, 4 ⚔, Piercing 1, Unforgiving 2
- **Bestial Visage (T):** Range C, 2 ⚔ mental, Stun

SPECIAL ABILITIES

- **Cunning Mimicry:** Thak can remember complex interactions, manipulations, and tasks by studying others. Whenever attempting to operate some mechanism or device, he can re-roll a single d20 if he has seen the activity performed before. This does not extend to combat.

DOOM SPENDS

- **Inhuman Vitality:** Once per encounter, Thak can shrug off 1 Wound by spending 1 Doom.

YAG-KOSHA (NEMESIS, HORROR)

In the dim and primordial time of history, long before humanity rose for the first time, before the rise of the Seven Empires and the Cataclysm that ended them, a small number of powerful beings landed upon the Earth. They were almost demigods in nature and power, soared through stellar gulfs and across nigh-unto-infinite blackness of space on wings of extra-terrene matter. Exiled from their green and verdant jungle home world of Yag, they sought to make the Earth their new home. This became a necessity, as the substance of their wings could not bear the harsh, acidic atmosphere of Earth's early environment and withered from their shoulders.

> *Conan stared aghast; the image had the body of a man, naked, and green in color; but the head was one of nightmare and madness. Too large for the human body, it had no attributes of humanity. Conan stared at the wide flaring ears, the curling proboscis, on either side of which stood white tusks tipped with round golden balls. The eyes were closed, as if in sleep.*
>
> — "The Tower of the Elephant"

Yag-kosha — once called Yogah — was one of these Yaggites, and he and his kin battled the primeval monsters inhabiting much of the Earth, whether the ancient empires of the serpent folk, the dinosaurs, or the ancient and terrible Old Ones and their servants. Eventually, the Yaggites sought refuge and seclusion in the steamy jungles of the East, inhabiting the lands now known as Khitai and Vendhya. As humanity rose and sought gods, the Yaggites cultivated worshipers among these early humans, creating early cults that served and venerated the Yaggites.

Humans built temples around them and worshiped them as gods. In return, the Yaggites taught their magical arts to human sorcerers, instilling upon them an understanding of the occult and mantic principles that governed the natural universe, and how will might be marshaled to altering the very substance of reality, pulling back the veils between this plane and others. Eventually, only Yag-kosha was left, the last of the Yaggites on Earth.

Hundreds of years ago, Yag-kosha's own jewel — "The Heart of the Elephant" — was seized by his greatest worshiper and apprentice, a human sorcerer named Yara. Yag-kosha had taught Yara the secrets of white magic all too well, but Yara desired the knowledge of blackest sorcery, and for that he betrayed his patron and enslaved him, inflicting inhuman levels of cruelty and torture upon the alien demigod over the centuries.

Yag-kosha's topaz eyes were blinded, his body contorted on the rack, his flesh seared with flame, and his magnificent tusks sheared short and tipped with golden balls for Yara's mocking amusement. Over years, Yag-kosha's muscles atrophied and his flesh is now rugose and loose, a scarred map of centuries of torment. Once he was worshiped as a god, but now his serene beauty is gone, leaving a crippled, broken thing, an object of pity rather than awe.

Despite his ruined nature, Yag-kosha still has considerable magical potency. Using Yag-kosha's magic, Yara has made himself virtually immortal and raised the Tower of the Elephant out of raw elements in the span of a single night. For three centuries, Yara dwelt in Zamora and held sway over the city, cowing even kings with threats of his sorcerous retribution. Though Yag-kosha is unable to wield his Heart — withheld tantalizingly from Yara's magic — the Yaggite is able to see the patterns of time and reality, and understands the workings of Fate. He bides his time and crafts a mighty spell, waiting for a moment when the sorcery of the Blood and the Jewel might come to its fruition, and he might be avenged upon his tormentor.

Yag and Yaggites are described in additional detail in *The Book of Skelos*, and Yara and the Tower of the Elephant are described on pages 28 and 26, respectively. Yag-kosha's attributes below reflect his ruined and decrepit state. A healthy Yaggite — should one still exist — would be far beyond the scope of these rules to describe adequately.

ATTRIBUTES

Awareness	Intelligence	Personality	Willpower
13	12 (2)	12	10
Agility	**Brawn**		**Coordination**
6	7		8

FIELDS OF EXPERTISE

Combat	—	Movement	—
Fortitude	1	Senses	3
Knowledge	5	Social	3

STRESS AND SOAK

- **Stress:** Vigor 8, Resolve 11
- **Soak:** Armor 1 (Tough Hide), Courage 3

ATTACKS

- **Cosmic Tragedy (T):** Range C, 5 🦅 mental, Non-lethal

SPECIAL ABILITIES

- **Inhuman Intelligence 2**
- **Slave to the Jewel:** Yag-kosha's use of sorcery is intrinsically tied to the Yaggite jewel described in *The Heart of the Elephant* (following).

DOOM SPENDS

- **Sorcery of the Eons:** Yag-kosha knows all mortal spells, along with countless others he is loath to use, though he has been forced to do so by Yara. For all practical purposes, Yag-kosha can accomplish any magical effect he is commanded to, with the gamemaster determining the Difficulty and Doom cost.
- **Bound by Yara's Will:** Yag-kosha is enthralled by Yara, a domination so complete that though his Heart is left within reach, he is unable to reclaim it. Whenever Yag-kosha wishes to act against Yara's bidding, he must pay 3 Doom and succeed in a Willpower test with the Difficulty based on the degree of his disobedience, with Average (D1) being speech only, ranging up to Epic (D5) for outright attacks (magical or physical).

THE HEART OF THE ELEPHANT

Intrinsic to each Yaggite's magic is a powerful jewel, an extension through which the Yaggite might focus any sorcerous abilities. Yag-kosha's own jewel is known as "The Heart of the Elephant", after his appearance. Using the Heart for any other Sorcery tests allows the sorcerer to roll an additional d20, and any roll of less than the Sorcery Expertise acts as if it were a roll under Focus, yielding an additional point of Momentum per success.

Without the Heart, all Sorcery tests Yag-kosha attempts are increased in Difficulty by four steps. Conversely, the jewel itself is bound to Yag-kosha, and anyone possessing it finds that any spells directed against Yag-kosha are decreased in Difficulty by four steps, making him virtually defenseless against one who has possession of the Heart and wishes him harm.

CHAPTER 6

HITHER CAME CONAN...

> *He saw a tall, strongly made youth standing beside him. This person was as much out of place in that den as a gray wolf among mangy rats of the gutters. His cheap tunic could not conceal the hard, rangy lines of his powerful frame, the broad heavy shoulders, the massive chest, lean waist and heavy arms. His skin was brown from outland suns, his eyes blue and smoldering; a shock of tousled black hair crowned his broad forehead. From his girdle hung a sword in a worn leather scabbard.*

— "The Tower of the Elephant"

Made curious by tales from his grandfather of the wealthy and decadent lands of to the South, Conan leaves the lands of the north behind, putting Cimmeria, Nordheim, and Hyperborea at his back and closing the earliest chapter of his life, a period addressed in *Conan the Barbarian*.

Out of the Savage North

Striking southward from Hyperborea, he passes across the western ridge of the great mountain range that makes up Brythunia's eastern border, and finds his way down to the thief-city of Accursed Zamora. Though penniless, the Cimmerian quickly discovers a taste for the decadence of civilization. Finding refuge in the rough-and-tumble district of the city known as the Maul amidst other foreigners and adventuresome types, Conan quickly learns the Zamorian language. He survives the easiest way he can, as a thief, putting his considerable climbing skills to use scaling walls, buildings, and even towers, and liberating the owners from their valuables. Spending long hours squatting in the courtyard of the philosophers, he becomes familiar with the myriad of strange and outlandish gods of the south, as well as the bizarre and meaninglessly abstract codes by which these civilized folk govern their lives.

The Tower of the Elephant

It is only a matter of time before he becomes interested in tales of the jewel-encrusted Tower of the Elephant, hearing tell of its enigmatic master Yara and the priceless jewel known as the Heart of the Elephant. Striking out after a vigorous disagreement within a Maul taproom, Conan attempts to scale Yara's tower to steal the Heart. While inside, he meets and teams up with the master thief Taurus, but Taurus does not survive the burglary, killed by a giant venomous spider. Conan makes his way into the Tower, but encounters a scene of cosmic tragedy in the form of the alien god Yag-kosha, broken and humiliated under Yara's cruel dominance. Ashamed for his race, Conan aids the humbled being in its vengeance, resulting in the deaths of Yag-kosha and Yara, the loss of the Heart, and the utter destruction of the Tower of the Elephant.

The Hall of the Dead

Though he earned almost nothing from the exploit, Conan continues as a thief for a while, embarking on a daring series of robberies that earn him the enmity of the noble class and authorities. The ruling class puts a Gunderman captain named Nestor onto Conan's trail, and Conan escapes them, heading out into the nearby mountains following a rumor of a ruined city filled with undisturbed treasure. Nestor and his company pursue, but all of the guards are killed in an avalanche, part of a trap set by Conan. Infuriated, Nestor follows Conan to his destination, the mysterious ancient city on a mountain plateau, and they fight once more. Knocked unconscious and left for dead, Nestor awakens and tracks Conan into the city, but the Cimmerian thief is able to convince Nestor to split any loot they find. In a throne room guarded by giant skeletal warriors, the two men discover a vast sum of wealth, including a jade serpent, which Conan wins in a coin toss. When Conan tries to take the artifact, the skeletal warriors rise and attack, but are destroyed when sunlight falls upon them. A sudden earthquake, likely caused by the unleashing of the old enchantment that kept the skeletons at their vigil, separates the two men, and they each make their way back into town.

While Conan celebrates at a tavern in the Maul, a magistrate accompanied by a squad of guardsmen, seeking his arrest, interrupts him. They learned of the exploit from Nestor, who had unwisely gotten drunk and inadvertently revealed the source of his new wealth before escaping. The magistrate reaches into Conan's loot sack and is bitten by the jade serpent, now brought to hideous life. Conan escapes in the following tumult.

Rogues in the House

Conan eventually befriends Nestor, the Cimmerian and Gunderman putting aside their cultural hatred in place of a grudging respect, and the two men make their way to Shadizar the Wicked, the second-most infamous city in the decadent kingdom of Zamora. They head to the Maze, a den of thieves and cutthroats similar to the Maul. When Nestor is captured and hung for desertion and other crimes, Conan risks imprisonment to avenge him upon the judge, a priest of Anu. Conan kills the priest but is betrayed by a supposed ally and captured soon after. He is sentenced to death and left chained to rot in a cell until his execution.

Meanwhile, a young noble, Murilo, fearing the reprisals of a powerful enemy — Nabonidus, the Red Priest — for various acts of treason, decides to seek out an assassin to dispatch his blackmailer. His chosen assassin is Conan, who readily agrees. Murilo bribes the jailer and goes home to await news of Nabonidus' death. Instead, he learns that Conan is still imprisoned and that the bribed jailer has been arrested. Desperate, the young nobleman decides to take matters into his own hands and trespasses into Nabonidus' home, attempting to murder his foe himself.

He instead encounters the red-garbed priest, but is knocked unconscious. Conan, meanwhile, sets himself free and goes to finish the task he was hired to do. He encounters Murilo in the tunnels beneath the Red Priest's house and, soon after, the two men find the unconscious Nabonidus, stripped of his robe. Waking the priest up, they learn that the priests' bestial manservant, Thak, a man-ape from the wilds of eastern Zamora, now masquerades as Nabonidus

in crude approximation of his human master. After some more of Nabonidus' enemies break into the house and are dispatched by Thak, Conan and the others kill the beast. When Nabonidus tries to betray them, Conan kills him. Realizing his days in Shadizar are numbered, the Cimmerian prudently leaves Zamora.

The God in the Bowl

Conan strikes north and west, arriving in the Nemedian city of Numalia, where he continues his career as a thief. The resourceful Cimmerian soon gains a reputation for thievery. He is hired by the governor's very nephew, Aztrias Petanius, to steal a jeweled goblet from Kallian Publico's Temple, a gallery of artifacts and priceless objects of art. Entering the Temple, Conan encounters a watchman who has just discovered the body of Kallian Publico himself, mysteriously strangled. Other guards are summoned, along with Demetrio, the chief inquisitor of the city. They discover a large open urn sent from Stygia to the priest Kalanthes of Hamumar, an enemy of the cult of Set. Publico had the urn diverted from its intended recipient, thinking that it might contain a treasure known as the diadem of the giant-kings.

> *Arus saw a tall powerfully built youth, naked but for a loincloth, and sandals strapped high about his ankles. His skin was burned brown as by the suns of the wastelands, and Arus glanced nervously at the broad shoulders, massive chest and heavy arms. A single look at the moody, broad-browed features told the watchman that the man was no Nemedian. From under a mop of unruly black hair smoldered a pair of dangerous blue eyes. A long sword hung in a leather scabbard at his girdle.*
>
> — "The God in the Bowl"

However, when the investigators examine it, they find that it is empty, apparently opened by Publico before his death, its contents missing. Though the urn itself had been sealed for millennia, the outside bears a marking indicating it came from Thoth-Amon, a Stygian sorcerer and agent of Set. After Demetrius interrogates Publico's servants, Conan's patron Aztrias arrives and pretends not to know Conan, consigning him to death. Enraged, Conan kills the foppish young noble and strikes at the other watchmen and at Demetrius. In the fracas, he wounds most, and one of Publico's servants escapes into a side-room, emerging moments later screeching in pain about a long-necked god, dying immediately thereafter. Curious, Conan enters the

chamber and encounters an impossibly beautiful woman standing behind a neck-high standing screen.

She attempts to seduce him in an ancient, alien tongue, but he reacts reflexively, striking her head off with his sword. He peers behind the screen and beholds a scene of pure horror — a writhing serpentine body where the woman's own form should have been. Conan flees the Temple and the city itself.

Leaving the Way of the Thief

This ends Conan's career as a thief, leaving him in Nemedia to seek another means of making his livelihood, a period detailed in *Conan the Mercenary*. Despite putting this thieving ways behind him, Conan finds the skills he learned from this period of his life invaluable in his later exploits.

CONAN THE THIEF

As a thief, Conan is just coming into his own, expanding his repertoire of combat and survival skills to include stealth and some languages. He is learning the ways of civilization and how to survive in society, as well as whetting his boundless curiosity. If encountered during his career as a thief, he is likely working out of the Maul or the Maze, or some similar district of ill-repute, and selling his services as a thief or even, on rare occasion, as an assassin. Conan will become stronger, cannier, and more skilled at dealing death and destruction, but even at this young age he is still far stronger and fearsome than any the civilized southern folk have encountered before. He is a formidable foe, but, in his naivety and openness, liable to win the loyalty and friendship of those who recognize the gleam of bloody destiny in his eye.

Of course, this innocence leaves the young Cimmerian open to the predatory gazes of those who manifest the subtleties of civilization with none of the learning that should accompany it. However, taking advantage of anyone with Conan's highly attuned senses and instincts is liable to be fatal. Driven by a cheerful amorality and a yearning to see and encompass all the lands of the continent stretching before him, Conan begins to fill the enormous outline he will one day assume. He might not be there yet, but every day he stays alive he grows nearer to doing so.

This represents Conan after he has been a thief for a year or two, dwelling among the so-called civilized people to the south of his homeland. After a variety of exploits, he's amassed and spent a few thousand experience points, and has invested them in new Skill Expertise and Focus, improved some existing talents, and added a few more. Most importantly, he has improved his Coordination through necessity. Traits from *Conan the Barbarian* are summarized where necessary.

Due to Conan's restless career path, he has not earned any additional Renown, and his Social Standing is unchanged. He has very little wealth to show for his time as a thief, spending or losing it as quickly as he gains it.

> *A few long strides brought him to the door, and as his hand fell on the lock he stifled an involuntary grunt. His practised fingers, skilled among the thieves of Zamora long ago, told him that the lock had been forced, apparently by some terrific pressure from the outside that had twisted and bent the heavy iron bolts, tearing the very sockets loose from the jambs.*
>
> **— The Hour of the Dragon**

CONAN THE THIEF

AGILITY — 10

Skill	TN	Focus
Acrobatics	13	3
Melee	14	4
Stealth	13	3

AWARENESS — 9

Skill	TN	Focus
Insight	10	—
Observation	11	1
Survival	11	2
Thievery	11	2

BRAWN — 13

Skill	TN	Focus
Athletics	16	3
Resistance	14	1

COORDINATION — 9

Skill	TN	Focus
Parry	12	3
Ranged Weapons	10	—
Sailing	9	—

INTELLIGENCE — 8

Skill	TN	Focus
Alchemy	8	—
Craft	8	—
Healing	8	1
Linguistics	11	1
Lore	9	1
Warfare	8	1

PERSONALITY — 7

Skill	TN	Focus
Animal Handling	9	2
Command	7	—
Counsel	7	—
Persuade	7	—
Society	7	—

WILLPOWER — 8

Skill	TN	Focus
Discipline	9	—
Sorcery	8	—

BACKGROUND

- **Homeland:** Cimmeria
- **Caste:** Barbaric
- **Caste Talents:** Savage Dignity, Uncivilized
- **Story:** Born on a Battlefield
- **Trait:** Born to Battle
- **Archetype:** Barbarian
- **Nature:** Proud
- **Education:** Educated on the Battlefield
- **War Story:** Defeated a Savage Beast
- **Languages:** Cimmerian, Nordheimer, Aquilonian, Hyperborean, Nemedian, Zamorian

SOAK

Armor	—
Courage	1

FORTUNE POINTS

STRESS

Vigor	
Resolve	

HARMS

Wounds	
Trauma	

ATTACKS

- **Broadsword (M):** Reach 2, 8 🔱, Unbalanced, Parrying
- **Dagger (M):** Reach 1, 6 🔱, 1H, Hidden 1, Parrying, Thrown, Unforgiving 1
- **Brawl (M):** Reach 1, 5 🔱, 1H, Improvised, Stun
- **Steely Glare (T):** Range C, 3 🔱 mental, Stun

SOCIAL

Social Standing	1
Renown	1
Gold	2

TALENTS

- **Ancient Bloodline (Atlantean):** Conan's bloodline, like that of many Cimmerians, reflects the heritage of ancient Atlantis. He may even have direct lineage from Kull, the famed Atlantean king, a mighty warrior who shares many of the same characteristics. Conan is quick to anger, fierce and indomitable, and he often experiences glimpses into the vastness of time, insights at times of extreme peril or danger.
- **Agile**
- **Courageous**
- **Deflection**
- **Hardy**
- **Healthy Superstition**
- **Human Spider**
- **Master Thief**
- **Nimble as a Cat**
- **Savage Dignity:** Conan may roll an additional d20 for any test to resist being intimidated, persuaded, or impressed by a "civilized" person.
- **Strong Back**
- **Thief**
- **Traveler's Tongue**
- **Uncivilized:** Unaccustomed to civilized ways, Conan suffers one step of Difficulty in social tests when dealing with people from more civilized countries. However, his Upkeep is reduced by 2 Gold.

OTHER BELONGINGS

- Broadsword
- Dagger
- Rough tunic
- Loincloth
- Sandals
- 5 Gold

CHAPTER 7

THE WAY OF THIEVES

"By Bel, god of thieves!" hissed Taurus. "I had thought only myself had courage to attempt that poaching. These Zamorians call themselves thieves — bah! Conan, I like your grit. I never shared an adventure with anyone, but by Bel, we'll attempt this together if you're willing."

— "The Tower of the Elephant"

In every city across the continent there are thieves, stealing to feed themselves, to make themselves rich, or just for the purest thrill that, for a true master thief, can only be found filching something that isn't yours from somewhere which might cause your death at any moment. The world respects skilled thieves; those who are truly artists in the purloining of items which do not belong to them are venerated, their deeds recorded in songs and tales, recounted in admiring tones by those lesser proponents of the larcenous arts. Of course, this doesn't mean that, if caught, unfortunate thieves won't be beaten, tortured, and executed in short order. Becoming a legend requires constant risk, the imminence of death. But, unlike most professions available to the brave and the bold in the cities of the Hyborian epoch, thievery may make you rich and your fate rests entirely in your hands: plan carefully enough, cleverly enough, and you need never be caught.

Of course, the opposite is also true; breaking into an alchemist's laboratory searching for precious metals without making a careful escape plan could leave you without much of a face left. A thief must be constantly alert and aware — guards lurk behind corners, booby-traps lie concealed under flagstones and secreted within the very items you're attempting to steal. And that's before we get to your comrades in the underworld, many of whom would love to make you smile. Or make your throat smile, at least — a big, broad, red smile — if they thought they could get away with it. And you need to keep an eye on the guilds, of course. There's safety and protection there, but only for the right price. Thieving in Aquilonia, in Gunderland, in Shem... there are riches to be found and fortunes to be made, but you're going to need to be smart, fast, and blessed by Bel himself if you choose to take the way of the thief.

THIEVING CAMPAIGNS

Running a campaign influenced by the time that Conan spent as a thief is very different from an adventure modeled on any other stage of the legendary barbarian's career. For one thing, while violence, or at least the threat of it, is definitely an important tool in a thief's kit-bag, it isn't the main one. If the players express an interest in creating thief characters, remind them of this — there are moments when fighting their way out of a situation is necessary, but this shouldn't be their first instinct as thieves.

Instead, speed, stealth, and intelligence are even more important in securing their survival than the strength of their sword arms. This might be something of a change for your players, used to playing soldiers and barbarians

WE LUCKY FEW

Conan's thieving career only lasts two or three years, at best, but they are some of his most memorable stories. He refers to his thieving career in Zamora in later stories and also learns much about the workings of civilization and bureaucracy during this time — skills and attitudes that help him at several points in his long and colorful career.

However, he was one of the lucky ones. Shevatas, master thief of Zamora, accidentally frees an ancient evil while attempting a heist in "Black Colossus", instigating an invasion that kills thousands. Taurus, too, is killed by one of the many dangers lurking inside "The Tower of the Elephant". Conan's Gunderman friend Nestor is captured and hanged in "Rogues in the House". The life of a thief during the Hyborian Age can be exciting, dangerous, and short.

Whether player characters begin their careers as fledgling thieves or fall into this rough trade during their wanderings, playing a series of thief adventures is a great way to increase wealth, renown, and experience. Whether it's a one-time job, or an avowed career, it requires forethought and cunning, and a bit of luck if the player characters are to stay one step ahead of the gallows.

who plunge into the thick of the battle. The gamemaster might have to allow a little leeway for the characters, at least initially. Thieving is a very different, complex art and learning it, for both players and player characters, may not be easy. But it is a lot of fun. After all, living by one's wits doesn't only depend on pilfering a few coins from short-sighted market vendors.

A thief's life is made of grand adventures spent obtaining fist-sized jewels; it's clambering up obsidian walls to snatch a gold tiara from the throne room of an arrogant princeling. *The Way of Thieves* explores the means by which the gamemaster can render a thief campaign an entirely unique experience, exploring an array of additions that can be brought to any game to give it a hint of the underworld. The gamemaster is, of course, free to use these ingredients in any way desired. Thieves, and the lifestyle of the underworld, cut across many worlds, and a game in which the player characters are scouts visiting a border outpost might also involve a thriving black market site at said fort. Someone must traffic in Pictish charms and treasures, after all.

These ingredients help create an exciting, authentically Howardian Conan game in which the player characters are thrust into the dangerous, clandestine world of thievery — so now get them planning their next heist!

SETTING SOME CONDITIONS

It's not a coincidence that the stories detailing Conan's career as a thief take place in large cities. Things happen in cities. In a city, surrounded by people, bombarded with information, and swamped by the endless drama of human lives, the player characters can listen, think, plan, and decide on the actions they want to take.

In the wilderness, things happen to the player characters. In the city, they can make things happen. They can visit a priest who, between ministering to his congregation, is a famed fence. There they might hear the latest gossip of the enormous diamond which was given to the city's ruler in exchange for his daughter's marriage to a neighboring dignitary. Perhaps this priest mentions a palace guard who owes the local crime lord a large sum of money as part of a gambling debt. The guard, once found, is amenable to giving the player character's details of the keep in exchange for the gold to pay off what he owes. From here, the player characters can begin to build their heist.

A good thief game needs the incessant life and energy of a city to provide the opportunities for larceny, as well as the wherewithal to carry that larceny out. That said, this doesn't mean limiting your setting to only cities. They dot the map, but off the parchment, where few tread, are other, smaller, urban locales. They might remain hidden from the cartographer, but needn't be hidden from the imagination.

> *"He was like most men, half blind in the dark. A good thief should have eyes like a cat."*
>
> — Taurus, "The Tower of the Elephant"

The Price of Doing Business

A thief-based game may be best set in the city, offering the right admixture of scope, and most importantly, limitations. But what other considerations need to be made? The first thing to emphasize is the tone of the game.

While the temptation might be to make a thief game lighter than a game set on the frontier of Pictish Wilderness, the gamemaster should try to avoid the impulse. An urban location lends itself to more personal interaction and the broad, knock-about exuberance of tavern brawls, but remember that the player characters always involve themselves in a dangerous world with dangerous people. A tavern brawl might provoke laughter around the table — never a bad thing — but, if the players begin to approach a thief game as something of a farce, the gamemaster may wish to disabuse them of this notion. Perhaps have a crime lord of the city kidnap one of the player characters (or one of their allies) and break the fingers of one hand for jeopardizing the fragile peace that crime lord has managed to create. Perhaps have the owner of the tavern found face down in the river, garroted, for having let the fight occur. It might be that the city watch does not care overmuch for player character revelry, and makes life extremely difficult for those who support or aid them. The gamemaster wishing for a more serious campaign should let the player characters learn that recklessness is likely to be punished — not by the gamemaster but by the world they have entered into as thieves.

There are checks and balances, relationships between certain criminal elements and the authorities, codes of honor and pacts struck years ago which render some places untouchable for thieves — breaking these treaties can and should be dangerous. The player characters are the protagonists of the adventure, certainly, but they are not the only thieves who wish to avail themselves of the riches on offer. Whole guilds of highly trained and ruthless men and women dedicate themselves to thievery. See *Thieves' Guilds* on page 105 for more detail on such organizations.

Dressing the Part

Conan the Thief contains an extensive list of supplementary equipment of the kind which thieves conducting raids, burglaries, and other nefarious escapades might need. However, being a thief in the cities of the south, for example, requires more careful consideration than simply choosing a lockpick and finding the right doorway. In "The Tower of the Elephant", when Conan encounters Taurus of Nemedia,

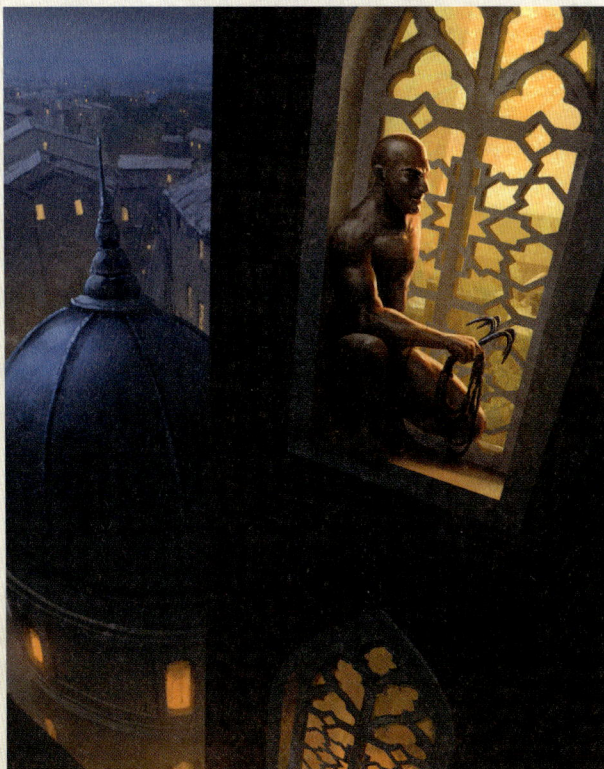

they are both dressed in ways you might not expect. Conan is scarcely dressed at all. Wearing only a loin cloth and sandals, Conan meets the Prince of Thieves who, himself, wears nothing on his feet at all and is also half-naked. Thieves must be nimble and dexterous.

Player characters wishing to undertake the dangerous path leading to the sort of mastery boasted by Taurus of Nemedia must learn to eschew armor and any but the lightest of protection. The thief strives to be undetectable. The jingling of mail makes that impossible. Unlike the player characters in more combat-oriented Conan games, protected from swords and arrows by trusty layers of leather and steel, thieves must do without such things if they wish to escape alive from the adventures upon which they embark.

Again, adjusting to this can be something of a tough ask for both players and gamemasters alike — the adventures should emphasize that combat is a risky option, especially if it is unplanned and or executed without the quiet celerity of trained assassins. The player characters should be aware that armor is a hindrance, and that Athletics and associated skills are therefore more important. This is not to say, of course, that a combat specialist isn't extremely useful at certain points, but even then, the "muscle" of the group fights in a very different way to the equivalent in a mercenary group and against very different threats. It is the difference between escaping the palace with the loot and being overwhelmed by the guards as the player characters try to flee. However, a thief need not outrun the guard… only the thief running alongside.

No Fit Night

One of the main differences in a thief-focused **Conan** game is the increased importance of the environment, and its condition, during a heist. Heavy rain can turn what might have been a climbable surface into a slickened death trap. The wind can dislodge a closely located grappling hook or change the course of a drugged dart so that what was bound for the neck of a guard suddenly strikes the wall, alerting him to the player characters' presence. The gamemaster should be conscious of climactic and environmental conditions and impose additional challenge levels where dramatically appropriate. Rules for this are provided in the *Weather and Thievery* table (next page) along with a table which allows the weather conditions to be randomized.

As always, the gamemaster is encouraged to pick the weather conditions that best suit the desired scene, properly setting the tone. Alternatively, if the player characters are smart enough to take the weather into account, then the gamemaster might think of letting them choose the conditions as a reward. These rules could be ignored, but they do provide an easy way of adding tension and danger to robberies, capturing that heightened, dramatic tone which Howard's stories strived for.

		WEATHER AND THIEVERY	
Roll	Weather Condition	Effect	Complication
1–3	Thunderstorm	It as though the Gods themselves fought above you! Rain sweeps down in sheets and thunder echoes like iron being hammered into shape. All tests are increased by one step of Difficulty, except for those tests involving either sight or hearing, which are increased by two steps.	Lightning Strike! A bolt of lightning spits from the writhing black clouds and hits the earth. All player characters must make an Athletics test or take 3 🦅 damage. All player characters act as though Stunned for the next turn.
4–6	Thick Fog	*Mist swamps everything around you, making the world unsettling. You can scarcely see your own sword at your belt.* All checks with a visual component are increased by two steps of Difficulty.	The blind leading the blind. If one player character fails an Observation check, everyone must then attempt an Athletics test to avoid tripping over or otherwise making a sound detectable to any nearby guards.
7–9	High Humidity	*The air shimmers before you, your palms are slick with sweat, and your own tools warp with the heat even as you try to use them.* All equipment provides one step less assistance to any test made using them, to a minimum Average (D1).	Any complications lead to the tool being used breaking. A 2-point Momentum spend can prevent this breakage, resulting in the user merely dropping the tool.
10–13	Clear and Dry	*Bel has turned his face to you and smiled. Clearly, your theft is blessed!* The weather is bright and crisp and perfect for almost any undertaking — including crime.	The complications should be decided and administered as normal by the gamemaster.
14–16	Fierce Winds	*The gusts of wind are ferocious, making the sturdiest edifices shake and tremble. Trying to land your grappling hook is somewhat trickier.* All tests made in order to use a ranged weapon or tool are increased by two steps of Difficulty.	Any complications incurred during this weather condition result in the player character that failed losing a random item of equipment, chosen by the gamemaster. The item is caught by the wind and sent flying away, or blown over, falling out of reach.
17–20	Too Much Light	*The sun blazes with the intensity of a blacksmith's forge. This may help or hinder your theft — depending upon how wily you are.* The brightness of the sun and the fact that it is fixed on the location where the theft is about to take place can be used by the player characters. If they spend 2 points of Momentum, then they may have the sun shine into the faces of the guards, reducing the Difficulty of any tests relating to Stealth or concealment by one step. If the players choose not to spend the Momentum, or do not have Momentum to spare, then all Observation tests are increased by two steps of Difficulty. If the player characters shield their faces, then this is limited to one step.	Complications might involve conspicuous sunburns, or tools being too hot to handle from the direct sunlight heating them.

Covert Operations

Playing in a manner which emphasizes stealth and guile might at first seem quite difficult or even intimidating, but it shouldn't be. Just as Conan's career encompassed many roles, Conan as a game encourages many approaches to adventure, and the dramatic sneaking and creeping of the professional thief is well suited for a player character pursuit.

As a gamemaster, one of the best ways to create the right level of tension and claustrophobia is to make ready use of the Doom and Momentum pools. These resources are not just combat enhancers, but also provide a means of adding drama to every encounter. In any story in which a heist takes place, there is always a moment when success or disastrous failure hangs on how many guards are on hand, or whether a watchman was able to call for help before being subdued. Did a guard captain think to call for more reinforcements before responding to a cry for help? Did a guard notice something suspicious, or did they bring a pack of hounds rather than just coming alone? Is that apparently unguarded treasure actually warded with a trap? And did the player character notice it being set off? Doom simulates these sorts of possibilities in a thievery-based endeavor.

The gamemaster should create plenty of opportunities for players to spend Momentum to be especially daring, encouraging them to spend it in the service of being bold or remarkable even when not in combat. In some cases, it is even more necessary than in combat, where a missed blow can be parried.

A missed leap, for example, is only countered with gravity. A thief that makes a false step and alerts a nearby guard to his presence can spend 2 Momentum to make an almost impossible athletic leap upwards, to the concealment offered in a narrow window.

The gamemaster can inspire players to see Momentum as something to be generated and used freely to make things go right. Likewise, the gamemaster can use Doom and Complications not to simply introduce extra enemies in a fight, but as a way of posing further problems, further difficulties which the player characters must overcome.

THIEVES' GUILDS

Thieves live dangerous lives. The forces arrayed against them are numerous and formidable — there are watchmen prowling the dark streets armed and quite willing to break heads or rifle pockets themselves, and the kind of people who own houses worth robbing often have something approaching private armies to call upon. And, if a thief is particularly unlucky, these guards might be able to call on far worse things than their fellow guards or even hounds. Some temples and dreadful places have guards more terrible than anything this mortal can offer.

The criminal elements in a city tend to band together into rough alliances: loose affiliations of men and women with nothing in common save for the fact they make their living by preying upon others. What keeps them together is self-preservation and the fact that no one else is going to tend a thief's wounds when a job goes badly wrong. Like any group of people united by something which divides them from the rest of a populace, these confederacies begin to develop their own character: they develop secret languages and rituals to identify one another and demarcate membership; leaders emerge and establish bases of power and new traditions. This is how the first thieves' guilds began to grow — emerging from the chaos, filth, and degradation of a city's underworld and becoming a parody of the societies which formed them.

Of course, there are many cities spread across the continent, each unique as each human being within their walls are unique — and each infested with death and squalor. Each thieves' guild is just as different.

Following are some ways in which a gamemaster might use such an organization in their games.

THE FABRIC OF THE PLACE

Thieves' guilds should reflect the city they are based in. That is, the brash, arrogant guild based in Zamora — confident as they are of their supremacy and the fact that the nominal authorities in the city are too scared of the Maul to ever enter it — are going to be very different from any guild that manages to flourish in the well-ordered cities of Aquilonia or the oppressive conurbations of Stygia. If the player characters engage with a thieves' guild as part of an adventure — or if they are members — the gamemaster should bear this in mind.

There are no hard and fast rules about this; Howard played loosely his own details from time to time, in order to best serve the story he was telling, and the gamemaster should do likewise. However, matching player characters' thieves' guild to their locale can add interesting dynamics to the campaign and to how the players respond.

HOW BIG IS IT?

Is the guild a vast network of carefully organized professionals, guided by the invisible hand of the guild master? Is it a group of thugs who decided they had a better chance of making themselves rich if there was no one else muscling in on their action? The answer is whatever the gamemaster (and player characters) want it to be. The exact answer depends entirely on the adventure the gamemaster is trying to run. The size of the organization is also going to give a strong indication of how the guild views outsiders, interlopers, and even its own membership.

A small but ambitious guild will likely try to build up its power and solidify its position in the city. It will view a small party of strange thieves as an opportunity; if these outsiders — likely the player characters — agree to follow the rules and offer up the necessary percentage of their bounty, they'll be courted and given assistance, maybe invited to join. If they reject this offer, the reprisals are brutal. A young guild has to make an example of anybody who flaunts the laws or it won't last long. A bigger, more established guild might take little notice of a handful of new thieves among the throngs of people entering a city every day — at least that's how it might appear. This kind of guild expects the players to come to them, to ask for permission before attempting any major crimes, and to pay a commensurate fee for the privilege of thieving in their city.

Failure to do this results in repercussions, but likely they will not be of the lethal kind. Instead, a hand might be cut off, or an eye put out. This might make thieving more difficult, but is still a better fate than losing one's life. There is always begging, and hopefully the beggar's guild is more forgiving.

ALCHEMISTS

Thieves' guilds, and individual thieves, are amongst the chief patrons of those alchemists who ply their trade in the cities of the era. After all — while a knife and a rope are all some thieves might need to undertake a daring heist, others rely on more spectacular means of completing their robbery. For some, it might be the use of a *sutli* bomb to disorient and distract those who protect a treasure chamber; for others, it might be oils or unguents to make catching them that much more difficult — all of these are best produced by alchemists. An amateur thief might endeavor to make their own tools in this fashion, although this can have unfortunate consequences. Wrongly proportioned mixtures have a tendency to injure those who make them, and the injuries can leave a thief permanently crippled.

The richest guilds maintain their own alchemists, keeping them ever at the ready should a strange substance be required to melt the lock from a vault's door, or swamp a room with raging flames which do not burn those who touch them. All of this is possible for the alchemist — though their work rarely comes cheaply. And it doesn't always work as one might hope…

YOU'LL KNOW WHERE TO FIND THEM…

Some guilds might be able to afford lavish buildings with impressive facilities for those members deemed sufficiently important. Others operate out of a single room at the back of a butcher's shop. Again, these locations influence how the players and their characters perceive the guild and how they interact with them. In the same way, a guild can also offer the player characters a place to hide, to plan their next theft, and to recover after a dangerous heist.

Choosing the right location helps put these ideas into the player characters' minds and introduces new doors into an adventure. It is also a useful linking device for a thief campaign. Moving from city to city, adventure to adventure, and guild to guild introduces its own structure. Varying the kind of guild the player characters visit keeps things fresh and makes sure that players don't become complacent, but it also ensures that they feel a part of an underworld that holds a mirror to the societies and cultures to which they may be more accustomed.

WHAT WORK AND FOR WHO?

Any organization composed of criminals with the intention of acquiring as much money as possible is likely to have a leader. In some guilds, this is simply the biggest and meanest member, the one who takes his percentage by force if he has to and scares any thieves that dare to question. As the guild grows and matures, leadership passes to those who are the cleverest — those that can dream up the most enterprising and successful ways of carrying out heists, the men and women who can see the way through any locked door and over any high wall. But even they can be replaced.

Those possessed of a different kind of cleverness end up replacing them; the kind of leaders that *know people* and can make them do things without ever realizing they are doing them. Such people are the kind that run the big guilds in the capital cities of the continent. They forge relationships with those paid in gold to catch and kill them, they convince the brutish thieves that their skills are best deployed elsewhere, and they put the clever thieves to work being clever. The world is, to this kind of thief, a puzzle in which different parts have to be fitted in different places. Each of these three extreme examples of guild leadership has a host of underlings, but they are organized differently — is the guild rigidly hierarchical, with different ranks of thief determined by merit or seniority? Is there just a series of thieves who do as they want, when they want, governed by one or two of their own number who can be trusted to look to the protection of the whole? Again, no organization is the same. They all act differently and will respond differently to the players.

There is no need to define all of the various tiers of the guild — but having a rough idea of how guild members interrelate gives the gamemaster a good idea of how they will respond and relate to the player characters. More importantly, it defines what the player characters have to do in order to find favor with the guild: who they have to kill to take over... and how many.

JOINING A GUILD

The thieves' guilds of the Hyborian Age may be violent and corrupt, but they fulfill a useful function for any trying to live outside the law. There is comradeship to be found, a degree of security, and, most importantly of all, information. Information about which merchant has recently arrived in the city, at the head of a caravan laden with gold and silk; details about the number of guards surrounding a greedy priest's temple stash; the most intimate details of a noble lady's bedroom habits, including when she is absent from it, visiting a young commoner's abode. All of this can be found out through membership of a guild and such vital facts might be the difference between acquiring vast wealth and the painful insertion of a knife between your ribs.

No two guilds are the same, and the entry requirements for each guild reflect this. Some guilds require existing, trusted members recommend each new candidate. Others instead require a demonstration of loyalty — perhaps a branded symbol, the removal of a toe or a finger; whatever it is, it is usually painful and permanent. Another path to full guild membership is the trial job — a particularly dangerous robbery the completion of which indicates sufficient skill to justify adding a new member to the guild's ranks. Whatever the case, it should be difficult. Thieves' guilds are, essentially, secret societies. While it is true that part of the joy of belonging to an elite organization is being able to boast about it, some aspects of such groups must be clandestine in order to ensure that the group survives.

Once, or if, the player characters gain entrance into a guild, there is much to learn: passwords, places of safety where a member can escape to should a job go badly wrong, which members of the watch have been paid off, and how to alert these enlightened men and women of their affiliations. It isn't necessary to produce an endless list of such possible features — the gamemaster just has to ensure that any of these background elements contribute to the story, provide some fun for the players, and are consistently deployed. Other than that, there is only one final thing to remember — thieves operate thieves' guilds. Joining one comes with an entrance fee.

Player characters are not obliged to join a guild at all. However, committing a big theft in a guild-controlled city without paying a sizable fee to that organization is asking for trouble. The gamemaster is encouraged to think of

THIEVES CANT

An intriguing fact about criminal underworlds is their frequent development of a new lexicon to describe their crimes. These invented languages, designed to obscure the true meaning of a conversation, and hopefully confuse potential pursuers, are an easy and amusing way to add an extra layer of depth to thief campaigns and adventures. Even a couple of words, dotted here and there in a conversation, add extra color and verisimilitude. Perhaps this can be one of the few things connecting the disparate thieves' guilds spread across the continent. Or perhaps the very opposite, with each city's dialect entirely unique. The gamemaster may allow player characters with the *Cosmopolitan* talent to recognize these dialects, even without speaking them, and the Linguistics talents encompassing these cants as readily as they do languages.

suitably unpleasant ways of making the player characters' lives difficult. Are the palace guards mysteriously aware of the player characters' presence despite no one making the slightest sound? As the player characters approach the city's main gate, saddle-packs loaded with gold, do the doors slam shut and armed men surround them? Ignore the guild at your peril!

ONLY BY REPUTATION

Of course, certain thieves and certain crimes are more impressive than others. Taurus of Nemedia was known to Conan when he met him in Zamora. The master thief is recognized for his deeds across the continent — both for their daring and the skill with which they were carried out. The same might be true for the player characters, or it might one day be true for them.

A thief's reputation has an impact on how he is treated when he enters a city where thieving is controlled by a guild. Reputation is mechanically the same as Renown, though the response it generates from other thieves is quite distinct and worth going over in some detail.

The *Guild Recognition* and *Treatment* table (below) presumes that Renown has been awarded for actions committed as thieves. The table can be used for individual player characters, comparing their Renown individually and treating each member of the player character group separately, or can average the Renown values of the player character group if it is particularly tightly-knit, treating all members equally. There is precedent for both approaches: in good times a group might be rewarded equally, while in bad times

GUILD RECOGNITION AND TREATMENT

Renown	Guild Treatment	Expected Tithe
−2	Whatever it is the player characters did to warrant such universal disgust, it has reached the ears of the guild. It might be hypocritical for a guild of thieves to be picky about ugly pasts, but the evil reputation which follows the player characters is bad for business. Generally docile authorities are being pressured to act by growing popular outrage. The guild wants things back to normal; it wants the watch to take the bribes and be quiet. The best way to do that is to kill the player characters and leave their bodies hanged from the nearest improvised gallows. In addition to the usual penalties for having −2 Renown, any thief the player characters come into contact with reacts immediately, usually violently. This is the case in all cities where there is a thieves' guild.	None. If the player characters were guild members, they are no longer. The guild may attempt to exact 100% of anything the player characters have taken, or even more.
−1	There might be some reluctance, but the guild knows that having people around with the reputation of the player characters draws attention. There is some sympathy from low-ranking guild members that have perhaps heard the stories and think that, under the circumstances, they might well have done the same thing and been in the same position, but are unlikely to stick their neck out and risk being excommunicated from the guild. Any thieves the player characters come into contact with will report their presence to any nearby authorities — city watch, palace guard, or similar. If the player characters have been particularly obstreperous, the guild thieves may try and restrain the player characters and deliver them into the hands of the law themselves. This only applies in the first city they enter which has a thieves' guild and not in any subsequent cities they visit. However, these conditions continue to affect the player characters in the first city until their reputation improves.	None. If the player characters were guild members, they are no longer.
0	The player characters are treated by the guild as any low-ranking member or non-member might be. Contributing to the guild brings commensurate rewards, and transgressions the appropriate sanctions, but these are caused by a player characters' actions — not simply by their presence.	If the player characters are guild members, the tithe on all earnings is 25%.
1	The player characters are known and recognized by a few faces around town. These aren't the kind of people who run the guild, the kind of people with political influence, nor are they the wet-behind-the-ears cutpurses. Fellow thieves know the player characters and trust them. Fellow thieves willingly discuss potential jobs with the player characters.	The guild tithe on all earnings is 20%.
2	The guild's leadership knows the player characters and trusts them — and expects discretion. The player characters aren't elevated to the higher circles yet, and the guild hasn't started asking for their advice, but they know who the player characters are and appreciate the quality of their work. Fellow thieves willingly discuss potential jobs with the player characters and offer support in any fight or altercation, where appropriate.	The guild tithe on all earnings is 15%.
3	The player characters are welcomed into the inner circle of the guild. They know how things work now, who to bribe and with what, who to call on when things get tough, and where to run when things get too tough. The player characters are considered an asset to the guild leadership and trusted with missions of the highest importance. They get access to all the little whisperings of the guild's various contacts. Any fellow thief discusses potential jobs and helps in any conflict, where appropriate. Additionally, when confronted by a member of the city watch (or equivalent), all Persuade tests are reduced by one step of Difficulty.	The guild tithe on all earnings is 10%.

Renown	Guild Treatment	Expected Tithe
	GUILD RECOGNITION AND TREATMENT	
4	Every thief in the city knows who the player characters are. Those that don't admire the player characters and court their influence at least respect them, and those that show no respect have only fear. No one is likely to interfere with the player characters' claim to the choicest of jobs and the biggest cut of the profits. The player characters' names inspire fear in the local guard — though this makes them a target for the most righteous and ambitious of these law-abiding fools. Any fellow thieves, in any city, discuss potential jobs and help in any conflict, where appropriate. Additionally, when confronted by a member of the city watch (or equivalent), all Persuade tests are reduced by two steps of Difficulty.	The guild tithe on all earnings is 5%.
5	Such is the player characters' reputations in the underworld that they are lauded wherever they go. Whichever city they enter, every thief knows them and can recount the tales of their boldest escapades. Every guild inveigles the player character to join, every potential robbery is offered as a mark of respect. The player characters are veritable criminal royalty. Any fellow thieves, in any city, discuss potential jobs and help in any conflict, where appropriate. Additionally, when confronted by a member of the city watch (or equivalent), all Persuade tests are reduced by two steps of Difficulty and automatically generate 1 Momentum.	The guild tithe on all earnings is 2%.

members of the guild might seek out the player character with the highest Renown and intervene on his behalf, hoping that this one "good apple" might sway the behavior of the batch, or be spared the punishment of the rest.

The gamemaster is free to ignore these and impose other types of treatment, depending upon preference. The table also includes suggested tithes the guild might expect from members, depending upon their position in the guild and the scope of their criminal accomplishments. Naturally, also, the player characters can try and short-change the guild. Who has claimed that "honor among thieves" was universal?

GUILDS AND GANGS OF NOTE

Following are examples of guilds that inhabit the various major cities and locations the player characters are likely to travel. These are far from the only examples of such organizations and are provided here as examples of how to put together new guilds, if desired. Guilds each have their own unique flavor, purpose, and structure — and each offers the player characters a very different kind of threat, should they ever inconvenience one or more of

them. That's certainly not to say that smart player characters couldn't end up joining one of these guilds, finding respect and power there, and ascending the ranks... that might happen, as well.

KHORSHEMISH

If the public, iron fist of Strabonus is not enough to discourage a gathering of crooks, the secret machinations of Tsotha-lanti (described in *Conan the Mercenary*) certainly are. There is little room in Khorshemish for more than a crew to operate. One such crew is detailed below.

Baruch's Bastards

Under the withering eye of the king and the sorcerer who plays him, there are few crews that last more than a season or two. Koth is no place for thieves, or at least not Khorshemish. Baruch and his "Bastards" prove this wrong. For years, they have operated under the noses of the king and Tsotha-lanti, but, to be fair, they have often had to take to the road for a time as a result.

Their home is Khorshemish and they've cut out a space for themselves that few others can. Ostensibly, they are simply tenacious. In reality, they have absolutely no fear. There is not a soldier on any battlefield who can say they care less about death than this motley lot. They pull the most daring heists and the most dangerous. As a result, their ranks are constantly in need of new blood. The list of their dead comrades is long — allegedly carved on the underside of a table in an alehouse somewhere in the city.

Baruch is a Meadow Shemite, and his companions are Meadow Shemites, Pelishtim, and former members of nomad clans. One is even an outcast *asshuri*, and another hails from Vanaheim, of all places. How they came together is the subject of many legends. Some even claim Taurus, Prince of Thieves, ran with the Bastards. This is likely untrue, but it does make for a great tale of an evening.

- **Size:** There are nine Bastards, never more or less. They won't take on a job without nine members. The Bastards have a superstition about this. When one leaves — or is more likely killed — the crew is dormant until a replacement is named.

- **Specialties:** The heist is an art to the Bastards, and they have mastered it. Some say they stole the Star of Khorala, while others claim they looted the treasury of the king of Ophir. Certainly, slightly less remarkable crimes are reliably ascribed to the Bastards. They are unflinchingly loyal to each other... mostly.

- **Joining:** How one joins the Bastards is never the same twice. They work with other thieves from time to time, and keep their eyes watchful for those few thieves who might join them should their number fall below nine. None have ever told what they did to get in with Baruch and his Bastards.

LUXOR

Luxor is a curious case, for the real power in all Stygia lies in the priests and, through them, dreaded Set. Yet there is a group of highly organized thieves whose existence may be the oldest of any guild. In the long shadows of great obelisks, this guild works for means beyond mere treasure.

Set's Tears

The name of this guild is itself a way of excluding foreigners. Any Stygian knows Set bears no tears, and the saying "Set's Tears" mean to deceive or express false grief. The guild itself is old, impossibly so for a network of mere thieves, but these are not simple scoundrels.

The guild itself traces its history back to the previous dynasty and endured under the rule of many Kings and priests. Once, Set's Tears existed in Khemi but were exterminated by the theocracy there. Today, they have a presence in other Stygian cities but are nowhere so powerful as Luxor.

Their prime source of income is the lotus trade. Smuggling the drug under the eyes of the king's taxmen is a dangerous business in most kingdoms and doubly so in Stygia. There exists a sacred relationship between Set and the lotus leaf, to say nothing of the economic value to the crown and priesthood. Selling this drug under the king's nose is punishable by summary execution.

Set's Tears also conduct the more routine operations of guilds found in other cities. They kidnap and ransom, extort and steal. Nearly every job done in Khemi passes some portion of its haul to Set's Tears. The guild is wealthy, but, given the power of both crown and cobra, not overly powerful. They also harbor a deep secret.

Set's Tears began as a guild of thieves bound together due to the harsh laws of Stygia, which left little room for their ilk. Somewhere between the formation of the guild and the present day, another faction merged with them — the worshipers of Tarawet. In Old Stygia, it is said Tarawet worship was on the decline. In contemporary Stygia, it is illegal. Tarawet opposes father Set, for she is the god of life and fertility. Tarawet devotees believe the two gods were once lovers, but Setites dismiss this as blasphemy. In the last half millennium, Tarawet worshipers have been persecuted and crucified relentlessly. Few still exist.

It was during these purges that the two outlaw groups found common cause. Today, a member of Set's Tears is very likely a worshiper of Tarawet and at least an opponent of the current theocracy. If they are not true faithful, then they are rebels. As such, they would be ruthlessly hunted were the guild of thieves not there to serve as cover. Few suspect the two groups are enmeshed. Further, Set's Tears has an arrangement with the Luxor elite who siphon off profit from the illegal activities of the thieves. The thieves, in return, receive a certain leeway and also serve as spies for those elite who nominally worship Set but believe the priesthood has become bloated and overly powerful. Were it known that Set's Tears is in effect a group of rebels against crown and god, they would find few allies.

- **Size:** Set's Tears is a large guild. They number more than five hundred, though not all members are privy to their deeper purpose. A guild member can find compatriots in most Stygian towns and cities save Khemi. Set's priesthood alone rules there.

- **Specialties:** Smuggling, particularly of black lotus, is the specialty of the guild. They are also proficient in all manners of theft and many forms of poisoning. Moving good across the Styx is very dangerous, as Stygian patrols frequent the area both looking for enemy troops and smugglers. No smuggler who actually moves the product knows of the guild's connection to Tarawet.

- **Joining:** Any notable thief, however lowly, can join Set's Tears. On the surface, they operate as any other large guild — profit and power their only concerns. However, being initiated into the secret ranks, those who rebel against Stygia and Set, is open only to those who have thrice proven themselves loyal. One must either truly hate the crown, the priesthood, or Set, else they must be fully devoted to Tarawet. All others are looked on with suspicion, for Stygian spies could be among Set's Tears already.

SECUNDERAM

The largest of Turan's easternmost cities, Secunderam hosts an even greater portion of cultures which come from those mysterious places those in the west only hear of. In Secunderam, there are professional thieves aplenty, but one group takes professionalism to the level of ritual.

Thugra

The Thugra are a band of thieves and ritual murderers who sanctify their deeds by dedicating them to their dark eastern god. Hailing from somewhere in Vendhya, these men (for they are all men) wear beards and turbans. Of course, such is the fashion of many men in Turan, and it is thus difficult to spot any Thugra. This is not an accident.

The Thugra is one of the few gangs that travels. While their base is Secunderam, at least this far west, they befriend travelers, serving as porters, guides, and scouts, only to turn on them in the night and kill them all. Each death is given to their dark god as offering. They are, curiously, therefore a mix of fanatic and filcher, a strange brew to be sure. They are not specifically territorial, but there are few who challenge their power in the city who do not wind up strangled with the silken red scarves of sacrificial murder the gang leaves on their victims. It is both a warning and a sign of devout piety.

Thugra use guile and deceit to get close to their prey and, whenever possible, kill anyone they rob. Simple pickpocketing can maintain them, but it does not satisfy their god nor slake their bloodlust. They are unusually loyal to one another, being bound by religion, as well as crime. Thugra are occasionally hired as professional murderers, and it is said old King Yildiz once employed them against various would-be usurpers. Still, Turanians do not trust the Thugra, and the city of Secunderam looks warily at darker-skinned travelers because of the gang.

Within the city, and anywhere the Thugra travel, they are a valuable source of information. They broker such as a sideline and are bought by various despots for some small while. One must never mistake them for mere killers-for-hire, though. To their fell god are each of them promised. They do not drink. They do not engage in intimate relations. And they refuse the lotus. What brings them to the west is unknown, but Turanian cities evidence the worship of elder eastern gods now more so than ever.

- **Size:** The Thugra is medium in size, perhaps numbering a few hundred members. Speculation suggests they are far more numerous in Vendhya, but few have reliable tales from that far-off land.

- **Specialties:** Murder and robbery, not always in that order, are the twin specialties of the Thugra. They hire out on occasion but largely work for themselves.

When hired, they are usually good to their contract but demand all valuables acquired unless otherwise specified. They do not speak of their god nor their rituals to any outsider. Finding a Thugra to hire is a matter of some difficulty.

- **Joining:** Only those of direct Vendhyan descent and proper religious belief can join the Thugra. Because they are insular, little is known of their rituals or their god. Astreas opines, *"Of the Thugra I can say this — they are expert murders and leave bodies in their wakes strangled with eyes open toward the sky. That they traffic with demons is accepted as fact and I, having seen the dead behind them, shall not argue with this supposition."*

SHADIZAR THE WICKED

Shadizar the Wicked has earned its name over hundreds of years of debauchery and greed and cruelty. It is a city of wealth and the stark absence of it. It functions, if it indeed does function as a city, as a result of the thousands who slave and strive at the most menial and enervating of tasks so that the wealthy may pursue their vices and indulge their appetites. Visitors to the city — and there are many who come to sample the various lascivious pleasures of Shadizar — wonder how it is that such a place can exist, built on the back of so many who so rarely have the opportunity to share in the city's bounty. One answer to this question — and many are proposed — is the Crypteia.

Crypteia

This shadowy organization deals in slaughter and terror from the shadows; bands of young men leap from the darkness, killing and maiming and leaving that strange word scrawled on the walls of burned-out houses: Crypteia. No one is certain of its origin, save that is not of Zamorian etymology. Of course, whether the Crypteia even exists is a question quite able to provoke denials and queries about the inquirer's mental health; the city watch (such as it is) refuse to countenance its existence and scholars scoff at the notion. Only the victims testify to the reality of the entity — and only as eloquently as a corpse can. It is said that the Crypteia is not of Shadizaran origin — that, in fact, it was created in another nation entirely. Some claim Aquilonia, others say Argos, and still others claim Nemedia as its point of origin. The Crypteia, whisper these voices, was created by the nations of the world who wish to ensure that Shadizar never realizes its full power as a city, as a state, as a potential empire. The Crypteia keeps the city docile, its citizens drunk or deceived. Or simply dead.

- **Size:** From the very little that is known, it is supposed that the Crypteia is small and deliberately so;

tightly knit cells of young men and women who are dispatched to sow chaos and fear. Typically numbering only two or three people at a time, though bands as large as six or seven have been known, the Crypteia skulks through the dank streets of Shadizar, protected by its secrecy and the small, clandestine patrols which constitute its only manifestation.

- **Specialties:** The Crypteia specializes in murder, in the spreading of fear, in the quiet exertion of brutality, and the application of the knife in the most creative of ways. It has been said that, while the Crypteia is undoubtedly a foreign organization (what Shadizaran would plot like this?), its members are local thieves. Their knowledge of the streets, the alleyways, the rooftops, and the sewers is too precise and too exhaustive to be gleaned by outsiders. The Crypteia, some claim, is the test by which Shadizaran apprentice thieves may graduate to full thief-hood.

- **Joining:** Who knows? One is not approached to join the Crypteia and approaching a suspected member is most likely to earn a swift blade to the stomach rather than instructions on joining. Doubtless, there is some path through which one might join the Crypteia — perhaps it requires the privilege of having been born with Shadizar itself. There are many possibilities; just hope that finding the true one does not cost one's life in the process.

TARANTIA

The gangs of Tarantia are well known to be the bane of every Aquilonian king, long before Vilerius, for he has yet to stomp them out. Some city dwellers call them "urban Picts" as a way both to denigrate the thieves and the king who cannot vanquish them. The city is simply too large, too corrupt, and too fixated on the expansion of empire to squash every gang. There are no guilds here, though, they have long since been rooted out. The gangs are tolerated, as far as it goes. Two vie for the crumbs left by more stately men.

The White Feathers

When the king crushed the guild, a number of gangs rushed to fill the void — the White Feathers beat nearly all of them out of sheer viciousness. "The White Feathers are worse than Picts", writes one palace scholar, "for at least a Pict has the manners to kill you before eating you". This is, perhaps, overly hyperbolic, but the gang is known for their extreme violence. Severed heads, slain families, and crimes of which we will not here speak are all part of their toolkit.

Terror is their greatest weapon — citizens fear the gang. They respect the Threadbare Knights, but the White Feathers are insane. They revel in violence. The comparison to barbarians is, for city folk, not far off the mark. The brutality the White Feathers inflict is epic.

The sheer force of their will pushed them to overcome their rivals — all but the Knights. There, chaos met order and stalemate ensued. Currently, the two gangs vie for power. Where the White Feathers act from instinct, their rivals measure that instinct with a dose of thought. The two opposing ways clash head on in Tarantia's streets... at least they do until the king cracks down on both sides alike.

- **Size:** The White Feathers Gang is slightly smaller than their rivals, numbering perhaps seven hundred men and women. Their ferocity makes up for this deficit in numbers.

- **Specialties:** Violence, pure and simple. Tarantia's Maul is known for bloodshed, and the White Feathers Gang is no small reason why. They bully and terrorize people into submission. Their heists rely on force rather than finesse.

- **Joining:** One must be a capable thief and heartless killer to join this gang. The latter is more important, and the ranks of the White Feathers have more raw thugs than their opponents.

The Threadbare Knights

Unlike true knights, Threadbare Knights are neither virtuous, loyal to the crown, nor willing to give their lives for others. Nor are they especially threadbare, as they favor gaudy clothes as displays of their ill-gotten wealth. They are, however, one of the two gangs that vie for the streets of Tarantia.

The Threadbare Knights is what's left of the city's old thieves' guild. That lot, stamped out by the king, was hung in the great city square, their bodies left to rot along the banks of the river. The gang uses the gibbet as their symbol, and most members wear it as a tattoo. In fact, being so branded is a rite of passage and a firm commitment against the crown. Anyone found with such a tattoo is automatically thrown into the city's dungeons for five years, the tattoo and its surrounding skin removed painfully.

Roughly speaking, the Threadbare Knights control the eastern city underworld, while the White Feather Gang controls the west. In practice, this divide is not at all precise, and the two gangs control areas in what would otherwise be considered their rival's territory. So-called "rat wars" are common between thieves' guilds.

Because the Threadbare Knights are composed of some the defeated guild, they are more organized than their rivals. This gives them some advantage when it comes to dealing with the watch, proper extortion, and fencing. They lack the raw blood thirst of the White Feather Gang, though, and have lost territory out of an inability to be as wantonly destructive as the White Feathers.

One should not mistake them for the guild from which they descend. The Threadbare Knights are a well-organized gang, but a gang nonetheless. They traffic lotus into Tarantia, run prostitution rings, and extort local merchants. However, given the king's desire to see them utterly obliterated, they are not as powerful as gangs in other, less rigidly controlled, cities.

- **Size:** Somewhere under one thousand thieves and throat-slitters are members of the Threadbare Knights. The numbers shift based on prosperity and the king's wrath.

- **Specialties:** Strategic planning is the hallmark of this gang. They consider things before acting, though they do not consider them overly long. Action, not thought, is the first weapon of a gang, and it is only by virtue of their elder members, once guildsmen, that they organize their "business" as efficiently as they do.

- **Joining:** Any thief of worth can join the gang, but only on a probationary basis. The king's spies are everywhere, and turncoats have betrayed the gang on more than one occasion. Once they prove themselves as loyal, or the closest thing a thief can boast, the prospective initiates become full members and take the tattoo of the gibbet to mark their inclusion.

YEZUD

Spider-haunted Yezud, home to cults and killers, pressgangs, and priests. In this old city, Zhemri blood runs deep, and worship of old gods is common. The guild which controls the underside of Yezud is powerful, well connected, and much more than they might initially appear.

The Children of the Spider-God

The Children of the Spider-God are as much dedicated cultists as they are thieves. Even then, the truth is that, beyond being a thieves' guild, they represent the spy apparatus of the Spider-God's priesthood. There is also an aspect of a secret police force to the Children — they are ruthless in their pursuit of apostates or other traitors to the cause and their main focus of power is Yezud itself.

Run by a faceless individual known only as "Many Eyes" (see page 84), the Children of the Spider-God operates according to an informal cell network. Each has limited knowledge of the other and is able to operate entirely on its own, with little to no support or direction from the priesthood, or Many Eyes himself. It is this ability which has allowed the Children to operate, so effectively, as an information gathering tool, throughout the continent. Able to quickly take root in any city and blend into that place seamlessly, the Children are almost impossible to detect. Until, of course, they begin to preach. This may not happen for years, decades even, but, at some unknown signal, the Children will cease their surveillance and gradual accrediting of valuable knowledge to filter back to the temple in Yezud and, instead, begin to proselytize. This fact has long baffled those beyond the Spider-God's cult, when trying to determine where exactly the cult ends and the guild begins.

The Children of the Spider-God have long been suspected of carrying out assassinations at the whim of Many Eyes, who is a political genius, as well as a fanatic, able to tease the threads of political power throughout the continent with the same preternatural skill a spider can weave the skeins of its web. Of course, part of this preternatural skill is never leaving any evidence of the assassinations having been carried out. Some assert that Many Eyes carries them out. Of course, anything is possible where Many Eyes is concerned; like the god Many Eyes worships, the person is suspected by many to be naught but myth.

- **Size:** While the Children of the Spider-God maintain numerous agents, true members are small in number. Perhaps no more than three hundred people swell their ranks. No one in Yezud can say for certain who might be listening, and the underworld is shot through with eddies of paranoia and suspicion.

- **Specialties:** Spying and information-brokering mark the specialty of this guild. They traffic in valuable knowledge. However, there is that which they learn which is for the ears of their superiors alone. Not all information is for sale. Some is earmarked for their foul, arachnid god.

- **Joining:** There are many who would like to join the Children of the Spider-God. Some of these people already unwittingly work for the organization. No thief in Yezud can truly know if they are independent, or if Many Eyes has been secretly guiding their movements, their heists, and their earnings all along. Those who prove especially adept at carrying out the orders of Many Eyes may be given the opportunity to join the Spider's priesthood and, for the very, very few, may join the ranks of Many Eyes' chosen — though what this entails is impossible to guess. No one has ever confessed to being a member.

ZAMORA THE ACCURSED

The self-proclaimed "City of Thieves" earned its reputation generations of ago. It is a well-known truism that Zamorians are the best thieves as a people, and those from the Accursed City the best among them. Indeed, it is sometimes difficult to tell whether the king rules over the guilds or the other way around. There is no city so corrupt as Zamora and no guilds so influential anywhere in the west.

> *"Know that in Zamora, and more especially in this city, there are more bold thieves than anywhere else in the world, even Koth."*
>
> — Kothian kidnapper,
> *"The Tower of the Elephant"*

The Guild

It has no other name, no nicknames whispered conspiratorially over a dwindling candle. It is, and has ever been, simply "the Guild". The Guild is old, older than Zamora the Accursed, for it claims to have come with the Zhemri. Whether this is true or not, the Guild's stature makes many believe it so. In Zamora the Accursed, there is the king and there is the Guild. The smart fear the Guild, goes a Zamorian truism.

Zamorians have larceny in their blood, and the guild recruits from those ranks, though not exclusively. While Zamorians have privilege inside the Guild, any kingdom's castoffs may join should they display the requisite skill.

There is little separation between the authorities and the Guild in Zamora. The skein of relationships between the two is all but inextricable. While the populace leans toward believing the Guild is truly in charge, it is far more likely that power sways pendulously between the royalty and the thieves' guild.

Certainly, nothing criminal is like to occur within the walls of Zamora without their knowing it. Everyone is on the take. Everyone has an angle. Zamora the Accursed chews up the weak and spits out their bones. Hill-folk are like to meet their end in the gutter here, and the Guild will likely have sanctioned the murder. The city is a hub of trade, legal and otherwise, and the Guild skims off the top of everything. There is not a merchant in town who does not pay them protection, and there is no die rolled on a bet from which they do not demand a cut of the wager.

- **Size:** It is impossible to say how many citizens of Zamora the Accursed are members of the Guild, but a claim of one in ten of the population of the city is not out of the question. The Guild is the most professional and exacting criminal enterprise west of the Vilayet and possibly beyond.

- **Specialties:** The Guild does not specialize, for that would limit their reach. Instead, they count specialists of many nefarious disciplines among their number. Numbers and bloody murder — the Guild has the best working on it. They control all illegal trade in the city and no small portion of the legal trade. They wield power no other criminal group can boast.

- **Joining:** Any thief, killer, kidnapper, or charlatan can join the Guild. There are various jobs such would-be members take on and, if successful, become members... if the job isn't a set-up. No one that is not already a member can trust the Guild, and even then, doing so is a dubious prospect.

THE FINE ART OF THIEVERY

The guidelines in this chapter are intended to be a series of ideas for running a thief-based campaign which captures something of Howard's unique approach to storytelling as it unfolds. It is far from exhaustive and the gamemaster is encouraged to search for ideas in as many different places as possible. There are, however, a few final things to mention when begin putting together light-fingered adventures. The first is to always bring out the best in the player characters, letting them shine.

This piece of advice is emphasized in the **Conan** corebook, and counts doubly here, for the very good reason that a *Conan the Thief* campaign needs a bit more finesse on the gamemaster's part. Quick violence should not be the immediate source of peril. Instead of a failed Athletics test resulting in the player characters being plunged into combat as the guards rush in, they should instead lose a vital piece of equipment. Armed conflict is still an essential element of adventures, but should be used sparingly, a potential consequence to be avoided, rather than an inevitable means of solving problems.

It should also be reiterated that the gamemaster is the one who decides what works for a specific adventure or campaign. If the ideas presented in *Conan the Thief* are useful, use them. If they aren't, they should be ignored and others introduced.

CHAPTER 8
HEISTS

"You spoke of the Elephant Tower," said the stranger, speaking Zamorian with an alien accent. "I've heard much of this tower; what is its secret?"

— Conan, "The Tower of the Elephant"

The main type of adventure in a thief campaign is the heist. In a heist, the player characters infiltrate a setting and make off with something that doesn't belong to them. These stories can have a lot of variations and complications, rather than simply being about the illicit acquisition of wealth. There are many different reasons for stealthy intrusions: spies might break into a home and plant false evidence rather than steal a treasure; kidnappers might be hired to capture a valued noble; and righteous thieves might be motivated to infiltrate a tyrannical governor's estate and relay a threat.

The player characters may certainly undertake and initiate their own heists and capers, or they may rely on the gamemaster to supply them with the news of the next wealthy target. In either instance, certain questions must be asked and answered:

■ Who is the target? Who owns the thing that is to be stolen? Also, who hires the thieves to do the work?

■ What is the object of desire? What's the target?

■ Where is the item located?

■ What makes this item secure from casual thieves? Why are the player characters involved? How has the item been secured?

■ What's the payoff or reward? What do the thieves get if they complete their job?

There are a number of unknown factors in play, as well. Player characters can investigate and make tests to find hidden dangers and determine hidden agendas from their employers, or they may try to make the job easier on themselves in other ways. The gamemaster should encourage the player characters to spend Momentum, if available, in any of the usual ways. But unless the player characters are extremely lucky, they may not be able to uncover all there is to know about the job at hand. This is where Doom comes in. Doom can be spent to create additional challenges for the thieves in any of the ways listed in the **Conan** corebook.

The gamemaster should always encourage and support the player characters in spending Momentum as freely as they like, encouraging their creativity and allowing them more leeway than in other circumstances. This chapter

describes ideas for how the gamemaster might go about this, and how the player characters might want to spend their Momentum... and even fill the gamemaster's pool with Doom.

TURNING THE TABLES

In the face of overwhelming odds, a double-cross, or a flat-out botched caper where all seems lost and the end is near, a player character might spend a few points of Momentum and declare something to the effect of: "Of course, I knew this was going to happen. The clues were so obvious. So, before we got here, I took the precaution of..." Then the player may describe a scene prior to the current scene that effectively alters the situation to give the player characters a fighting chance.

The solution to this varies on a case-by-case basis, but the more simple and elegant a solution, the better. It could be anything from spending Gold to hire reinforcements to show up right after the bad guys show up, turning the scene into a mass melee, or sneaking into the barracks and cutting all the archer's bowstrings, thus taking out missile fire before it starts. This requires a bit of finesse, however, as players may be tempted to bypass any risks or create increasingly far-fetched "preparations" that they could not have reasonably foreseen. The gamemaster can override any plan that puts too much advantage on the player characters' side and may work with them to devise a suitable turn for the plot.

> *"At least we'll try; it's the chance of being turned into a spider or a toad, against the wealth and power of the world. All good thieves must know how to take risks."*
>
> — Taurus, "The Tower of the Elephant"

Spotted!

If the gamemaster spends 2 Doom, the thieves are spotted at some point in the job. Who spotted them is always important; was it a city guard in the wrong place at the wrong time? Was it a citizen that might make an excellent witness? Was it another thief, looking to horn in on the job and snatch the goods from the player characters? This creates a specific complication that may not actually affect the current job but carry over into the next one.

HYBORIAN AGE HEIST GENERATOR

These tables are designed to quickly and easily provide a general outline that the gamemaster can customize to fit the needs of the particular campaign or adventure. There are several categories used to build this outline, including specialized tables for certain factions. Examples of each outline can be found at the end of this section. It is not necessary to use all of the categories when creating a heist for the player characters, especially if they already have their own motives or answers to some of the necessary questions. These tables can help the gamemaster fill in the blanks quickly by rolling some dice or simply choosing an appropriate entry.

Every heist has a set of components to it. These components, strung together, create a scenario that suggests a plot with twists and turns and a generally — but not always — favorable outcome. The main components to the heist are detailed below.

- **Who:** This set of tables creates a non-player character connected in some way to the job — either the victim of the heist, or possibly the client.
- **What:** This is the thing being stolen by the thieves. It could be something incredibly valuable or a mundane item with an unknown purpose in a larger scheme.
- **Where:** These are the known risks, the things that are going to make the job more difficult for the player characters.
- **How:** These are the unknown risks. Some cautious thieves may be able to uncover one or more of them, but there is always something that the player characters don't know about when they undertake the job.
- **Why:** What's in it for the thieves? What do they get out of this heist?

These broad categories can be combined to create an infinite number of plots and schemes for a single adventure or linked to form larger campaigns.

WHO

Roll a d20 and consult the *Who* table to determine the Who's profession. If desired, roll a second time for a description. Gender can be determined with a roll of a d20: 1–10 = man, 11–20 = woman. The gamemaster should roll a 🜏 to determine if the Who is from the area the player characters are in, or is a foreigner.

WHO			
Roll	Profession	Description	Nationality
1	Servant	Anxious	The Border Kingdom
2	Peasant	Bitter	The Barachan Isles
3	Laborer	Charming	Brythunia
4	Merchant	Distraught	Nemedia
5	Soldier	Enigmatic	Corinthia
6	Acolyte	Fearful	Ophir
7	Minor Civic Official	Furtive	Argos
8	Artisan	Impatient	Zingara
9	Tradesman	Impulsive	Shem
10	Politician	Jealous	Koth
11	Minor Noble	Mischievous	Zamora
12	Court Official	Mysterious	Aquilonia
13	Diplomat	Paranoid	Stygia
14	Priest	Reckless	Kush
15	Royalty	Shrewd	Punt
16	Master Thief	Suspicious	The Black Kingdoms
17	Temple Antiquarian	Treacherous	Turan
18	Assassin	Unhinged	Hyrkania
19	Spy	Vengeful	Khitai
20	Unique Character	Zealous	Vendhya

1–2 or Effect: National — a person native to the kingdom the player characters are in.

Blank: Foreigner — a person from a kingdom other than the one the player characters currently inhabit. Roll the d20 and consult the *Who* table if a nationality is required. If the result is the same as the one in which the player characters are located, roll again or choose the closest neighboring kingdom to the current location.

This table can be used multiple times for different parties involved in the heist. Page 48 of the **Conan** corebook and page 18 of this sourcebook provide a variety of suitable names.

The gamemaster can also pick a desired result, and is encouraged to re-roll if a result is unsuitable or implausible.

Professions

Servant: This can either be a slave, an indentured servant, or simply a lowborn family in the service of a noble house or rich family.

Peasant: The working poor. Maybe a once-great family name, now reduced to poverty. Or perhaps ambitious people looking to pull themselves up to higher social strata.

Laborer: Farmers, smiths, carpenters, etc. Anyone that makes a living with their hands. They may be successful or struggling.

Merchant: Caravan owners, traders, and anyone that buys and sells goods and services made by others is a merchant.

Soldier: Soldiers could also be mercenaries or members of the city guard. They make their way in the world on the strength of their sword arm.

Acolyte: Any lowly position within a church, temple, or cult falls under this category.

Minor Civic Official: This can be the captain of the guard, a tax collector, or a bureaucrat within the political system.

Artisan: The person is similar to a laborer, but the works he creates are known and this person's standing in the community is much higher than most. An artist, a dancer, a poet or minstrel, or even an actor would also be considered an artisan.

Tradesman: Similar to a merchant, but a tradesman is responsible for an industry or large organized group. The head of the brewer's guild is an example of a tradesman.

Politician: Anyone that works within the civilian government behind the scenes to ensure that his district, or his constituents, or his own position of power is justified, is considered a politician.

Minor Noble: The very wealthy, someone appointed to court by the king or governor, or someone that was given a title and lands for service to king and country is a minor noble.

Court Official: Magistrates, prefects, heads of state, envoys, and anyone that keeps the council of the ruling class is a court official.

Diplomat: Someone assigned to court or invited to court by another head of state is said to be a diplomat. They are the eyes and ears of their own government.

Priest: Any high official in a church, temple, or cult can be considered a priest.

Royalty: This need not be the king or queen. Any member of the royal house, a princess, a second cousin, or even an unknown bastard is considered royalty.

Master Thief: This person is most likely Zamorian, or has a great story explaining why he is considered a master thief.

Relic Hunter: Almost certainly in the service of Mitra, this relic hunter may or may not have intense loyalty to his faith.

Assassin: Roll on the table a second time. The result is the assassin's cover identity. Whether or not this is revealed depends entirely on how the adventure unfolds.

Spy: Roll on the table a second time. The result is the spy's cover identity. Whether or not this is revealed depends entirely on how the adventure unfolds.

Unique Character: This can be any character that doesn't fall into the above categories, or it can be a renowned character from this book, the corebook, or other Conan sourcebooks.

WHAT

The gamemaster should roll a d20 to determine if the What is a mundane item or a rare item. If the result is a 1–10, the item is mundane, meaning that it is ordinary, though it may be quite valuable. If the result is 11–20, the item is rare, unique, or it may be a scarce and/or valuable commodity. Another d20 roll can determine the exact description of the What, and another roll provides a description.

As with prior tables, the gamemaster is encouraged to choose a desired result, and to ignore (or re-roll) results that are implausible.

Metal items might be made of tin, copper, bronze, brass, iron, steel, silver, gold, platinum, or another precious alloy. The item's basic type can determine this, though the item might be distinguished by being uncharacteristically made of metal, instead of its normal substance.

Mundane Items

Commodities: Anything from building materials such as wood or steel, to raw components, such as bolts of silk, are commodities.

Currency: This could be a military payroll, a personal debt payment, or any other excuse to fill coffers with coins of the realm.

Jewels: These could be uncut stones from far away mines or refined and polished jewels intended for merchants or artisans to use. Optionally, jewels could be a way of hiding vast wealth in a small place.

Antiques: This broad category includes furniture, personal items, decorations, and even fixtures. They are distinguished by their age, the materials used to make them, and their design which reflects far older cultures.

Equipment: Swords, armor, helmets, and even clothing could be considered equipment. Such things would be valuable to military encampments, mercenary groups, or garrisons.

Components: Magical or thieving components tend to be valuable and always in demand to the right people.

Artwork: Paintings, tapestries, rugs, statues, etchings, and other artwork can be quite valuable.

Food: In war-torn regions, bread and cheese can be more valuable than swords and shields.

Wine or Spirits: Rare vintages, exotic potables, and other such alcoholic beverages can be quite profitable.

Treasure Cache: This is a small stash of more than one of the above. The gamemaster should roll a 🜟, with the following results: 0 = roll again, 1 = one item, 2 = two items, Effect = three items. Roll again on the list equal to the number generated or simply choose up to three items that can be found in a storage room, a warehouse, or even buried or hidden somewhere.

Rare Items

Important Papers: Deeds, letters with incriminating content, contracts, or a bill of sale could all be considered important papers. Possession or publication of them would cause a power shift in some way.

Chest or Strongbox: This heavy container is full of... something. But it's sturdy and locked, so the odds are high that whatever is in there is important.

Grimoire: This book can be a grimoire, or it may contain information necessary to the heist. Optionally, this could be a library that aids with skill tests or research of some kind.

Statue or Carving: This work of art is small enough to be carried by one or two people, depending on the composition of the material used. What it depicts or perhaps what's inside of it may be of use later in the story.

Gems or Jewelry: This ancient gem is larger and older than the ones being mined currently and may have other properties, as well. Or it may be part of an antique piece of jewelry, such as a ring or an amulet.

Religious Artifact: A symbol of the old gods, or perhaps some recording of the spiritual word in book or tablet form. Of great interest to followers of the particular faith.

Legendary Item: Here is a sword with a storied past, or a cursed signet ring, or the jeweled goblet of the last of the Zhemri queen. As long as it has a story attached to it, and rumored (or confirmed) additional properties, it can be a legendary item.

Treasure Hoard: A hoard is similar to a cache, except that there's more of it. The gamemaster should roll 3🜏 — with the following results: 0 = roll again, 1 = one item, 2 = two items, Effect = three items. Add the values together to determine how many mundane or rare items, then roll a d20 for each. This hoard is always well protected in some way, whether by humans, guard animals, traps, or even supernatural methods.

Prized Possession: This is a mundane item, but not necessarily worthless. Nevertheless, it holds great meaning and significance for someone, and if it were stolen that person will do anything to recover the item. There may be additional repercussions associated with the loss of the item.

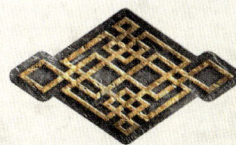

WHAT			
Roll	Mundane	Rare	Description
1	Commodities	Important Documents	Ancient
2	Commodities	Important Documents	Bejeweled
3	Currency	Chest or Strongbox	Carved
4	Currency	Chest or Strongbox	Dangerous
5	Jewels	Chest or Strongbox	Decorated
6	Jewels	Grimoire	Dirty
7	Antiques	Grimoire	Disguised
8	Antiques	Statue or Carving	Exotic
9	Equipment	Statue or Carving	Engraved
10	Equipment	Gem or Jewelry	Encased
11	Components	Gem or Jewelry	Fake or Forged
12	Components	Religious Artifact	Finely Made
13	Artwork	Religious Artifact	Glittering
14	Artwork	Legendary Item	Glowing
15	Food	Legendary Item	Metal (see page 118)
16	Food	Treasure Hoard	Rusted
17	Wine or Spirits	Treasure Hoard	Sealed
18	Wine or Spirits	Treasure Hoard	Shattered
19	Treasure Cache	Prized Possession	Tainted
20	Treasure Cache	Prized Possession	Unusual

WHERE

The Where of a heist can be determined with a roll of a d20:

1–10: Urban — a target located within the walls of the city, or optionally in another city.

11–20: Rural — a target located in an outdoor or wilderness area.

Then gamemaster should then roll another d20 to determine exactly where the heist takes place.

WHERE		
Roll	Urban	Rural
1	Private Residence	Abandoned House
2	Private Residence	Abandoned House
3	Public Building	Ruins
4	Public Building	Ruins
5	The Market	Burial Mound
6	The Market	Burial Mound
7	Local Business	Sacred Site
8	Local Business	Sacred Site
9	Under the City	Camp or Oasis
10	Under the City	Camp or Oasis
11	In Transit	Village or Trading Post
12	In Transit	Village or Trading Post
13	Warehouse or Storage	Fort or Outpost
14	Warehouse or Storage	Fort or Outpost
15	Government Building	Cave
16	Government Building	Cave
17	Palace or Mansion	On the Road
18	Palace or Mansion	On the Road
19	Private Residence	Homestead or Farm
20	Private Residence	Homestead or Farm

Urban Locations

Private Residence: The What is located inside the dwelling of a private citizen.

Public Building: The What is stashed in a place to which the masses have access or regularly gather, such as a church or temple.

The Market: The What is somewhere in an open-air market, very likely the largest and busiest one in the city.

Local Business: Any named business, such as a tavern, an inn, a gambling house, etc. is where the What is located. This could also be a service trade, like the blacksmith, city stables, or the local tailor.

Under the City: If the city has sewers, or ruins, or even a series of discontinued tunnels from a previous occupant, this is where the What is located.

In Transit: The What is currently in the city, but won't be for long. It's being loaded onto a caravan/wagon/ship and will be gone within a short span of time.

Warehouse or Storage: The What is somewhere within a warehouse or storage facility that may be in use, abandoned, discontinued, or filled to the rafters with other items.

Government Building: The What is located inside any building owned by the city or state, such as the jail or court of law.

Palace or Mansion: The What is located in a private residence with guards and/or servants, multiple rooms, and other unknown defenses and fortifications.

Rural Locations

Abandoned House: This home is now empty, its occupants long gone. There may be a good reason for this.

Ruins: Ancient, crumbling walls and columns are a great place to hide something. Who knows what secrets are found below?

Burial Mound: The What may be buried with the dead, or on top of the dead, or in place of the dead. There may be more than one burial mound at a given location.

Sacred Site: Strange idols, glyphs carved into rocks, crude altars stained with the ichor of ancients... this site is sacred to someone and may still be active.

Camp or Oasis: The What is here at this permanent watering hole or campsite. The occupants of the camp or oasis may well know that The What is there and have other plans for it.

> *Not for naught had he gained access into darksome cults, had harkened to the grisly whispers of the votaries of Skelos under midnight trees, and read the forbidden ironbound books of Vathelos the Blind.*
>
> — "Black Colossus"

Village or Trading Post: The What is located somewhere in this small village or trading post. Someone here knows of it... or do they?

Fort or Outpost: The military build forts, and businesses and guilds build outposts. They are extensions of the will of the people in charge. The What is somewhere within this structure.

Homestead or Farm: The farmer and their family may have the What, or may not know that they have it. Getting them to trust strangers is the first priority.

On the Road: A band of pilgrims, a gypsy caravan, or merchants on the Road of Kings may have the What in their possession and have specific plans for it.

Cave: Back in the hills, a cave set into the rock walls is the perfect hiding place for people, places, and things.

HOW

No heist is easy. Outside of the most general risks undertaking a heist involves — being caught and punished as the main concern — even the smallest burglary can have a range of potential dangers and problems that the player characters will have to successfully negotiate, if they want to get out alive, intact, and richer. Thieves call these wrinkles and hitches — the former being an unanticipated twist that must be planned around, and the latter being complexities or obstacles that must be overcome if you want to stick to the original plan.

The gamemaster should roll 1 to determine how many wrinkles and hitches there are, with a result of 0 or an Effect = 1. Once the number of each is determined, the gamemaster should roll 1d20 to determine each wrinkle and hitch, consulting the *Wrinkles and Hitches* table (page 122) and can ignore, re-roll, or choose wrinkles and hitches that complement each other. Wrinkles and hitches can and should support one another. *For example, rolling a 7 on the Wrinkles column yields a result of "Poison" while a roll of 15 for Hitches is "Beast." The gamemaster can interpret this as a pit full of cobras, which is both a beast and a poison hazard.*

Wrinkles are always mentioned or alluded to in the set-up of a heist. These are the things that the player characters know about the job from the outset, learned from the patron, contacts, or through their own research.

Hitches should not be revealed unless player characters think to do research on a target and make a successful Daunting (D3) Lore test, with an Obtain Information Momentum spend to learn about additional hitches. Other skills may be used, such as interrogating a former guard with Society, Persuade, or Insight, or careful surveillance beforehand using Observation. Optionally, the gamemaster may decide that there is simply no way for the player characters to learn what the hitches are ahead of time. In these cases, no amount of research or study reveals the hitches.

Wrinkles

Trapped: The Where is rigged or booby-trapped in some way. This may be known, such as: "The floor is a maze of covered pits, to thwart thieves"; or an unknown factor such as: "All who reach for the jewel have their fingers sliced off in mid-air"! This is a mechanical apparatus that can be discovered and disarmed.

Poisoned: The What or the Where is poisonous in some way. This can be gas from the swamp, noxious spores from an unknown fungus, or a subtle oiled coating that is absorbed through the skin. Figuring out what the poison is and what it does is critical to the job. Poison need not be lethal — but it usually is.

Guarded: The Where and/or the What is guarded by armed fighters, or optionally by armed commoners. Gaining access to the prize involves neutralizing the guards in some way.

Beasts: The Where and/or the What is guarded by animals, domestic and trained or wild and held captive. In either case, they are lethal to the thieves and attack on sight. Note that giant versions of natural creatures, such as giant spiders, are considered beasts.

Monsters: Any creature not of this realm, undead, from another plane of existence, or the product of foul sorcery is considered a monster.

Sorcery: The Where and/or the What is enchanted in some way that is almost always harmful or detrimental to the thieves. Entering a room could trigger a spell or several spells. Turning the key in the lock may summon something from another plane of existence.

Limited Window: The What is only available for a certain fixed length of time. After that, it is unobtainable until the next limited window opens again. This could be something as simple as "only during daylight hours" or something keyed to a celestial event, like a lunar eclipse, or the first new moon of each month.

It's in Transit: The What is on the move, either through town, or down the road, and is now a moving target.

Before You Can Get It…: This is an additional condition that must be fulfilled in order to successfully complete the heist. Maybe the vault has a unique key that must be lifted from the captain of the guard. The wolves that prowl the perimeter have a special diet that must be accounted for if anyone is expected to survive the encounter. Whatever it is almost certainly necessitates additional skill tests.

Unknown Security: The What lies deep in the crypts below, or high in the castle tower, out of the sight of anyone attempting to ascertain its secrets. There is no doubt it is guarded. By who — or what — is a mystery that will only be solved when the thieves breach the walls.

WRINKLES AND HITCHES		
Roll	Wrinkles	Hitches
1	Trapped	Extreme Repercussions
2	Trapped	Other Interested Parties
3	Poisoned	Heightened Security
4	Poisoned	It's on the Move
5	Guarded	It's on Display
6	Guarded	It's in Public
7	Beasts	There's More Than One
8	Beasts	It's Not the Right One
9	Monsters	It's More Valuable Than Originally Thought
10	Monsters	It's Less Valuable Than Originally Thought
11	Sorcery	It's Not Here
12	Sorcery	Trapped
13	Limited Window	Poisoned
14	Limited Window	Guarded
15	It's in Transit	Beasts
16	It's in Transit	Monsters
17	Before You Can Get It…	Sorcery
18	Before You Can Get It…	It's a Set-up
19	Unknown Security	It's a Trap
20	Unknown Security	It's a Double Cross

Hitches

Extreme Repercussions: The successful theft of this item starts a chain reaction that could lead to a campaign-wide event. A kidnapped princess might plunge two nations into war, just as easily as a stolen necklace from the neck of the queen.

Other Interested Parties: The player characters are not the only people looking for the item. It could be another thief or group of thieves, or any other opposed force who want the item for their own use.

Heightened Security: Owing to the value of what is to be stolen, extra precautions have been taken. Additional guards, new locks — rendering the old stolen keys useless — or any other kind of unexpected and very recent security upgrade.

It's on the Move: As a security measure, the item is being moved to a different location. The thieves may find out about this in advance, or they may watch it as it's being carried out of the place they previously cased.

It's on Display: There it is, right there, in the great hall, or on the top shelf of the library. With people always around, stealing this item becomes much more difficult.

It's in Public: The item is in plain sight, and everyone can see it. Stealth is difficult, if not impossible, under the circumstances.

There's More Than One: Is the one in your hands a clever forgery? How would you know?

It's Not the Right One: This is a decoy. It's a bag of diamonds, all right, but they aren't the Sacred Tears of Inanna.

It's More Valuable Than Originally Thought: Something this valuable, this precious? It's going to be very hard to conceal, much less sell. And how much were you promised for this endeavor anyway? If this is selected for a mundane item, it becomes rare.

It's Less Valuable Than Originally Thought: It's junk. The item may have been great once but is now in disrepair. Or perhaps it was never good to begin with. If this is selected for a rare item, it becomes mundane.

It's Not Here: Your information was correct. But the item is just missing. There may be clues as to where it went or who took it, though.

Trapped: No one mentioned that lifting the crown from the dais would cause the floor to collapse under your feet. But that's what happened.

Poisoned: The item is guarded by visible or invisible gas or some other toxin, whether breathable, on a sharp edge, or even deadly to the touch. This does not need to be a man-made poison: many are the plants whose vapors or sap are deadly.

Guarded: There are guards that no one told the player characters about.

Beasts: There are beasts (spiders, serpents, etc.) that someone forgot to mention.

Monsters: That thing is not of this world and was also not mentioned in any of the records of this place. The gamemaster should decide if the item is what is keeping the creature there, or if the creature was brought there to guard the item.

Sorcery: The place reeks of dark magic, and it's active.

It's a Set-Up: This was all a big distraction, designed to pull focus away from what is really going on.

It's a Trap: This was all an ambush designed to capture the player characters for their past misdeeds.

It's a Double Cross: The player characters were set up and meant to get caught. This allowed the real caper to go off without a hitch. If desired, the gamemaster can consult the heist tables and determine a second heist, representing what was really going on.

WHY

After all the hard work — thieving is sometimes harder than an honest wage — the thieves are at last presented with their prize. The gamemaster should roll a d20 to determine what the reward is based on the rarity of what is being stolen, whether mundane or rare, as determined in *What* on page 118:

Pre-Arranged Payment: The person who hires the thieves sets the price for successfully obtaining whatever it is they desire. Player characters may safely expect to be paid up to half the cost of the item, if mundane, and up to two-thirds the cost of the item if rare. Greedy thieves can negotiate for a higher price with a Challenging (D2) Thievery or Persuade test. Every success also generates Doom that may be spent on additional hitches or wrinkles, or may be used by the person who hires the thieves to try and get out from the deal.

Fencing the Goods: These items must be sold to generate money. Whether the thieves or the person who hires them does it, stolen goods don't always fetch a lot of money.

	REWARDS		
Roll	Reward	Mundane	Rare
1–3	Pre-Arranged Payment	Equal to the ½ the value of the item(s) stolen	Equal to ⅔ the value of the item(s) stolen
4–7	Fencing the Goods	¹⁄₁₀ listed value	½ listed value
8–11	Keeping the Goods	Bonus to Gold (+1)	Bonus to Gold (+1)
12–15	Split the Take	Skill Tests	Skill Tests
16–18	Renown	+1 Renown per 5 Gold	+1 Renown per 2 Gold
19–20	Trade or Barter	—	—

A RANDOMLY GENERATED HEIST EXAMPLE

Once the gamemaster has determined a number of random heist seeds, it's time to put the pieces together and see what sticks, until something resembling a heist begins to coalesce from the murky ether of creativity.

Rolling dice generated the following list:

- WHO: A *Local* (in this case, Zamora) that is an *Anxious Merchant*.

- WHAT: A mundane *Treasure Cache*, which turns out to be a stash of alchemical components (2 Resources).

- WHERE: A *Rural* location, specifically *Ruins*.

- HOW: Two wrinkles mean that it's *Poisoned* and there is *Unknown Security*. One hitch indicates that *It's More Valuable Than Originally Thought*.

- WHY: The thieves have agreed to a *Pre-Arranged Payment*.

Below is an example of a heist constructed from the heist elements determined above.

Synopsis

An anxious merchant approaches the thieves. On the road into Zamora, he claims, he witnessed someone burying a chest in the old ruins. The merchant knows from the markings on his robe that this stranger was an acolyte of Set. The merchant asks the thieves to go recover the chest and bring it to him. The merchant is taking a chance, something he's never done before, and he needs to stay in town and in public to avoid suspicion. He agrees to pay the thieves a pouch of silver each, provided the chest is brought to him locked and the contents intact.

The thieves can learn that the priests of Set routinely smear the locks and hinges of their chests with a special poison to deter thieves. But there is also a pair of serpents in the ruins, placed there by the acolyte, as guardians. If the player characters recover the chest, they learn from the merchant that these alchemical components are, in fact, a shipment of black lotus, and someone will certainly come looking for that.

Player characters may use skill tests of a type and Difficulty determined by the gamemaster, to try and swing the odds in their favor. Any Doom generated by these tests can be used to create further impediments in the form of idle gossip, being spotted by the city guards, or anything else that would prohibit a clean getaway.

Keeping the Goods: As long as no one is expecting delivery, keeping what was stolen adds to wealth and may provide equipment or other assets.

Split the Take: After the items are sold, the thieves split the take with the person who put them on to the job in the first place. The person with the plan or the idea for the job always expects a cut of at least 1⁄10 of the overall haul, maybe more. The exact percentage of the loot is to be worked out by the thieves and their employer.

Renown: Sometimes, news of the thieves' exploits reaching the ears of their friends (and enemies) is reward enough. For a master thief, or someone wishing to become one, this is paramount. The gamemaster decides how much Renown to award.

Trade or Barter: The stolen items are leverage in a larger business transaction or, in lieu of money changing hands, the thieves could agree to steal something in exchange for equipment or a commodity that they desperately need.

The treasure was there, heaped in staggering profusion — piles of diamonds, sapphires, rubies, turquoises, opals, emeralds; ziggurats of jade, jet and lapis-lazuli; pyramids of gold wedges; teocallis of silver ingots; jewel-hilted swords in cloth-of-gold sheaths; golden helmets with colored horsehair crests, or black and scarlet plumes; silver-scaled corselets; gem-crusted harness worn by warrior-kings three thousand years in their tombs; goblets carven of single jewels; skulls plated with gold, with moonstones for eyes; necklaces of human teeth set with jewels. The ivory floor was covered inches deep with gold dust that sparkled and shimmered under the crimson glow with a million scintillant lights. The thief stood in a wonderland of magic and splendor, treading stars under his sandalled feet.

— "Black Colossus"

HEROES OF THE AGE

Rogues, like honest people, shunned the shadowed ways,
gathering in foul-smelling dens, or candle-lighted taverns.

— Untitled Fragment

TYRIUS LEPIDUS

Born with a wanderlust, Tyrius was destined to leave Brythunia, his homeland, to find his fortune elsewhere in the world. Scarce had the boy realized this desire lay within him when deliverance came in the form of Pisceus, an elderly Zamorian envoy, with weathered skin, glimmering eyes, and a strange and insistent laugh. The stranger had saved the life of Tyrius's father, forever earning hospitality from the Lepidus family. Pisceus' every visit brought tales of adventure, danger, open roads and lands of enticing beauty. The world was ripe for the taking, Pisceus laughed, and after years of Tyrius' wheedling, cajoling, and sweet-talking, Pisceus agreed to take him as an apprentice.

Tyrius spent many years on the road, an eager pupil. While others seemed to come and go, only one other remained: Leysa, a young Zamorian woman. In every way Tyrius' equal, she matched him shot-for-shot in archery, length-for-length in horsemanship, trick-for-trick in games of wit. Their years together were full of joy — until one morning, he woke and she had disappeared.

He never found her again. All avenues were searched, all options exhausted. She was gone. Tyrius parted ways with Pisceus soon after, to forge his own destiny. In the years that followed, his wandering led him to adventure, bringing peace wherever he visited, by wit, word, or weapon.

BACKER CHARACTERS

Presented on the following page are characters created by backers for the *Robert E. Howard's Conan: Adventures in an Age Undreamed Of* Kickstarter campaign, provided here for use by the gamemaster or as player characters.

To this day, ambassador Tyrius Lepidus is the trusted voice of Asgalun, pride of the Shemitish coast, ally to Aquilonia, honored shield of Zingara, and loyal Lord-Protector and husband to Lady Karima of Asgalun. He cuts a striking figure among the nobles and diplomats. Confidence and self-assurance sit easily upon his shoulders, reinforced by his clear, bold voice. He carries himself as if born to command, earned from years of travel, and while the intricately carved longbow he bears seems a ceremonial weapon, it is a certainty that the ambassador is more than able to use it effectively.

ATTRIBUTES			
Awareness	Intelligence	Personality	Willpower
9	8	12	8
Agility	Brawn		Coordination
9	8		12

FIELDS OF EXPERTISE

Combat	1	Movement	1
Fortitude	—	Senses	1
Knowledge	—	Social	3

STRESS AND SOAK

- **Stress:** Vigor 8, Resolve 8
- **Soak:** Armor 2 (Leather), Courage 2

ATTACKS

- **Twisted Dagger (M):** Reach 1, 3 🔥, 1H, Hidden 1, Parrying, Thrown, Unforgiving 1
- **Ceremonial Longbow (R):** Range L, 6 🔥, 2H, Piercing 1, Volley
- **Commanding Voice (T):** Range C, 4 🔥 mental, Area

SPECIAL ABILITIES

- **Social Chameleon:** When impersonating other social castes, Tyrius can substitute his Persuade skill for Animal Handling, Craft, Insight, Society, Survival, or Thievery when convincing others of his expertise.
- **Accurate:** Tyrius may reroll 2 🔥 when making a ranged attacks.
- **Marksman:** Tyrius may take a Minor Action to aim, adding +1d20 to ranged attacks.

DOOM SPENDS

- **Pisceus's Finest Student:** By spending 2 Doom Pisceus's training lets Tyrius temporarily gain the benefit of one of the following talents for one round: *Nimble as a Cat, Heed My Words, Guardsman's Eye, Quiet Wisdom, Comforting Lies, Many Blades*. Tyrius can renewed the talent for another 2 Doom, or he can activate another ability for 2 Doom. Only one effect may be active at a time: activating one ends the other.

JAMIL THE THIEFTAKER

"Jamil the Thieftaker" is a name known throughout Zamora, a name both intoned in songs of praise and spat out, in venomous curses. Few names in Zamora invoke such a range of potent emotion. The reason for Jamil's fame, and infamy, hinges on the fact that none can properly guess Jamil's ultimate goal, or what he is prepared to sacrifice in its pursuit. Rumor has it that Jamil has his eyes on a title both prestigious and immensely important: that of royal thieftaker.

Jamil himself is a simple man, soft of voice and modest in garb. He prefers traditional Zamorian clothing, dressing plainly as any common trader or free-person. The sharp of eye, though, may catch a flash of mail beneath his robes, or hear the soft slide of metal ring on metal ring.

This deceptively humble-looking man made his first appearance in Shadizar a scant few years ago, a humble pilgrim looking to settle in the Wicked City and help its citizens retake the streets. He set himself up as a bodyguard and hired hand, offering protective services to local merchants, as well as shielding wares stored within the city walls and caravans and larger shipments needing safe passage through the streets.

He quickly made a name for himself. His fees were exorbitant, but his employees were well worth the price: ex-watchmen from Nemedia and Corinthia, trained guardsmen whose loyalty was unwavering. As Jamil's comfort with and knowledge of Shadizar grew, he began to expand his reach. All too quickly, organized crime in the shadows of the Wicked City found their plans thwarted before reaching fruition, their henchmen and runners captured and fed to the city's official authorities — all with a note from Jamil claiming credit for the arrest.

Criminals in the shadows have every reason to hate Jamil, and wonder how he is so well-informed. In this, the city authorities share a common curiosity and resentment with the felons they pursue: this man's success is starting to cause the everyday city folk to question the already-tenuous authority of the law here in this city of thieves.

STRESS AND SOAK

- **Stress:** Vigor 13, Resolve 11
- **Soak:** Armor 2 (Ringmail), Courage 1

ATTACKS

- **Long Knife (M):** Reach 1, 3 ⚔, 1H, Hidden 1, Parrying, Thrown, Unforgiving 1
- **Shortbow (R):** Range M, 3 ⚔, 2H, Piercing 1, Volley

SPECIAL ABILITIES

- **Eyes of a Hawk:** Any Thievery or Stealth test made against Jamil is made at two steps of Difficulty greater than normal.
- **Equally Despised and Lauded:** All social tests made by Jamil in Zamora are one step of Difficulty higher than normal but all successful social tests he makes gain 2 bonus Momentum.
- **Heard it Before:** Any player character spending Doom or seizing an opportunity on a social test against Jamil grants Jamil a number of d20s than the player character receives, minus 1d20.

DOOM SPENDS

- **Counter-ambush:** Whenever attacked in melee by an ambushing party, Jamil can spend 3 Doom to negate any bonus the ambush may have granted.
- **Leadership:** Jamil may spend 2 Doom to grant a bonus d20 to a single Mob or Squad within close range. This bonus die may be used on any single skill test attempted by the group before the end of its next turn.

There are some in this world, though, who know too many secrets, and for the right price, the correct questions might be asked. Is the Shaded Rose brothel really a drop-point for instructions? Does Madam Mishana hide a list of informants locked in her desk? What of the strange rumors of a lawman gone missing from Numalia several years ago, the man named Julius the Thiefcatcher? Whatever did happen to the Chief Prosecutor after he was found guilty of illegal gambling? Certainly, he disappeared — but wherever might he have gone? More dangerously still, those questions might be answered correctly, and Jamil's true identity revealed — who would risk their life to secure these answers is less obvious, but there are many who would profit from the fall of such a man within the Wicked city.

ATTRIBUTES

Awareness	Intelligence	Personality	Willpower
9	8	11	9

Agility	Brawn	Coordination
10	11	10

FIELDS OF EXPERTISE

Combat	2	Movement	1
Fortitude	2	Senses	1
Knowledge	1	Social	2

INARUS

To look at this grinning, tattooed man is to see and understand why the life of a pirate is so romanticized in song and story. For Inarus, his profession is evident in every aspect; his preferred garb is chosen for comfort and color, simple, brightly colored trousers, and plain sandals for his feet. In strong, deliberate contrast, shining jewels adorn his arms, gems sparkle from his ears and fingers, and gold rope chains glimmer enticingly around his neck. With each swaggering step, he tempts any challengers to face him.

Ask him his name, and he barks with harsh laughter. *"You do not know me? I am Inarus!"* He flashes an impudent grin, his voice seasoned by sea-salt and drink. *"Inarus, who stole the golden coins from the shadowed eye-sockets of long-dead Lord Iahmesu! Inarus, who wrested the favored vipers from the very shoulders of High Priestess Sabahat and left her weeping at the angry gates of the Styx! Inarus, whose deepest thirst is for adventure, for riches, for fame and glory!"*

One finds a more reliable accounting of tales about the man when he is not asked directly. Born to a Corinthian slave-woman, his father a mystery, Inarus grew up with constant reminders that he was destined only to die, either in servitude to a master worthier and wealthier than he, or to be bought and slaughtered, a sacrifice to power some mad sorcerer's blackest whims.

Little wonder that he used everything at his disposal to fight his way out of the life chosen for him. He promised any god that would listen that he would do whatever it took to please them, so long as he was able to escape this fate. One of those gods must have answered, for over the years, Inarus gained wit and finesse enough to escape his lowly position, flee his would-be masters, and find his way to freedom on board the *Errant of Khemi*, where he has become his own Prince of the Sea. Time and again he has found his fortune reversed, strange mishaps besetting his foes, or his errant wishes coming true almost instantaneously.

For as often as the man boasts of his own adventures, one is left wondering how many of his stories are actually true. Certainly, his charm and his boastful, swaggering manner are among his chief weapons, and he makes no secret of his distaste for those content to live straightforward lives as honest merchants or in the employ of the wealthy and indolent; as such, it is easy to believe he is a liar at heart. His swift skill with his scimitar, though, and the ease with which he dances in and out of his enemies' weapons, lends some truth to those tales.

ATTRIBUTES

Awareness	Intelligence	Personality	Willpower
10	8	12	8

Agility	Brawn	Coordination
12	9	10

FIELDS OF EXPERTISE

Combat	1	Movement	3
Fortitude	—	Senses	2
Knowledge	—	Social	1

STRESS AND SOAK

- **Stress:** Vigor 9, Resolve 8
- **Soak:** Armor 1 (Clothing), Courage 2

ATTACKS

- **Scimitar (M):** Reach 2, 3 ⬥, 1H, Cavalry 1, Parrying
- **Boastful Taunt (T):** Range C, 2 ⬥ mental, Stun

SPECIAL ABILITIES

- **Strength from the Sea:** Inarus is used to combat aboard ship and only suffers penalties in the fiercest of weather.
- **Boarding Action:** Pirates are experts at boarding unfriendly craft and know all the best places to seek cover. When boarding, Inarus gains 2 ⬥ Cover against missile weapons
- **Strength in Numbers:** Inarus's attack inflicts an additional +2 damage against any creature that has already been attacked this round.
- **Ambush Tactics:** Inarus is seldom inclined to fight fair, relying on sneak attacks and skullduggery to triumph. His familiarity with such tactics grants him 1 bonus Momentum on all movement tests made during a combat.

DOOM SPENDS

- **Chosen of a Mysterious God:** To this day, Inarus does not know who answered his prayers, but once per encounter, Inarus can spend 2 Doom to re-roll any failed dice roll, or he can force an opponent to re-roll any one damage roll.

INDEX

THE HYBORIAN AGE AWAITS YOU

BOOKS COMING SOON

Conan the Thief
Conan the Mercenary
Conan the Pirate
Conan the Brigand
The Book of Skelos
Conan the Wanderer
Conan the Adventurer
Conan the Scout
Conan the King
Nameless Cults
Ancient Ruins & Cursed Cities
Conan Monolith Boardgame Sourcebook
Conan and the Shadow of the Sorcerer
Legendary Beasts & Otherworldly Horrors

ACCESSORIES

Gamemaster Screen
Geomorphic Tile Sets
Doom & Fortune Tokens
Q-Workshop Dice
Card Decks
Stygian Doom Pit
Fabric & Poster Maps
Character Sheet Pad
Conqueror's Bag

MODIPHIUS ENTERTAINMENT

2D20

CABINET

ROBERT E. HOWARD OFFICIAL LICENSE

HYBORIA

modiphius.com/conan